Political Parties in Post-Soviet Space

Recent titles in
Political Parties in Context series
Kay Lawson, Series Editor

How Political Parties Work: Perspectives from Within
Kay Lawson, editor

The Organization of Political Parties in Southern Europe
Piero Ignazi and Colette Ysmal, editors

Cleavages, Parties, and Voters: Studies from Bulgaria, the Czech Republic, Hungary, Poland, and Romania
Kay Lawson, Andrea Römmele and Geogi Karasimeonov, editors

Political Parties in South Asia
Subrata K. Mitra, editor

Political Parties in Post-Soviet Space

Russia, Belarus, Ukraine, Moldova, and the Baltics

EDITED BY ANATOLY KULIK AND SUSANNA PSHIZOVA

Political Parties in Context
Kay Lawson, Series Editor

PRAEGER

Westport, Connecticut
London

Library of Congress Cataloging-in-Publication Data

Political parties in post-Soviet space : Russia, Belarus, Ukraine, Moldova, and the Baltics / edited by Anatoly Kulik and Susanna Pshizova.
p. cm. — (Political parties in context)
Includes bibliographical references and index.
ISBN 0–275–97344–1
1. Political parties—Former Soviet republics. 2. Former Soviet republics—Politics and government. I. Kulik, Anatoly. II. Pshizova, Susanna. III. Series.
JN6598.A1P557 2005
324.2′0947—dc22 2005023265

British Library Cataloguing in Publication Data is available.

Library of Congress Catalog Card Number: 2005023265
ISBN: 0–275–97344–1

First published in 2005

Praeger Publishers, 88 Post Road West, Westport, CT 06881
An imprint of Greenwood Publishing Group, Inc.
www.praeger.com

Printed in the United States of America

The paper used in this book complies with the Permanent Paper Standard issued by the National Information Standards Organization (Z39.48–1984).

10 9 8 7 6 5 4 3 2 1

Contents

Series Foreword

Political Parties in Post-Soviet Space is the fifth book in the series "Political Parties in Context" for which I serve as the Series Editor. Like all the other volumes to date, this one draws exclusively from the work of indigenous scholars, authors who live and work in the countries about which they are writing, and who know their political development and their contemporary party systems from personal experience as well as academic study. The goal is always to permit such scholars to discuss their nations' political parties as they see fit—to give the essential basic information, but also to give the fullest and most honest interpretation of the meaning of the history and the structures they discuss. They have not been asked to follow anyone's theory of political parties (though they draw on various theories that interest them); they have been asked to tell the truth as they see it.

That may seem a simple enough goal, and an easy plan to carry out. But those who know anything of the tumultuous times these nations have lived through in the past three decades, and the impact such times have had on the lives of scholars as well as on the lives of political parties, will understand that producing this volume has been anything but a simple task. Nonetheless, Editors Anatoly Kulik and Susanna Pshizova have found and guided scholars from all seven nations who have been willing to take on this challenge, and who have met it handsomely.

A unique feature of this volume is the organization of Parts II and III, both of which begin with overview chapters, permitting readers to see the individual party systems in their sub-regional as well as national contexts. In addition, the introduction and conclusion give each of the individual editors the opportunity to place the work they have gathered in their own interpretive contexts, and further enrich the understanding we gain from the seven generously detailed nation-specific chapters.

The question these nations pose today is the question of democratization. Is it taking place, and if so—or if not—what role are political parties playing? The unusual wealth of information and contextual interpretation these studies offer lead us to new answers, springing from within.

Kay Lawson
Series Editor

Acknowledgments

Many people in different countries have made contributions to this book. The idea of the comparative research of political parties in post-Soviet space belonged to Andrew Degtyarev, professor of political science of Moscow State University of International Relations and Moscow High School of Social and Economic Sciences. He received encouragement and support from Professor Kay Lawson, well known for her works on political parties. They met in Moscow in 1998 at the conference devoted to the 100th anniversary of the first publication of M. Ostrogorsky's classic book *Democracy and Political Parties* and discussed possible ways of cooperation between rebuilt Russian political science and the Committee on Political Sociology of the International Political Science Association, headed at that time by Kay Lawson. Since that moment Kay Lawson became the good genius of the project.

The idea of such cross-national study looked very tempting, and nobody could imagine all the difficulties of the venture. It was not a matter only of the stormy political developments in all post-Soviet countries. During the first years after the destruction of the Soviet Union many ties between parts of the former single country were lost, and it was not so easy to find a contributor for each chapter, to reconstruct connections between colleagues, and to adjust normal cooperation. We are very grateful to all authors of the volume for their response to our call to participate in this project.

A very important point on the path toward completion was the International Workshop "Political Parties and Party Systems in the Baltic States and Commonwealth of Independent States" in March 2000, in Kaunas, Lithuania. We wish to thank our colleagues in the Kaunas University of Technology for their hospitality and help in the organization of the workshop. Algis Krupavičius, Director of the Policy and Public Administration Institute of Kaunas University of Technology and Associate Professor in Political Science at the Vytautas Magnus University, merits a special note of appreciation. He was the real motor of the meeting.

It is a pleasure to acknowledge the "Open Society" Institute (The Soros Foundation) for the financial support that had allowed many of us to meet at the workshop in Kaunas.

Our thanks also to English-speaking colleagues for their help in the preparation of the book, including Jane Shamaeva, Courtney Ranson, Olga Mindrul, and Eliza Hammer, who did a remarkably careful job with the editing of the final version of the manuscript.

We are also indebted to Praeger Publishing Group and especially to our editor Hilary Claggett for great patience and trust.

CHAPTER 1

Introduction: The Multidimensionality of the Context of Post-Soviet Transformation

Anatoly Kulik

The development of political parties in countries of the post-Soviet space has been much less explored than that in the post-authoritarian countries of Southern and Central Europe, Latin America, and many others regions of the world.

All of the Newly Independent States (NIS) that have appeared in the post-Soviet world purport to be "electoral democracies," and in them parties are presented as one of the most important attributes of the political system. However, while parties in the West emerged in the middle of the nineteenth century as a product of natural modernization and have since traveled a long path to current patterns, the majority of parties in the post-Soviet space were created in the late twentieth century under fairly different conditions. They differ from parties as they first appeared in the West, and, at the same time, they are not like contemporary parties in liberal democracies, even if they have much in common in organizational structures and declared goals.

The purpose of this volume is to present contemporary scholarship on party politics within each of the independent states that emerged in 1991 from the Soviet Union, particularly in its European part and the Baltics, and that have undergone in subsequent years deep political, economic, and social transformation. In the transition paradigm, the development of political parties is assumed to be a constituent process of democratic consolidation that contributes to strengthening links between the political elite and society, and to deepening the political participation of the population and the democratic accountability of governments. Parties and "free and fair" elections are widely believed to be the foremost institutions that set into motion parliamentary democracy by transforming societal conflicts into political division.

Undertaking this research we intended to emphasize the involvement of new parties in politics—"the process that determines who will occupy roles of leadership in government and how the power of government will be exercised, the authoritative allocation of scarce resources throughout a polity."[1] Therefore, we have sought to stress the broad multidimensional context that affects the emergence of parties, their evolution and performance in government, and, eventually, their place in the system of power and in the society, making clear the role they actually play in the wide-ranging process of transformation.

Already by the early 1980s, it was evident that the model of governance established by communist rule in the former Russian empire under the name of the Union of the Soviet Socialist Republics had outlived itself. In the epoch of late-industrial development, this rigid hierarchical model, based to a large extent on coercion, obviously lacked the efficiency of Western democracies in the global challenge of liberal capitalism versus real socialism. It had exhausted the limits of socioeconomic development and could no longer bear the arms race, finance anti-Western regimes and movements all over the world, and at the same time provide even modest living standards for the majority of the population. The dramatic changes in the political landscape of the world, including the fall of right-wing authoritarian regimes in southern Europe, the replacement of many military dictatorships by elected civilian governments in Latin America, and the apparent decline of authoritarian rule in some countries of East and South Asia, alerted some part of the Soviet ruling elite to the urgency of modernization.

Early 1985 marks the outset of the irreversible transformation of the Soviet empire. When the first attempts to improve "real socialism" without any challenge to the domination of the Communist Party of the Soviet Union (CPSU) in state and society proved futile, the reformist wing opposing hard-liners in the Soviet ruling establishment endorsed party democracy as the best form of government ever elaborated by human civilization. The fact that political parties played a key role in democratic development in countries of the first wave of modernization inspired many to believe that depriving the CPSU of its power and replacing the one-party state with a multiparty system would consolidate society and allow the country to follow the shortest path to a prospering democracy. In the early 1990s, many democratically oriented scholars and politicians in the Soviet Union believed that processes of transition, once launched, would unfold naturally, driven by their own internal logic and impetus. The great expectations for an inevitable and smooth transition to democracy rested in large part on the newly emerging party system, which was expected to serve as a powerful engine of political modernization.

Of course, the post-Soviet states were not alone in their firm faith in the transformational capacity of political parties, given that there is no nonparty representative democracy in the world. For them, as for many other political scientists and promoters of democracy all over the world, a constitutional representative democracy controlled by a multiparty system through competitive elections provided the main reference point in post-authoritarian transformation.

In March 1990, the Constitution of the Soviet Union was amended by the Congress of people deputies of the USSR to cancel the legal monopoly of the CPSU on power, and in October 1990, Mikhail Gorbachev, the first president of the Soviet Union and the CPSU general secretary, signed a law on popular associations that allowed emerging parties to register. Yet, the efforts for perestroika, undertaken by Gorbachev to promote fundamental changes in the political system and economy of the inflexible 70-year-old regime, which lacked working mechanisms for social self-regulation, had already gone wrong by 1991. In August 1991, a group of top state functionaries attempted a coup d'état in order to reverse the spontaneously accelerating process of decay and to preserve the Soviet Union. However, this attempt was supported only by Azerbaijan and a few republics of Central Asia, whereas most of the fifteen national republics constituting the Soviet Union disapproved or refused to recognize the schemers. In the course of regime liberalization, the slackening central power gradually lost control over national elites. National communist bureaucracies enlarged their rights and achieved a significant autonomy vis-à-vis Moscow. They did not want to lose what they had acquired.

The failure of an attempted riot brought about the final collapse of the Soviet empire and its underlying model of government. The attempt to democratize the Soviet Union that began from the top soon got out of control and resulted in the breakdown of the main pillars of the ruling regime. The Central Committee of the CPSU under Gorbachev had to declare its self-dissolution, and the cabinet of ministers accused of involvement in the plot was dissolved as well. Thus, the foremost state- and-party binding structures that had held the Soviet Union together so long now collapsed, and centrifugal trends in the policies of most republican elites broke free of any limits. Gorbachev himself was forced to resign the presidency. The Union of Soviet Socialist Republics that, according to official ideology, composed a so-called united family of Soviet peoples, disbanded surprisingly easily. The 15 national republics headed by republican state bureaucracies gained full sovereignty. As new independent states, they joined the vast and heterogeneous "third wave" of democracy that has encompassed numerous nations all over the world.

The decay of the communist regimes in the USSR, and in nations of the socialist block in Central and Eastern Europe as well, meant the end of the communist project as a state ideology. For the countries that emerged in the post-Soviet space, as for other post-authoritarian societies in any cultural or geographic region of the world, constitutional representative democracy controlled by multiparty and contestable elections served as the only landmark of transformation. So, the ruling ethnic elites in former Soviet republics had no other option but to declare a parliamentary democracy with a free-market economy, civil society, and the rule of law as the destination point of forthcoming transitions. They presented themselves as eager Western-style reformers. The hope of getting recognition and democracy-promoting aid from Western governments and nongovernmental organizations served as an additional encouragement. This declared goal made the substitution of the hegemony of republican communist parties with legal multiparty systems inevitable. Thus, the institution of political parties was artificially implanted, rather than emerging naturally, at least in majority of new independent states.

Therefore, all the new independent states had a common point of departure for transformation and most of them declared the same goal. However, as the following brief summary amply indicates, it soon became apparent that they were pursuing quite different political trajectories with quite different outcomes.

On the one hand, the National Fronts in the Baltic republics that emerged in the course of Gorbachev's perestroika worked purposefully from the very beginning to re-establish both state sovereignty and democracy. They demanded an inquiry into the secret Molotov-Ribbentrop Pact of 1939 that enacted the annexation of Lithuania, Latvia, and Estonia by the Soviet Union. They insisted on the recognition of the illegal nature of this pact, which would mean the reinstatement of their lost sovereignty. The impact of communist rule on Baltic society, limited as it was in the post-war period, was not as deep as in other republics. The collapse of the Soviet Union made them free to restore national state institutions and democratic order, which had been established as early as the inter-war period. The past experience of democracy and independence contributed strongly to the consensus of major groups in the national political elite on the goals for post-communist transformation. In the founding elections, pro-independence forces received an absolute or relative majority of seats in the constituent parliaments.

The process of democratization unfolded along the regular sequence of stages supposed by transitology: after liberalization comes the collapse of the regime and that in turn is followed by the establishment of a democratic institutional structure, and further democratic consolidation. The Baltic countries have established parliamentary democracy as the only game in town with a relatively stable party system, allowing for a smooth transfer of power as even several changes in government occurred in the midst of political scandals. National elites agreed on the indefiniteness of outcomes with definiteness of rules. In 2004 they joined the ranks of the European Union (EU), and this landmark in their post-Soviet development acknowledges that significant progress was achieved by these countries in building the infrastructure of democratic and market-oriented societies. This progress in their post-communist development was predetermined essentially by the fact that they had retained essentials of civil societies throughout the communist era, as well as by their favorable geographic location.

At the other extreme in the array of NIS are the countries of Central Asia with strong archaic biases. Turkmenistan, for instance, had no past experience with either statehood or democracy. Annexed by Russia between 1865 and 1885, the territory of Turkmenistan became a Soviet republic in 1925. However, the Soviet period did not change the traditional nature of power. As a result, the dissolution of the USSR and subsequent independence opened the way to the solidification of an autocratic regime of power. The first secretary of the Central Committee of the republican Communist Party, and simultaneously the chairman of the republican Supreme Soviet in early 1990, Saparmurat Niyazov, easily became the president through a popular vote, with the support of 98.3 percent of the population. In December 1999, Turkmenistan's People's Assembly named him president for life. The initial impulse for political openings had no chance to develop there.

Between these two poles there is an immense gray zone of countries falling in between outright dictatorship and full-fledged liberal democracy. So, for instance, despite having established all the main formal institutional structures of representative democracy, Russia was assessed by experts of Freedom House in its annual survey 2003 as a "Transitional government or hybrid regime."[2] Here, as in other countries of the Commonwealth of Independent States, or CIS (the 12 non-Baltic states of the former Soviet Union), the survey continued to note a worrisome level of antidemocratic practices and insufficient commitment on the part of national leaders to reverse negative trends. Many of these CIS countries remain at the same level of democratization as in the early 1990s, and many actually have regressed in recent years—Russia's score for "Democratization" dropped from 3.80 in 1997 to 4.88 in 2003.[3] As in previous years, the ratings and scores by *Nations in Transit 2003* indicate an ever-widening gap between the countries of the CIS and those in Central and Eastern Europe.

Thus, in a decade after the collapse of the Soviet empire it became clear that the word "post-Soviet" had essentially lost its relevance as an identifier. The fact that the NIS share a common Soviet past explains very little about the trajectory of development they have taken since then.[4] Further transformation of the NIS has generated a great variety of political regimes that formally correspond to such criteria of democracy as regular elections and political parties in opposition. However, while a relatively small number of them enjoy a certain positive dynamic, others have hardly democratized at all, and many have taken on only a modicum of democratic features, like a multiparty system, but show few signs of further democratization. As Thomas Carothers asserts, the core assumption of the transition paradigm, which articulates that after the collapse of authoritarian rule any country moves toward democracy according to some predictable democratization script, has been called into serious doubt.[5]

The collection of essays in this volume comprises seven case studies limited to the European region of the former Soviet Union. However, even in this particular geographical region, the countries under examination differ greatly in pre-Soviet history, duration of Soviet rule, ethnic composition, culture and mentality, and levels of socioeconomic development. This array of cases with a rich variety of national contexts gives readers an opportunity not only to become familiar with newly emerged parties and party systems, but also to track and compare how particular contexts shape party politics in a particular state, and to reject or uphold some conceptual assumptions about the development of parties in post-authoritarian transformations.

By now there is no one universal theory that could help describe and make sense of the variety of post-Soviet party politics. Contemporary party theory is a rather loose and mobile sphere of theories and hypotheses, each with its own particular sample of objects, assumptions, and limitations. Hence, parties may be investigated on the basis of a number of alternative theoretical frameworks developed in different times by such prominent scholars as M. Duverger, S. M. Lipset and S. Rokkan, G. Sartori, A. Panebianco, K. Lawson, K. Janda, R. Katz, A. Ware, and P. Mair. However, any particular theoretical framework chosen as the tool of analysis almost inevitably reduces the continuum of political reality to a limited set of issues that are deemed crucially important by the underlying theory and therefore neglects or underestimates the rest as unrelated. By exploring the same reality with different theoretical frameworks we would arrive eventually at different conclusions. This is the problem of the measuring device and of the error of measuring. In our case a question arises, whether a theory of parties originally developed in a Western or West-European context and tied to a particular time period will be workable when applied to the ambiguous context of post-Soviet transformation, and will not lead to simplification and misinterpretation of the nature of party politics in the countries under examination.

The researcher looking for a conceptual framework to analyze party politics in the NIS also faces another, related problem. That is the problem of conceptual equivalence or the "traveling capacity" of borrowed concepts from established democracies to transitional countries. In other words, whether observation of the same variables means the same things in different contexts.[6]

So, for instance, the framework developed by Seymour Lipset and Stein Rokkan identifies the crucial lines of cleavages that have structured emerging party systems in Western democracies. According to the framework, the divisions between *Center and Periphery* and between *State and Church,* in particular, gave rise to parties representing the ethnically, linguistically, or religiously distinct populations of the peripheries in the developing nation-states of Europe.[7] It would seem very attractive to apply this framework in an analysis of the emerging party systems in the NIS under consideration. However, a researcher of Russian party politics, for instance, comes upon the problem that the 2001 "Law on Political Parties" forbids the creation of parties advocating racial, national, or religious, as well as professional, interests.

The development of party politics might also be explored from different methodological approaches; the process-oriented approach and the structure-oriented approach are among those most often cited. The first approach views the development of party politics as dependent mainly on political processes, procedures, and decisions by political actors, or as *path-dependent*. Parties are supposed to respond rationally to the opportunities provided by formal institutional settings within a given social environment. The alternative perspective sees parties as dependent mainly on long-lasting traditions and legacies of society; electoral behavior; political cleavages that should channel mass demands into leadership representation; and the general quality of the political elite.

However, if the separate application of these approaches may be helpful as an analytical practice to test some particular hypotheses, it appears to be inappropriate to describe, interpret, and explain the multidimensional phenomenon of party politics in various countries undergoing post-Soviet transformations. In their seminal work *A New Handbook of Political Science*, Robert E. Goodin and Hans-Dieter Klingemann refer to the concept of "new institutionalism" as an integrative approach that seeks to combine alternatives, actors, structures, interests, and institutions instead of placing them in opposition to each other, in order to eliminate the disadvantages of either particular approach. They also stress that particular case studies are no less valuable than large scale, cross-national comparative studies.

The theoretical and methodological problems of studying party politics in the NIS were extensively discussed at the International Workshop "Political Parties and Party Systems in the Baltic States and Commonwealth of Independent States" that took place March 25–26, 2000, in Kaunas, Lithuania, under the aegis of the Research Committee of Political Sociology, International Political Science Association. Many contributors to this volume took part in the discussion. The participants came to the conclusion that, given the scarcity of theoretical insights into the mechanism of parties' emergence and operation in the NIS, a rigid theoretical framework would distort and misinterpret the incongruous real picture. Therefore, at the present state of knowledge, a loose, theoretically neutral, and more descriptive than analytical framework would serve the purpose of this study better.

The multidimensionality of the context that shapes emerging parties and impacts the development of party politics in post-communist transitions is widely recognized. However, the set of meaningful internal and external contextual variables that should be taken into consideration—its values, weights, and inter-reliance in affecting the development of party politics—varies from country to country even in the same region. Moreover, if at the initial phase of transformation such variables as the political will of elites, the personalities of politicians, and procedural characteristics usually play a leading role, over time structural factors become more significant. Besides, the qualitative nature of most variables, like the Soviet legacy that has dominated informal institutions at the level of both government and mass behavior in most republics, makes it hard to identify and almost impossible to measure their impact.

So, instead of imposing a unified and operationalized research template and a formalized procedure of analysis, we have left it to the authors to decide what dimensions are salient in a particular national context, and how they shape electoral and mobilization activities of parties, their relations with civil society, their transactions in the party system and efficiency in the legislature, and in the government as well. All chapters are written by authors who are current or at least recent residents of the country whose party politics they had to consider. The position of included observers lets them see from the inside problems that otherwise could be underestimated or misinterpreted. At the same time, to provide due comparability of separate case studies, the authors agreed at the workshop to follow a rather broad general framework, not bound to any explicit hypotheses that would be applicable to different cases but would leave freedom to elucidate deviating particularities. Therefore, case chapters, besides the overview of particular party systems and parties' efficiency in the government, should be focused mainly on the following issues constituting such a framework:

- the impact of the cultural and socioeconomic legacy of pre-communist development and that of communist rule on the renaissance and institutionalization of political parties
- the way the new regime came to power after the collapse of communist rule and the effect of the constituting elections
- the constitutional design and legal terms, including the electoral system, in which parties emerge and operate
- voters' attitudes toward state institutions, parties, and politics, as well as their voting behavior
- socioeconomic dynamics, cleavages in society, and parties' response to them
- the base of party competition, campaign techniques and strategies, dynamics of electoral support, and output of parties
- the institutionalization, internal organization, and sources of financing of political parties
- personalities of top politicians, informal rules of doing politics

- the impact of electronic mass media and electoral technologies on the electoral success of parties
- the impact of the external actors on domestic party politics
- the functions parties perform in post-Soviet politics and civil society
- trends in the development of party politics and prospects for party democracy consolidation in transforming the NIS

Another crucial problem discussed at the workshop referred to what we mean when we speak about parties, that is, what is the main object of our study? What definition are we using, a broad or a narrow one? The choice depends primarily on the goal of our study. Since we seek to investigate party politics in concrete national contexts of post-Soviet transformation, we have to consider not only those public associations that fit into the requirements of national laws on political parties, but also all those who are legally eligible to nominate candidates and take part in elections to parliament on "party lists," and who participate in elections separately or as a part of an electoral block.

To make the results of the case studies comparable, the contents of the volume are structured in three parts. The first part renders the case of Russia. Russia, the constituting nation of the former Russian Empire and ancestor to the Soviet Union (SU), due to its geopolitical location and dimensions, population size, and economic potential, dominated in the formally equal Union of Soviet Socialist Republics. Transformation processes in the Russian Soviet Federal Socialist Republic gave birth to changes in other parts of the SU and at the end resulted in its disintegration. But also at the present time, when former republics have become independent states, internal processes in Russia continue to impact the politics of many of them significantly. So, as Jacques Rupnik asserts, "The fate of democratization in Ukraine, Belarus, and Moldova will to a large extent depend on what happens in Russia."[8] After Russia's President Vladimir Putin came to power, Russia's influence on the other CIS countries grew even more pervasive.[9] That is why Russia is presented in a separate part.

Discussions of the three Western countries of the Commonwealth of Independent States (CIS) mentioned by Rupnik comprise the second part. According to the *Nations in Transit 2003*, "Belarus has the grim distinction of being the sole dictatorship in Europe";[10] the Republic of Moldova has come, in the 11 years since the collapse of the Soviet Union, full circle—from declaring its independence in 1991 and opening the way to establishing a democratic system of government, to the communists' return to power in the elections of 2001;[11] and Ukraine has succeeded in establishing the basic framework of a presidential-parliamentary democracy, where, for example, parliamentary elections in March 2002 marked the first post-independence victory for opposition forces other than the Communist Party.[12]

The most coherent area, the Baltics, where political parties are playing an essential role in the consolidation of new democracies, is presented in the third part.

Both the second and third parts are preceded by introductory chapters that seek to sum up and explore subregional similarities and particularities of the development of party politics from a cross-national perspective. Overall, this structure is expected to contribute to the consistency and cohesiveness of the contents.

This collection of analytical essays on the development of parties in countries of the European part of the former Soviet Union and the Baltics, produced by distinguished experts indigenous to countries they write about on the basis of a common framework, should reveal how much the national context influences national party politics. It allows for an efficient comparison of different trajectories of development and therefore provides a great opportunity to test existing theoretical models in a variety of contexts.

Many sources on party politics in the countries involved are issued in national languages by national publishers and thus are hard for many Western readers to access. That is why we have included in the list of references some Internet sources in English of both a general and a specific kind, including annual analytical country reports by Freedom House under its *Nations in Transit* Project, items of national affiliations of the International Foundation for Election Systems (IFES) in the NIS, national constitutions, laws on political parties, electoral codes and other legal acts regulating party politics, poll results on citizen awareness and participation, and so on.

We hope that this volume, despite all its imperfections, will be informative and make a noticeable contribution to a better understanding of party politics in the NIS, introduce fresh ideas regarding the strength of context in shaping party politics in countries undergoing transformation, and moreover, will raise the question whether the institution of parties by itself, in the absence of a developed civil society, rule of law, and stable market-oriented economy is able to change the authoritarian nature of power, and lead to democratic transformation.

Our volume is addressed to a wide range of scholars and practitioners dealing with post-Soviet politics and party systems; faculty and advanced undergraduate and graduate students in political science, sociology, comparative politics, transitology, and regional studies.

PART I

Russia

CHAPTER 2

Political Parties in Post-Soviet Russia: An Agent of Democratic Transition?

Anatoly Kulik

Even during the initial phase of perestroika, it became evident that no advancement in the envisaged reform of the decaying communist regime was possible without the development of a system of social self-regulation and self-management. In the late 1980s Mikhail Gorbachev, then the general secretary of the Communist Party of the Soviet Union (CPSU), endorsed creating mechanisms of "freedom of formulation and disclosure of the interests and demands of different classes and social groups." However, he rejected the very idea of political pluralism with a multiparty system, which would have challenged the political and ideological domination of the CPSU.[1] Nevertheless, with the first relatively free and partially alternative elections to the USSR Congress of People Deputies in 1989, some rudimentary arrangements appeared and fielded candidates against nominees of communist *nomenklatura*. Shortly thereafter, political developments in 1990 brought about the amendment to the USSR Constitution that deprived the CPSU of its dominant position in the state and society. Some time later a law on public associations of citizens opened the way to the institutionalization of numerous emerging political parties.

After the final collapse of communist rule and the decay of the Soviet Union in 1991, Russia became a sovereign country and thus, along with other former Soviet republics, joined the growing "third wave" of democratization. At the time, many Russian scholars and some politicians accepted the universal transition paradigm, popular in the West, according to which a country that has left an authoritarian regime is predestined to transition to democracy. The populist rhetoric of the new ruling establishment, whose members vowed fidelity to democratic values, added to the cogency of the axiom of Russia's transition to democracy. In this vein, a multiparty system and regular elections were widely regarded as a universal tool of democratic transformation.

A decade later, after the 2000 presidential election, analysts of the Carnegie Endowment for International Peace evaluated the ongoing transformation as a transition "from the Soviet decorative democracy to the Russian manipulative-decorative one."[2] And further, the author of Russia's country report for *Nations in Transit*, a project of *Freedom House* measuring progress and setbacks in political and economic reform in Central and Eastern Europe, came to the conclusion that Russia experienced more regression than forward movement over a five-year period of study.[3]

In this chapter I will attempt to trace the post-Soviet development of the Russian multiparty system, which culminated in the complex structural and institutional context of today's Russia. I will focus on such context variables as the heritage of the pre-Soviet and Soviet past, constitutional design, legal framework and informal rules of politics, personalities of post-Soviet rulers, dynamics of socioeconomic development, and mass political attitudes and electoral behaviors. It will be asserted that the contemporary party system emerged in a post-Soviet country with centuries of autocratic government in its past, no practical experience of how party democracy makes politics public, and a weak civil society, which remained mostly indifferent or unsympathetic to parties. This party system, having neither strong roots in the unstructured post-Soviet society (except for the Communist Party), nor real power capacity in the constitutional design, developed as fully dependent upon the president, who is the only substantial center of power in Russian politics. It has been engineered to preserve the concentration of power in the president's hands while providing formal legitimacy to the ruling regime inside and, even more, outside the country. Moreover, its dependency has increased in the course of the transformation of Boris Yeltsin's "democracy of disorder" into the "managing (or manipulating) democracy" under Vladimir Putin. The latter is being fitted onto the model of an authoritarian-bureaucratic "neo-corporatist" regime where the party system constitutes one of the agents of presidential rule, the others being business associations, trade-unions, and even NGOs, all of which are licensed by the Kremlin in exchange for their compliance.[4] Parties have no option except to agree to this "only game in town" imposed by the Kremlin. They have been assigned the function of stabilizing the political elite and society under the ruling regime; however, this party system is deprived of the crucial potential for democratic development.[5]

EMERGENCE OF THE RUSSIAN MULTIPARTY SYSTEM

One of the components of perestroika initiated by Gorbachev in the summer and fall of 1986 was the "instigation of the human factor"[6] that assumed a moderate extension of popular activities under the control of the CPSU. However, the process spontaneously evolved into a mass informal movement. The reference book *Rossiya: partii, associacii, soyuzyi, klubyi* comprises data on 457 political or politicized organizations, as well as references to another 657 that existed in Russia by early 1991. Among them were such organizations as "Orthodox Russia's Monarchial Order" with the goal of "restoring the Monarchy in the borders of the USSR" on the one pole, and "Movement 26 July," a "militant organization of internationalists who share the ideas of the great revolutionary Ernesto Gevara," on the other.[7] Some of them took part in the 1989 campaign of election to the Congress of Peoples' Deputies of the USSR. However, the most popular and most efficient form of political participation was, at that time, mass meetings—mostly spontaneous and unauthorized.

The law on public political associations, signed by Gorbachev in October 1990, allowed registration of emerging parties. The law guaranteed the citizens' right to create parties that would "take part in creating the government and in performing the functions of power through their representatives elected to the soviets of peoples' deputies."[8] In January 1990, candidates to the office of Peoples' Deputies from 22 regions of Russia founded the first electoral bloc "Democratic Russia" whose main demand was to deprive the CPSU of its monopoly on power. This demand was supported by more than half of Russia's population. At the same time the proponents of radical reform of the Communist Party from inside created the "Democratic platform in the CPSU." In March 1990, the 3rd Congress of Peoples' Deputies of the USSR ratified amendments to the Constitution of the USSR canceling the right of the CPSU to monopolize political power, and in May, the first political parties opposing the CPSU emerged. Most of them united in the movement "Democratic Russia" on the general basis of anti-communism. In the struggle against the CPSU, the parties that designated themselves as democratic radically rejected not only communist rule, but also any socialist perspective for Russia, ignoring the lasting cultural and historical legacy of Russia. They took as their motto "No communism, no socialism." This choice was vigorously supported by the independent mass media, the child of Gorbachev's *glasnost'*.

By the late 1980s the glamorous image of the West overshadowed the dull everyday socialist reality. Public opinion, disaffected with official ideology, immediately turned to mass sympathy toward the assumed Western democracies, which had been associated mostly with a high level of consumption. In 1990, public opinion, when faced with a choice between different Western patterns as the final goal of Russia's transformation, opted for the U.S. model by32 percent, whereas the German model gained only17 percent, and the Swedish only 14 percent.[9]

Benefiting from the weakness of the central power, which gradually lost control over political developments, Russia, the first among the republics, declared its sovereignty in the Soviet Union, thus opening the following "parade of sovereignty" that led eventually to the breakdown of the Soviet Union. Within a few days, in mid-June 1990, the multiparty system was legalized through amendments to Russia's constitution. Soon after, in August 1991, the failure of the coup d'état, attempted by top officials in Gorbachev's close circle in order to reverse the seemingly spontaneous process of decay, brought about the final collapse of the Soviet Union and realignment of the Russian political elite around Yeltsin, the rebellious former secretary of the Central Committee of the CPSU.[10] In order to eliminate the most powerful challenger and to free the way to consolidation of the new regime of power, Yeltsin immediately banned the CPSU in Russia and confiscated its property.

The fiasco of Gorbachev's reforms, creating "socialism with a human face," made it obvious that the possibilities for Russia's transformation on the socialist foundation were exhausted at that point, and that the new ruling regime, to justify its coming to power, had no alternative to offer to society as a new social project but the market economy and a multiparty political system.

MULTIPARTY SYSTEM UNDER YELTSIN'S "REGIME POLITICS," 1991–1998

After the elimination of the communist monopoly on power, the cleavage in the political space along the communists—anticommunists line lost its significance. As Russia acquired state sovereignty and established the institution of the presidency, such problems as economic reforms, distribution of powers between legislative and executive powers, and building of statehood and federalism advanced to the forefront in the alignment of parties. Since Russia had lost its Super Power status, and the entire system of sociocultural symbols that had developed during more than 70 years of communist rule had been destroyed, the search for a new national identity made for another political distinction.

The key to the strategy that brought victory to Yeltsin was the promise of a rapid transition to the market economy without any significant worsening of life conditions and the preservation of the former system of social protection. However, even the first step of the government headed by the market economist Egor Gaydar—liberalization of prices—immediately pushed the majority of the population below the poverty line as prices soared to more than 10 to 12 times their original levels. Privatization of state property, which was intended to create a large middle class of shareholders who would support reforms, failed. An abrupt reduction of state financing inflicted great damage to cultural, scientific, and educational institutions, where the initial enthusiasm for reforms had been the most intense. During the course of one year, the wild privatization produced extreme inequality in the distribution of national income—by 1993 the income of the top four percent exceeded that of the lowest percent by a factor of 300. This provoked a strong mass feeling of frustration directed against the government, which had promised to advance reforms without a drastic decline in the quality of life.[11]

The parties on the left began the first opposition to the new government policy. However, the "new left," represented primarily by the Socialist Party and the Socialist Party of Workers, could not take root in society and remained limited to small groups of intelligentsia that had neither political will nor organizational capacity. The "old left" advanced much more effectively. The Russian Communist Workers' Party (RCWP) that emerged a few months after the ban of CPSU called for the dismissal of the government, cancellation of "exorbitant" prices, cessation of "anti-people" privatization, "re-sovietization" of the economy, and the immediate reconstitution of the Soviet Union. In February 1992 the RCWP managed to gather between 40 and 100 thousand people for street demonstrations in Moscow.[12]

The popularity of the original endeavor to achieve democracy at the beginning of Gorbachev's period gradually changed into discreditation of the worn out democratic symbolism and slogans, and, moreover, of the political institutions of democracy. In 1992, 49 percent of Russians did not sympathize with any political party, while another 40 percent did not know anything about parties or did not identify themselves with any of them.[13] The traditional path for a party into national politics is to nominate candidates in elections and to campaign under its name. However, until December 1993, there had not been any elections of that kind in Russia. Even if a campaigning candidate adhered to a party, he had to present a personal "program." Among the 1,032 Peoples' Deputies of Russia in January 1993, only 195 declared their party affiliations. Newly formed parties actually remained mostly outside of the mainstream of public politics—elections and running for public offices—and were doomed therefore to intrinsic struggle with each other accompanied with endless maneuvering, changing platforms, or noisy splitting and merging because scandals were the only way to attract the attention of the mass media. The disillusionment of the people with the capability of parties to change the course of development for the better resulted in the disappearance or reduction in size of many democratic parties and groupings.[14] The communist wing also split into many parties.

In an attempt to gain support from the regions, Yeltsin chose a policy of "Take as much sovereignty as you want." On the basis of opposition to this policy, procommunist and anticommunist adherents of the strong state (statists) consolidated into the national-patriotic National Salvation Front and National Sobor (community). Actually, by the end of the first year of reforms, not one progovernment party remained.

In fact, parties performed at that time only two functions—the self-actualization of political entrepreneurs and intra-elite communication. The political process mirrored not as much confrontation between supporters and adversaries of the declared reforms, but, in no less degree, the struggle for power and resources among the old elite and the different fragments of unconsolidated new elites. In order to mobilize support they tried to present their intra-group contradictions to public opinion as being caused by social cleavages in the transitioning society.

Having no legal instruments to influence politics, parties could not affect the worsening relations between Yeltsin and the Supreme Soviet on the matter of power and asset distribution. Because the legal separation of powers was so poorly defined, the legislative branch assumed the right to amend the Constitution and, benefiting from this innovation, began to take charge of state property in an attempt to rein in the president and the government. On September 21, 1993, Yeltsin dismissed the Supreme Soviet and announced elections to the State Duma, the new Russian parliament, seeking a renewed corps of deputies. The Supreme Soviet as well as the head of the Constitutional Court judged this move as a coup d'état, and the political collision evolved into a direct clash. The resistance of the Supreme Soviet was suppressed by armed troops with about 150 officially avowed victims. However, the public showed a complete lack of interest in the fate of parliament[15]

Constitutional Design, 1993

Yeltsin announced the popular referendum on the new Constitution that would establish the new parliament on the same day as the election to this parliament, thus excluding a priori any possibility of a negative outcome. The Constitution declared formally: "Political plurality and the multiparty system shall be recognized in the Russian Federation."[16] In fact, the Constitution really secured Yeltsin's victory by calling for the winner-take-all electoral system and predefined the further path of the party system's development. The president had become the head of the state and guarantor of the Constitution with wide-ranging yet poorly defined powers. He received much more power than any other president in known presidential republics and, at the same time, was practically unaccountable to any political or representative institution.

The president now held all the executive power—he appointed and dismissed federal ministers, whereas the Duma not only lost any capacity to affect the government composition, but was deprived of its oversight functions. For example, the president could now terminate the powers of the Duma ahead of time if it rejected the nomination of a prime minister three times in a row. Although the Duma had the power to issue a vote of no-confidence in the government, this power was countered by the threat of dissolution. The Duma never attempted to resort to this constitutional provision—the self-preservation instinct of MPs in the majority always took precedence.[17] Even the Duma of 1995, where communists and their allies controlled nearly half of the votes, never crossed this dangerous line. The legislative power of the Duma was also limited by a double veto—either of the president or of the Council of the Federation.

Parties in the First Electoral Cycle

In accordance with presidential decree, half of the 450 MPs in the State Duma had to be elected in the federal electoral district in proportion to the number of votes cast for federal lists of candidates nominated by electoral associations (established in the form of a political party, an all-Russia public organization, or a public movement whose charter provides for participation in elections) or electoral blocs (groups of two and more electoral associations). Electoral associations were also eligible to field candidates in single-mandate districts (SMD) for the remaining half of the seats. Yeltsin expected to provide a stable propresidential majority in the Duma by giving half of the mandates to electoral association lists, since another presidential decree on the measures of state and public safety during the election campaign actually excluded from the elections those parties, public associations, and movements that had backed the Supreme Soviet in the conflict with the president. At the same time he hoped thereby to reinforce the eroding legitimacy of his presidency.

To be registered for the ballot, a public association (a party, an organization, or a movement) or a bloc of such associations had to gather 100,000 or more signatures in a very short time. For most aspirants this was very difficult without the support of federal and regional authorities. However, the task was simple for the recent prime minister, Egor Gaydar, who headed one propresidential bloc, "Russia's Choice," and for the acting deputy prime minister Sergei Shahrai, who, together with some leading members of the cabinet, created another electoral association—the Party of Russian Unity and Concord (PRES). These were the first so-called parties of power created by government officials to ensure legislative support for the president and the government. Party leaders decided on the order of the names on the lists, and thus on the chances of nominees to receive MP mandates. From 35 pretenders, the Central Election Commission (CEC) admitted only 13, and only 8 eventually overcame the five percent threshold established by presidential decree.

Four parties were among the winners—the Liberal-Democratic Party of Russia (LDPR), CPRF, the Agrarian Party of Russia (APR), and the Democratic Party of Russia (DPR), whereas the other four, namely Russia's Choice, the political movement Women of Russia, Bloc Yabloko (Apple), and PRES, were all electoral groupings assembled just before the elections. For instance, Women of Russia had been constructed from The Union of Russia's Women, The Association of Russia's Female Entrepreneurs, and The Union of the Navy's Women. The RCWP boycotted elections. See Table 2.1.

Table 2.1 Results of Parties That Won Elections to the State Duma, December 12, 1993

	Votes		*Seats*		
	List	*SMD*	*List*	*SMD*	*Total %*
Valid Votes	50.6	50.6			
Invalid Votes	3.7	4.0			
Total Votes (% of electorate)	54.3	54.6			
Liberal Democratic Party of Russia	21.4	2.7	59	5	14.3
Russia's Choice	14.5	6.3	40	30	15.6
CPRF	11.6	3.2	32	16	10.7
Women of Russia	7.6	0.5	21	2	5.1
Agrarian Party of Russia	7.4	5.0	21	12	7.3
Yabloko	7.3	3.2	20	3	5.1
Russian Unity and Concord	6.3	2.5	18	1	4.2
Democratic Party of Russia	5.1	1.9	14	1	3.3

Source: Russia Votes 2003/2004—a Joint Project of Centre for the Study of Public Policy, University Strathclyde, and VCIOM Analytic Agency. http://www.russiavotes.org/

Many experts predicted that no less than 60 percent of the votes would go to pro-presidential Russia's Choice and PRES. However, despite the enormous efforts of the presidential team, they received only 89 seats in total. The list of LDPR with 21.4 percent of the votes came in first. A posteriori political observers explained this surprisingly fair performance in large part by the deep frustration held by the population. The LDPR leader Vladimir Zhirinovskii dissociated himself from both "democratic" rivals, whom he accused of destroying Russia's Super Power status, the worsening living conditions, and creating political instability, as well as from the communists due to their odious heritage. Lavish with promises, he gained the votes of many socially deprived people, who did not want to support parties related to either the former or the current ruling regimes, but who could not find a positive choice among the given set of parties.

So, these constituent elections were not fully normal, not perfectly free and fair, and not really party elections either. The results of the referendum on the new Constitution, as well as the results of the elections to the State Duma, have never been officially publicized in full, causing some observers to question their fairness. Nevertheless, parties became parliamentary and, therefore, attractive to the political elite who were thereby motivated to compete for votes as well. At the same time the new constitution defined the dependent status of parties in the system of power and strictly limited their role. The Duma was made up of party factions voting for the most part according to consolidated party decisions.

Political Development, 1993–1995

Having deprived the Duma of any real power, Yeltsin nevertheless considered it as a personal threat. The Duma constantly underwent public humiliation at Yeltsin's hands. Yeltsin also tried, a number of times, to withdraw the proportional system of representation or to lessen the number of seats filled by the party lists, but the party factions did not concede their acquired privileges. Neither did they agree to lower the five percent minimum vote requirement for party lists to the one to three percent proposed by nonparliamentary parties, thus demonstrating "cartel solidarity."

This first post-Soviet Duma was elected for only half the regular term, and the anti-Yeltsin opposition hoped to acquire a majority in the normal election of 1995, especially as Russia's Choice disintegrated after Gaydar left the government, and PRES was losing its influence as well. To counter the opposition, Yeltsin "ordered"—as he declared publicly—"the creation of two centrist blocs prior to the beginning of the electoral campaign." The prime minister, Viktor Chernomyrdin, was commissioned to establish the right-centrist bloc, and the Duma speaker, Ivan Rybkin, who by that time had drifted away from the communist wing toward the president—the left-centrist bloc. (The mass media nicknamed the two blocs the "parties of the right and left hands of power"). The evident purpose of this combination of a strong propresidential party and a soft opposition party of the social-democratic species had been to force the hardliners under the five percent minimum barrier and thus create a compliant Duma.

In May 1995 a loose conglomeration of 32 collective members—from Russia's Sport Association Spartak to the Union of Oil and Gas Industrials—was registered under the name of the all-Russian popular-and-political association Nash Dom Rossiia—NDR (Our Home is Russia). The social base of this "party of power" encompassed numerous bureaucrats from the presidential, governmental, and regional administration, those in business who profited from tight links with the administration, and a portion of the state-dependent employees who still maintained their paternalist expectations in regard to the state but did not want the resurrection of communist rule. The chief of the Russian Federation (RF) government's administration became the head of the NDR Executive Committee. However, the creation of the left-centrist bloc that, in theory, should have included the Agrarian Party of Russia and the Federation of Independent Trade Unions, failed completely. With the CPRF having solid support of about 20 to 30 percent of the constituency on the left, there were no significant actors who would risk supporting a new leftist bloc.

By that time more than 80 parties of federal scale were registered. Moreover, the laws *On Basic Guarantees of Electoral Rights and the Right of Citizens of the Russian Federation to Participate in a Referendum* and *On the Election of Deputies of the State Duma of the Federal Assembly of the Russian Federation* made it possible for 260 public associations—trade unions, professional associations, artist's unions, and so on—to compete in elections. During August to September 1995 numerous electoral blocs were emerging and splitting, with politicians jumping from one list to another in search of more profitable positions.[18]

Eventually, 68 electoral associations and blocs applied to take part in the elections, and 43 of them managed to collect the required number of signatures. Electoral manifestos of candidates had much in common; all of them promising social security to pensioners, increased earnings to workers, savings to depositors, incomes to entrepreneurs, and increased power to the state. The manifestos of the national-communists and national-patriots appealed to the habitual stereotypes of Russia's exclusive *sobornost'* (traditional devotion to communitarianism of the Russian genre) and of the Super Power legacy.[19] All rivals demonstrated their opposition to the acting government. Even NDR, whose leader, as the head of the government from December 1992, shared the responsibility for the current social-economic situation, joined with critics of the executive power.

Ordinary people usually perceived particular ideological clichés associated with a particular party or its leader as the "party program." In addition, voters often assigned their own beliefs to their favorite party. So, for instance, 11 percent of CPRF partisans, while answering the following question in a poll: "What political system do you consider to be the best?," indicated "Western democracy." At the same time, 21 percent of the right-centrist Yabloko voters, mostly intelligentsia and small entrepreneurs, chose "The Soviet system before 1991."[20] The public's knowledge about the basics of democracy and market economy was rather confused. Thus, people might approve of a transition to a market economy and, at the same time, favor rigid state control over prices.

Unlike the first electoral campaign, this second one was conducted by professionals rather than by party bureaucrats. Campaign managers and consultants with expensive electoral know-how as well as polls were widely employed by the main stakeholders. NDR gained obvious advantages for its candidates, such as the information, communication, and transportation resources of the federal and regional administration. The financial resources and access to the mass media that had been controlled mostly by the authorities since 1993[21] proved to be significant factors of its success.

Of the 43 parties, electoral associations, and blocs competing for the proportional representation (PR) half of the seats, 35 were entirely new for voters. Only four overcame the five-percent threshold, and these four gained in total 50.5 percent of the votes. CPRF, LDPR, and Yabloko succeeded in maintaining their former position in the Duma. Between 1993 and 1995, CPRF increased in size by 1.5 to 2 times and strengthened its image as a "genuine" communist party. LDPR won support from lumpenized layers of the population, playing on the traditional Russian negative attitude to politics that opposes "Power and Us."[22] The propresidential Russia's Choice was replaced by the propresidential NDR, which placed third with 10.13 percent of votes, a rather modest result, given efforts and resources spent by the administration. On the whole, party factions of winners acquired two-thirds of the mandates, leaving independent SDM deputies no chance to play any significant role in the process of legislation. The election demonstrated the failure of the attempt to reanimate the social-democratic idea. All the political groupings of social-democratic orientation combined gained in total only one to two percent of the votes because the socialist niche in the political arena was occupied by CPRF, whose partisans aspire to the restoration of the system of state-socialism. The attempt to mobilize the electorate under the banners of Christian democracy also failed: The Christian-Democratic Union—Christians of Russia gathered only 0.28 percent of the vote. See Table 2.2.

The presidential elections of 1996 concluded the first post-Soviet electoral cycle. They were not really party elections where voters could choose between alternative party programs and candidates. The election campaign was designed so that in its final stage voters faced a dilemma: to cast their ballot either for Yeltsin, thereby preserving some hope for further positive changes, or for the CPRF's leader Gennady Zyuganov, which would mean turning back to the past and risking an unpredictable outcome. The business and political elite that had emerged under Yeltsin did not want to risk its own wellbeing. It thus expended immense efforts to back him, in spite of the fact that at the beginning of the electoral campaign he enjoyed the support of only six percent of voters. Much of the population also preferred to maintain what they had, even if they felt nostalgic for times of state social security and scant, yet guaranteed incomes, as well as the privilege of identifying themselves as citizens of a Super Power. In the end, voter turnout was 68.8 percent of the population, and 54.4 percent of the turnout was in favor of Yeltsin. Zyuganov received 40.31 percent of

Table 2.2 Election Results for Parties That Won Elections to the State Duma, December 17, 1995

	Votes (in percent)		*Seats*		
	List	*SMD*	*List*	*SMD*	*Total %*
Valid Votes	64.4	62.9			
Invalid Votes	1.3	1.4			
Total Votes (% of electorate)	65.7	64.3			
CPRF	22.3	12.6	99	58	34.9
Liberal Democratic Party of Russia	11.2	5.4	50	1	11.3
Our Home is Russia	10.1	5.5	45	10	12.2
Yabloko	6.9	3.2	31	14	10.0

Source: Russia Votes 2003/2004—a Joint Project of Centre for the Study of Public Policy, University Strathclyde, and VCIOM Analytic Agency. http://www.russiavotes.org/

votes, and 4.9 percent of ballots were cast 'Against all'.[23] CPRF did not risk disputing the official election results, although it had strong reasons to do so. Evidently CPRF remembered the lesson of 1993.

Socioeconomic Context and Mass Political Attitudes

On the eve of the 1995 election to the State Duma, 47 percent of Russia's population did not feel capable of adapting to the new economic system, and another 28 percent failed to answer whether they could find a place for themselves therein.[24] The long-lasting inability or unwillingness of the regime to limit the social burden caused by the economic transition alienated people from the authorities. In mid-1994 the Institute of Sociology of Parliamentarism found that the most frequent feelings of Russians in regard to authorities were as follows:

Mistrust, fear	73 percent
Disregard	60 percent
Offense, opposition	63 percent
Apathy	50 percent

In answering the question "Who executes the power?" respondents indicated:

Criminal groupings, mafia	43 percent
Government	13 percent
Bureaucracy and state administration	30 percent
Federal Assembly	6 percent
President	24 percent
People	2 percent

Alienation permeated the entire sphere of politics. It was found that up to 40 percent of the adult population had no strong political beliefs, and that every fifth person was completely apathetic with respect to political developments in the country. A considerable part of the electorate was disaffected from political participation due to mistrust toward political parties, leaders, and ideas.[25] These findings were generally confirmed by monitoring data obtained just before the election.[26]

TRANSFORMATION OF THE PARTY SYSTEM IN THE "MANAGING DEMOCRACY" UNDER PUTIN

Parties in the Second Electoral Cycle

The second electoral cycle encompassed elections to the State Duma on December 19, 1999 and the presidential elections of March 26, 2000. Actually, it started with the financial catastrophe and political crisis of 1998, and the subsequent rapid changes of prime ministers. Elections to the State Duma were considered by main candidates to the office of the president as being crucial for the presidential elections. The high stakes of the elections ensured that electoral campaigns would be harsh and ruthless.

After Yeltsin dismissed Chernomyrdin and failed to reinstate him, Our Home is Russia lost any attractiveness for the regional politicians and federal bureaucrats who had made the party significant but now felt out of the game. Political crisis, multiplied by the default of August 1998, led to the weakening of the Kremlin. Once the "party of power" lost control over political developments, initiative transferred to the regional bureaucracy. Governors began to desert Our Home is Russia for Fatherland, a new political movement that Moscow mayor Yuri Luzhkov, a presumed candidate for the office of president, created on the eve of the forthcoming parliamentary elections. In August 1999, Fatherland and the second governors' block All Russia, headed by the president of Tatarstan and the governor of Saint Petersburg, merged under the popular politician, Evgenii Primakov. One of the key points of his political program supported the redistribution of power, namely, the transition from a presidential to a presidential-parliamentary republic.

The Kremlin responded to that threat to its power. In August 1999, Yeltsin appointed Putin, the director of the Federal Security Service (FSB), as the head of the government. Soon after, public opinion was shocked by the Chechen invasion in Dagestan and a number of explosions that killed numerous victims in some of Russia's major cities, including Moscow. The invasion and explosions created a strong popular demand for personal security and order, as well as for vengeance. The default of 1998 and concurrent blossoming of organized crime that, by 1999, controlled more than 40 percent of private business, 60 percent of state-owned enterprises, and from 50 to 80 percent of banks, further strengthened the popular sentiment.[27]

Putin's resolute antiterrorist actions quickly brought him growing popularity. The visible comparison of this young and determined politician to the infirm and discredited Yeltsin also worked in Putin's favor. Still, in September, Putin trailed all other presidential contenders in the polls.

A little more than two months before the elections, the presidential administration created its own stakeholder in the run for the State Duma, the interregional movement Unity/Bear (Medved'), led by Sergei Shoigu, minister for emergency situations and civil defense. Unity had no detailed program and was assembled from several minor political groupings. In reality, not one of these minor groupings had a chance to win more than one percent of the total votes if running as an independent actor. Putin publicly articulated his support for Unity, and the bloc fully profited from this publicity. Its rating rose along with the growth of Putin's reputation. The election campaign of Unity was neither programmatic nor ideological, its main mottoes being *"Strong state"* and *"Struggle against corruption and criminality,"* and its most sound raison d'être being *"We are the party of Putin."*

Unlike during the campaign of 1995, the Kremlin was wrestling for power not with the communists, but with another clan of the same state bureaucracy. Since there were no ideological divergences between the two rivals, the main factors of electoral success became "administrative resources" and PR technologies. The Kremlin's strategy was to discredit the Fatherland—All Russia (OVR) leaders. The attack was extremely brutal, often bordering on and frequently overstepping the bounds of acceptable practices.[28] Possessing the nearly unlimited financial resources and backing of the presidential administration, the media support of the two dominant federal TV channels (ORT and RTR) controlled by the Kremlin, and the intellectual support of an experienced analytical center, Unity won the information war against Fatherland—All Russia. Under the rigid pressure of the Kremlin, most regional heads changed their support from OVR to Unity.

In addition to these two main rivals, the CEC registered in total 26 participants for elections, six of which gained seats in the Duma. See Table 2.3.

The CPRF did not significantly change its electoral strategy and not only preserved its former constituency, but increased it from 15,432,963 to 16,196,024 votes. Yabloko and LDPR also maintained their former electoral strategies. The head of the LDPR propaganda department defined its constituency as follows: "Our voters are the mob, street dregs of society (lumpen), they are ordinary people. Furthermore, [they are] exceptionally russkiye (Russian)."[29]

Unity came close behind the CPRF with an outcome that no other new party had been able to achieve during the last decade. The governors' bloc Fatherland—All Russia trailed far behind. Union of Right Forces (Soyuz

Table 2.3 Election Results for Parties That Won Elections to the State Duma, December 19, 1999

	Votes (in percent)		*Seats*		
	List	*SMD*	*List*	*SMD*	*Total %*
Valid Votes	60.5	60.3			
Invalid Votes	1.2	1.3			
Total Votes (% of electorate)	61.7	61.6			
CPRF	24.3	13.4	67	46	25.1
Unity	23.3	2.1	64	9	16.2
Fatherland—All Russia	13.3	8.6	37	31	15.1
Union of Right Forces	8.5	3.0	24	5	6.1
Zhirinovsky Bloc (LDPR)	6.0	1.5	17	0	3.8
Yabloko	5.9	5	16	4	4.4

Source: Russia Votes 2003/2004—a Joint Project of Centre for the Study of Public Policy, University Strathclyde, and VCIOM Analytic Agency. http://www.russiavotes.org/

Table 2.4 Distribution of Seats among Party Factions and Deputy Groups

Party factions and deputy groups	*Seats*
CPRF	88
Agro-industrial Group (pro-communist)	42
Unity	83
Peoples Deputy Group (Narodnyi deputat, pro Kremlin)	58
OVR	48
Regions of Russia Group (pro-OVR)	41
Union of Right Forces (liberal)	32
Yabloko (social-liberal)	21
Zhirinovsky's Bloc (nationalist-patriot)	16

Source: McFaul, Petrov, Ryabov 2000: 394

Pravykh Sil—SPS) emerged on the right wing and encompassed different political groups adhering to the economic liberalism of the most unconditional breed. Unlike Yabloko, SPS declared full general support to Putin's policy, and particularly, to the military solution of the Chechen crisis. Profiting from the benevolence of the presidential administration and federal TV channels, SPS was able to gather 8.5 percent of votes.

The elections significantly altered the alignment in the State Duma, creating the composition illustrated in Table 2.4.

Once in the Duma, Unity transformed itself into a legal party. A top functionary of Unity, Sergey Popov, declared that 95 percent of the party's views mirrored those of the president, and that the party sought to help the president create an efficient system of executive power in Russia.[30] To further increase its supremacy over OVR, Unity, in spite of the customary principle of proportional distribution of committees among factions and groups, concluded a separate agreement with the CPRF, which remained neutral to the Kremlin's fight for control over power. This arrangement gave the CPRF the post of speaker and one third of the committees, while depriving OVR an appropriate share of the portfolios.[31] Some analysts compared this union to the Molotov-Ribbentrop Pact.[32]

Both the political and business elite accepted the Kremlin's victory. Many politicians and political groupings, including those who in the past had pretended to play "party of power," and those who struggled against Unity in the recent elections, sought to adhere to it now. Among them were Fatherland—All Russia, NDR, PRES, Russian Socialist Party, and the National-Patriotic Party.[33] Many of the regional leaders who had recently supported OVR hurried to demonstrate their loyalty to the Kremlin by creating local branches of Unity in their regions.

The Kremlin had successfully wrested back full control over the fragmented political elite on the eve of the presidential election. State-owned mass media and particularly TV channels were actually blocked for Putin's rare opponents in the election campaign.[34] The dominance of the Kremlin was convincingly confirmed three months later when Putin prematurely won elections in the first round with 52.9 percent of the votes. His real rivals were knocked out of the race beforehand during the elections to the State Duma.

The second electoral cycle of 1999–2000 completed the 11-year-long phase of Russia's transition to the new political regime that Lilia Shevtsova, a prominent Russian political observer, characterized as the "authoritarian-bureaucratic" regime.[35] The authors of a detailed analysis of the 1999–2000 electoral cycle concluded: "The question which needs to be asked now is whether any aspect of democracy has taken root and will survive."[36]

Putin's Reform of the Multiparty System

In fact, no elections in Russia were carried out according to standardized rules. However, the scale, significance, and results of the changes between 1999 and 2003 allow one to speak about a reform of the party system that in essence developed in Yeltsin's "democracy of disorder."

Putin inherited from his predecessor a grave legacy, including, as he mentioned four years later in his Speech to Campaign Supporters,[37] the degradation of state power. Hence, one of the foremost priorities of his internal policy during his first term in office became the consolidation of the "vertical (structure) of federal executive power" that aimed to overcome disorder, enhance the administration of the country, and bring stability. This goal supposed the further concentration of power provisions in the hands of the president and the strengthening of control over all the actors in the political arena—federal and regional bureaucracy, political elites, business elites, trade unions' establishments, and the independent mass media. The goal and the traditional authoritarian means that Putin preferred to use to achieve it determined the further development of the party system.

After Putin's victory, adherence to Unity, the party under the patronage of the president, became a sort of lottery without risk of loss for politicians and businessmen alike. Just after the presidential elections, the leaders of OVR came to the decision to merge into Unity, thus creating a dominating super-party that would obtain a strong majority in the next Duma. By the end of 2001, the founding congress declared the emergence of this new party, Unity and Fatherland or Unified Russia (Yedinaya Rossiya [YeR]). "We are going to build a mass party as a pillar that the president can lean on," declared the head of its General Council.[38]

Even before merging into one party, factions of Unity and OVR, in cooperation with the pro-Kremlin MP's group Peoples' Deputy and the OVR satellite MP's group Russia's Regions, formed the Coordination Council in the acting Duma. The total membership of the Council outnumbered that of CPRF with its left-wing ally Agrarian Group by 234 to 127.[39] By this move, the Kremlin, for the first time in post-Soviet history, obtained stable control over the process of voting in the Duma.

The alliance with CPRF had been necessary to enact the laws strengthening Putin's "vertical (axis) of power." Having got what it wanted from this pact, the Kremlin did not need it any more. In April 2002 the Coordination Council initiated a campaign aimed at redistributing the Duma's portfolios, this time at the expense of the CPRF. This move provoked a serious crisis in the CPRF top layer when the Duma speaker, Gennady Seleznev, who had been nominated to this post by CPRF, together with some other heads of committees from CPRF, left the party in order to preserve their offices in the Duma.

In June 2001 the Duma adopted the Kremlin-backed Federal Law *On Political Parties* that defined what kind of organization would be considered a party. To qualify as a political party an organization must have no fewer than 10,000 registered members and branches with no fewer than 100 members each in at least 45 of the regions constituting the Russian Federation. Evidently, only those who enjoy the strong patronage of authorities and support of business can afford to launch such a huge and expensive venture. The law forbids the creation of parties advocating professional, racial, national, or religious interests, and parties consisting of persons of one profession as well. The most recent amendment to the Law *On the Elections of Deputies of the State Duma* made parties the only kind of public association entitled to participate in elections independently or in election blocs with other parties.

The law on parties, the amendment to the law on the election of deputies of the State Duma, and amendments to other electoral laws—*On Basic Guarantees of Electoral Rights and the Right of Citizens of the RF to Participate in a Referendum* and *On the Election of the President of the Russian Federation*—shaped a new legal framework for the activities of parties. These laws raised the minimum vote requirement for party lists in Duma elections up to seven percent (effective in 2007), thus giving further advantages to the few large parties. Parties that have factions in the Duma acquire privileges over outsiders in that they do not need to collect signatures or to mortgage money as requirements for participation in elections. They also are exempt from the requirement to collect the two million signatures needed in order to nominate a candidate for the office of the president.

Equally important is the fact that no less than half of the seats (the upper border is not limited) in regional legislatures shall now be elected in proportion to votes cast for lists of candidates nominated by parties, that is, by *federal* parties, for no regional parties are legally admitted. Therefore, regional political elites are deprived of a significant instrument of influence on politics. To take part in elections and to be represented in the legislatures of different levels, they are now compelled to join a federal party and to obey the decisions of its central leadership in Moscow, which is tantamount to the dissolution of regional parties. Many among the regional political and business elites naturally chose United Russia as the most attractive option. Thus, the reform significantly strengthens the public and instrumental role of parties in politics in that they now have the monopoly on making up the federal and regional legislatures. At the same time, the reform made the registration of a party more complicated; it strengthened administrative control over party performance and over the sources of its income. For those who meet the requirements, annual financial support from the federal budget is provided, on the basis of the results of their participation in the last elections—to be eligible, parties or blocs must receive no less than three percent of the list or of the presidential vote, or win no fewer than 12 seats in single-member districts. Those that do not participate in the elections or fail to show significant results during five consecutive years are subject to liquidation. As a whole, this reform intensifies the control of the federal center over political parties and, in this way, over the legislative branch of power.

Elections to the State Duma, 2003: First Results of the Reform of the Party System

By mid-2002 YeR and CPRF were the most significant parties. However, YeR, led by Interior Minister Boris Gryzlov, was profiting from Putin's steady high rating. CPRF, on the contrary, was gradually losing its leftist electorate and potential to oppose the Kremlin. The Duma's peripheral position in the political system did not permit CPRF, or any other party, to work on its program even if it so desired. Ceaseless compromises of the communist faction with the Kremlin on the budget and other socially vital laws, as well as the disappointing results of CPRF activities in the "red belt" regions where it occupies key offices, contributed to the shift of state-paternalist expectations of those moderate constituents who cannot adapt to the ongoing transformation, from CPRF to the "party of Putin," of the "president of hope."

By the beginning of the election campaign of 2003, 44 parties met the legal requirements of the new law on political parties. However, a loophole included in the electoral law governing the 2003 State Duma elections allowed public associations to compete alongside the registered parties. Finally 19 parties and 4 electoral blocs took part in the elections.

Not only YeR but many other parties seeking seats in the Duma declared centrist positions and manifested unconditional loyalty to president Putin, since this position not only spared them the necessity of creating a proper program of their own, but also inspired expectations to deserve his benevolence.

The Electoral campaign was to a large extent shaped by the YuKOS (one of the most efficient oil companies) affair. When in October 2003 the General Prosecutor's Office detained Mikhail Khodorkovskii, the head of one of the most efficient oil companies, most politicians held their tongues, waiting for Putin's comments since it was evident that no action of that scale could be performed against his will. Having heard the message sent by the president, most parties based their mobilizing campaigns on the struggle against the oligarchs (typically understood to be moneyed businessmen who are assumed to get their capital through unfair means and use it to manipulate politics). They promised to give back to the people the money stolen from them through the oligarchs' exploitation of natural resources, to deprive the oligarchs of their incomes, and to spend this money for broad social programs.

The general populist anti-oligarchy climate of the campaign limited the potential of liberal parties, which, particularly in the case of YuKOS, advocated for the transparency of the rules of the game for both business and government. In addition, the personal ambitions of the leaders of the two liberal parties, Union of Right Forces and Yabloko, prevented them from creating a united right-wing electoral bloc. Union of Right Forces decided this time not to apply to the president for support and to take an independent position that they thought would give them no less then eight percent of the votes. Nevertheless, they abstained from a serious critique of the president and chose the strategy of winning over members of Yabloko's constituency. The first three names on the party list of Union of Right Forces included Anatoly Chubais, the most unpopular promarket politician, connected in public opinion with fraudulent privatization and constantly rising prices of public utilities. As a result, both parties lost all but a handful of SMD seats.

On the other hand, the information campaign against the oligarchs and YuKOS heavily weakened the positions of the communists. The mass media broadcast information revealing that YuKOS was a financial supporter not only of Union of Right Forces and Yabloko, but also of CPRF—and that places at the top of CPRF's list were contracted for oligarchs, as well as that CPRF had close contacts with the disgraced oligarch Boris Berezovskii. As a result, the share of the seats occupied by the Communist Party decreased from 113 seats in the 1999 election to 52 seats in the 2003 Duma.

Subsequently, both right- and left-wing oppositions in party alignment were weakened, and their votes shifted partially to the centrist United Russia, the "party of the President"; partially to LDPR, seeking support under the motto "We are for poor men, we are for Russians (russkie)"; and partially to Motherland (People's Patriotic Union), an electoral bloc of national-patriotic orientation created in Autumn 2003. Later, in February 2004, one of its leaders, Dmitry Rogozin, calling upon Motherland's adherents to vote for Putin in the presidential elections of 2004, attributed the bloc's success to the support of the president.

United Russia was, as in the previous elections, publicly endorsed by President Putin and refused to take part in electoral debates with the other competitors, evidently fearing it could only do harm to its high rating.

Table 2.5 Results of Elections to the State Duma, December 7, 2003

	Votes	*Seats*		
Total votes 55.75 %	*% List vote*	*List seats*	*SMD seats*	*% Total seats*
United Russia	37.57	120	102	49.3
Communist Party	12.61	40	12	11.6
Liberal Democrats	11.45	36	0	8.0
Motherland–People's Patriotic Union	9.02	29	8	8.2
People's Party	1.18	0	17	3.8
Yabloko	4.30	0	4	0.9
Union of Right Forces	3.97	0	3	0.7
Agrarian Party	3.64	0	2	0.4
Other parties	11.56	0	6	1.3
Independents	—	—	68	15.1
Against all	4.70	—	34	0.7

Source: Russia Votes 2003/2004—a Joint Project of Centre for the Study of Public Policy, University Strathclyde, and VCIOM Analytic Agency. http://www.russiavotes.org/

The outcome of the elections exceeded the expectations of the Kremlin. See Table 2.5.

United Russia received 222 seats compared to 141 acquired by Unity and Fatherland-All Russia combined in 1999. This success inspired 78 SMD deputies, nominated for elections by parties that had failed in the Federal district (People's Party, Union of Right Forces, Yabloko, and others) and independents, to join United Russia factions, thus increasing its strength to 304 members, that is, to a constitutional three-fourths majority. The faction members headed all 29 committees and occupied most of the deputy head positions as well. The faction organized into four groups, thus acquiring four seats instead of one on the Duma Council, which organizes parliamentary business.

The Deputy Head of the faction claimed in an interview that its members must vote in the Duma according to decisions taken by the faction.[40] The idea of the imperative mandate is very popular in the Duma establishment. This makes the Duma a sort of club of speakers, leaders of party factions, and MPs' groups who haggle over all important decisions personally, in fact, deputies do not participate in the decision making process but only make out the decisions taken by the leaders of party factions and the MPs groups.[41] Such an arrangement facilitates the Kremlin's control over the Duma's activities, because the results of the voting are often the results of bargaining done at the "zero hearing" level—directly between the presidential administration and these "nobles."

The parties that failed in the 2003 elections lost more than merely one electoral campaign. In the new electoral legal framework, it is much more difficult for them to return to the Duma without the support of the Kremlin.

A public opinion poll that was conducted by WZIOM-A Analytical Service less then two months before the elections revealed that 70 percent of Russians were convinced that the election could not change their lives for the better, and 59 percent doubted its fairness.[42] CPRF and Yabloko have claimed that the results of the elections were falsified. However, the Kremlin did not seem to need any outright fraudulent elections, because the relations between the system of power and the party system are constructed so that it is enough for the president to "quietly tilt the electoral playing field to ensure victory."[43]

Three months later, on March 14, 2004, Putin ran for a second term in office and won the presidential elections in the first round with 71.2 percent of the votes For and 3.46 percent Against all. Given that the CPRF and liberal parties failed in the Duma elections, and there were no real contestants, the outcome of the presidential election was predetermined. Therefore, the Kremlin's main problem was to ensure the turnout of no less than half of the voters included in the voter lists. Otherwise the election would have to be declared as not having taken place. The enormous efforts of the Kremlin, including administrative pressure on voters, mobilizing a campaign via state-controlled mass media, and even repeating appeals of the churchmen, brought a 64.3 percent turnout.[44]

WHAT IS THE MAIN RAISON D'ÊTRE OF THE PARTY SYSTEM IN POST-SOVIET POLITICS?

At present, the party system has become an indispensable feature of Russia's political system. At the same time, it is evident that neither Gorbachev's perestroika, nor Yeltsin's "regime system" has given rise to parties functioning as an interrelated institution that links together the constituency and the government.

Historically, power in Russia has always been personified and concentrated in the hands of one person, either a monarch or the CPSU General Secretary, in the Soviet period. It has always been self-sufficient, alienated from and independent of society. After a short interval between 1991 and 1993, the Constitution of the Russian Federation has brought post-Soviet Russia back to this traditional monocentric model of power. (Yu. Pivovarov, a well-known Russian scholar, identifies a very close correspondence between the *Constitution of the Russian Federation*, 1993, and the *Main Laws of the Russian Empire*, signed by the Tsar in 1906). In this model, the president is the dominant figure of politics, since the separation of powers is even de jure unbalanced, and de facto all branches of power serve as instrument of control in the hands of the president. There is no place left for either a genuine parliament endowed with powers equal to that of the executive branch, or for independent efficient political parties. Even those that are created by the Kremlin and call themselves *parties of power* are actually *parties under power.*

Since the Constitution makes no provision that new governments must be approved by either a parliamentary majority or a parliamentary coalition, which would thus take responsibility for its performance, such crucial rational choice criteria as the socioeconomic aftermath of the party's governing activities during its term in office cannot be employed. The connection between the outcome of voting and the alternation of current policy, as well as of the everyday life conditions of the voters, is highly questionable . Therefore voting in elections to the State Duma has largely become an empty ritual. When electoral success gives a party no chance to act upon its program, the programmatic component vanishes from the electoral contest of parties. This makes elections nothing more than a kind of competition of electoral projects, designed by different PR agencies on a contractual basis, under the control of the Kremlin. Moreover, when a group's ideological motivation for adherence to a party decreases, it is replaced with material incentives, thereby making party membership for an individual a sort of business venture.

In 2002, only five percent of the population assumed that the Duma was passing laws and decisions that are vital for the nation, whereas 27 percent believed that even if the Duma discusses useful acts, it is not in the position to make them work, and 50 percent were convinced that the Duma was mostly occupied with futile quarrels with the government.[45]

The peripheral place of the Duma in the political system determines the steadily marginal rank of parties in public opinion. In late 2000, 55 percent of respondents judged parties as being of no use for Russia, and the opposite opinion was shared by only 25 percent.[46]

Despite having granted the parties in parliament a rather significant public status and material privileges, the Kremlin did not relinquish any considerable share of power, and thus created a vicious circle. Without sizeable power, parties cannot establish stable linkages with constituencies, and without their support parties cannot play an independent role in the political system. The law on political parties deprived the party system of even the abstract possibility of developing along such lines of actually existing social stratification as professional, racial, national, religious, and regional differentiation, and representing the interests of appropriate social groups in the political process. Given that ideological cleavage that structured the emerging party system after the collapse of communist rule is exhausted, and that the trade union movement, which gave birth to social-democratic parties in Western Europe, is weak and dependent on the government,[47] the question arises, whose interests, with the exception of those in power, the party system is eligible to represent.

At the same time parliamentary status is extremely attractive for a party and its leaders as a crucial factor of collective and personal survival since it opens access to state resources (administrative, financial, informational, communicational, transportation, etc). It also makes it possible to hold on to the attention of the mass media, the loss of which means virtual (and physical) death for a party, since it has usually no other involvement in public life worth mentioning.

So, parties have much more to worry about with regard to their relations with the Kremlin, which holds control over regional authorities, electronic mass media, financial flows, and distribution of resources, than with regard to their constituencies. Even for CPRF and LDPR, opposition to the government serves mainly as an electoral brand, inasmuch as since 1995 both parties have mastered the tactics of compromising. When voting on the budget, no confidence in the government, or any other crucial issues, these parties simply appoint a sufficient number of members to cast their votes contrary to the officially declared position of the faction.[48] This suits the Kremlin perfectly, for they are thus able to attract and buffer protest attitudes—each of different layers of the population—that otherwise would go over to more radical organizations.

Given that expenses on election campaigns are steadily growing, the electoral success of a party depends heavily on its external financial sources. At the same time, the active involvement of the state in economics in the form of export quotas, licenses, particularized benefits, state guarantees, and so on, up to direct investments in business, in the absence of a legal procedure of lobbying, inevitably generates corruption and makes the Duma factions that are positioned close to the real centers of decision making as vulnerable to corruption as the state bureaucracy. When the Duma passes a law, the second rank in the system of priorities belongs to the interests of business while the first encompasses those of the Kremlin.[49] For more than a decade, the parties in the Duma have not passed any bills on lobbying.

The tightly interwoven institutional framework and mass political culture have shaped the nature of the post-Soviet party system in Russia, and it seems impossible to separate the cause from the consequence. However, at this point, it is worthwhile to present some polling data on the dominant political values, attitudes toward different political institutions, political participation, and electoral behavior, since they can be helpful in understanding what allows the powerful to shape parties according to their will.

One of the main impetuses of mass political participation in established democracies is the protection and promotion of individual and group interests before the government. In a nationwide poll in 1998, Russians were asked what means they use to protect their interests. In response, 36.5 percent indicated none, 32.2 percent said personal links, 18.7 percent admitted bribing, and only 1.4 percent cited involvement in party activities.[50] When there are no helpful political means to influence the ruling power, the stimulus for and the active interest in political participation disappear. According to an investigation by Russian Public Opinion and Market Research (ROMIR), nearly three-fourths of Russian people consider themselves as "passive observers of political life," whereas the active part does not exceed seven percent. Only 0.7 percent adhere to any party or political organization, and only 0.3 percent are actually engaged in their activities.[51]

Even if participation in elections is the most frequent form of political participation, voting, for many people, is simply an inherited custom. So, according to the VCIOM poll, habit was the main incentive to take part in presidential elections in 2004 for 45 percent of voters, whereas only 25 percent have demonstrated willingness to support a particular candidate.[52]

The political preferences of voters are highly volatile. Thus, in the presidential elections of 1996, 60 percent of voters in Tatarstan cast votes for Zyuganov in the first round, and the same 60 percent voted for Yeltsin in the second round. Twelve to fourteen percent of voters decided for whom to cast their vote in the last week before the day of election.

In 2002 VCIOM asked respondents in a national sample to rate 20 political actors according to their impact on the life of Russia. They placed the president on top. The State Duma got seventeenth place, and political parties the next to last place, just before trade unions (twentieth).[53] Hence, it is quite natural that 49 percent of Russians in 1999 were convinced that "Having a strong leader who does not have to bother with parliament and elections" is a "very good" or "good" way of governing the country.[54] People in Russia are much more worried about poverty and corruption than about the state of democracy. Only two percent of Russians have named development of democratic institutions (free mass media, popular associations) and political freedoms of citizens as a priority for Putin's second term in office, whereas 42 and 41 percent pointed out poverty and corruption in government as the main problem to be solved.[55]

In his speech to campaign supporters on the eve of the 2004 elections, Putin declared the need for "... civilized political competition in order to develop our state. Influential, large political parties that have authority and enjoy the trust of our citizens should be the main support in this work."[56] However, the reform of the party system and everyday practices of the presidential administration during his first term in office have made the party system one of various political technologies that are applied to stabilize the ruling regime. The party system is servicing the government by contributing to its formal legitimacy, by channeling protest attitudes and public demands into the ballot, and by maintaining control over the power ambitions of different business and bureaucratic clans. This system turned out to be efficient in stabilizing the regime of manageable democracy.

In party democracies, parties were created by maturing civil society and gradually changed the nature of power. Their raison d'être in the political system and their indispensability is that they do have power and are the main mechanism that sets in motion representative democracy. The Russian multiparty system has been shaped by the "regime system" in the atomized, post-Soviet society. The regime modified emerging protoparties so as to preserve the self-sufficient autocratic nature of power. Both parties of power and parties in opposition are assigned the role of simulacra of the political institution of democracy.

This conclusion seems self-evident. Unfortunately, there is no theory that would be helpful in the search for an answer as to whether any other party system might develop in the context of post-Soviet Russia, a country with a communist structural legacy.

There is another question waiting for an answer. Is it accurate today to describe and measure political development in Russia with the norms of democracy, elaborated by the culture of modernity for industrial societies, particularly when the very notion of democracy as a reference point of development is dimming in the post-industrial context?

PART II

Slavic States and Moldova

CHAPTER 3

The Peculiarities of Party Politics in Belarus, Moldova, and Ukraine: Institutionalization or Marginalization?

Andrei Tarnauski

INTRODUCTION

The Newly Independent States (NIS) that appeared after the collapse of the Soviet Union faced the necessity of creating their own democratic political systems in the first months of independence. Political parties, one of the key elements of systems of this kind, formed at a very high speed, and the multiparty system became common in all the post-Soviet states during the first years of their independent development.

If we try to analyze the political parties in Belarus, Moldova, and Ukraine on the basis of one methodological approach (institutional, structural, behavioral, neo-institutional), we can get the impression that a constructive process of democracy formation and the institutionalization of political parties has been taking place. It is possible to develop models, calculate coefficients, even support some hypotheses, for example, about the factors of the institutionalization of political parties, and so on. However, a more intense analysis of the context in which the political parties have been emerging, and of the peculiarities of the political and economic systems formed in the region, show that the parties formed here differ significantly from the parties formed not only in Western Europe, but also in Central and Eastern Europe. They are "torn away" from the voters and are able neither to protect nor to express the voters' interests. The new political systems were formed on the basis of the Soviet system that had been developing for dozens of years. The context in which the new democratic political institutions function—the elite's political culture, the methods of state governing and public control, the mentality of the population, and the economic system in general—are also based on that earlier system. As a result, political parties appeared much earlier than favorable conditions for their effective activity. The structural and institutional context greatly influenced the formation of the political parties. At present, in some of the countries of study, the unfavorable context is still determining the nature of political parties; in other countries, however, parties have been increasing their influence. Which condition prevails is determined by the specifics of the political regimes and the peculiarities of constitutional legislation.

Subsequent chapters, devoted to the analysis of the political parties in Belarus, Moldova, and Ukraine, cover in detail the peculiarities of how each state's parties function in every state. Here we focus on a comparative overview of the contexts in which the political parties of the countries of this subregion have developed, without which it is hard to understand the political processes that have taken place in each.

POLITICAL PROCESS IN BELARUS, MOLDOVA, AND UKRAINE: COMMON FEATURES AND COUNTRY SPECIFICS

Before the collapse of the USSR, Belarus, Moldova, and Ukraine were comparatively well-off parts of the country: a significant portion of the industrial potential of the Soviet Union was concentrated here, agriculture was relatively well developed, the level of education of the population was high, and there were no open ethnic or national conflicts. Transformation trajectories of the countries were not very distinct until the period of 1993–1998, which was characterized by deep economic changes and the active development of political systems in the Newly Independent States. At that time, differences started to appear, determined both by the influence of system factors and accidental, sometimes fatal coincidences. As a result of the influence of a complex of economic, political, social-psychological, and personal variables, the political systems of these countries gained a definite configuration, and their further development has been taking place to a large extent in correlation with this internal logic.

Belarus

The year 1996 was crucial for Belarus, since its further political development was determined when the conflict between the president and the parliament ended with a change to the Constitution in the president's favor and an increase of authoritarian tendencies in the country.

The predominance of state-owned enterprises, the preservation of the ineffective kolkhoz system and a structure of industrial production that does not correspond to the needs of the country, state control over the highly profitable sphere of business, the revival of command-administrative methods in managing the economy, the limitation of mass media freedom, the suppression of the opposition and civil society structures, as well as political and economic support from Russia—here are the main characteristics of the situation that developed in Belarus. Along with that, in Belarus, the level of unemployment is the lowest and the level of human development the highest in the NIS, free education and healthcare have been preserved, large enterprises continue to maintain the social infrastructure, and there are no international conflicts—these are the characteristics of socialism that have been preserved, and which remain attractive to the electorate.

Moldova

Moldova possesses a smaller economic potential than Ukraine or Belarus. Agricultural production predominates in the structure of production; exports are mainly oriented at NIS countries. In the first years of independence, political elites were attracted by the reunification with Romania (a part of the current territory of Moldova was annexed by Romania, and then returned to the USSR in 1940). Among the factors that slow down the process of integration in Moldova and Romania, the most important is the presence of numerous Ukrainian (13.8%), Russian (13.0%), and other (8.7%) national minorities that do not accept the prospect of "Romanization." The most tragic example of this problem took place in the so-called Pridnjestr conflict in 1992. The most industrialized section of Moldova, peopled mostly by Ukrainians and Russians, declared itself the Pridnjestr Moldavian Republic, and the armed conflict that erupted was terminated by Soviet forces, since then no real political solution has been found.

Unlike Belarus and Ukraine, Moldova managed to overcome the stage of confrontation between the president and the parliament at the end of 2000 and is now a parliamentary republic. However, the political situation changed significantly in February 2001 after the communist victory in the parliamentary elections. The communists, who represent the constitutional majority in the parliament, voted in their president and formed the government. This kind of dominance at all levels of power, along with unformed democratic traditions, creates the danger that authoritarian tendencies will develop.

A number of deep social contradictions remain in Moldova. A powerful ethnic factor is still present—the Pridnjestr conflict is not settled yet, the national minority of Gagauzia also strives for self-determination and independence, and the language issue is very sensitive. The economic crisis is deepening, the recession continues, and the demographic situation is deteriorating.

Ukraine

Ukraine possesses the largest economic potential in this subregion. As soon as independence was gained, a myth of future blooming and of the speedy development of the Ukrainian economy free from the Soviet Union, with its significant industrial potential and qualified working force, was widespread among the national political elite. It did not, however, take place. Moreover, an economic recession connected with the breakdown of economic links present in the USSR, and worsened by the local elite's incompetence, led to a very deep crisis. Phased privatization was not finished, and agrarian reform began only 10 years after independence was proclaimed. Starting in 1996, economic groups (clans) started to form. Using the support of executive authority representatives, they gained access to profitable contracts and credits, as well as privileges in taxation and privatization of state property, which let them accumulate a large amount of capital. The clans are integrated into the political system and have a significant influence on its functioning. To defend the interests of their businesses, economic groups seek their representation in the parliament, develop controlled mass media, create "pocket" political parties, and strive to increase their control over the structures of the state governing apparatus. An attempt at introducing systemic market reforms that had an appreciable positive effect in 2000 involved the interests of large capital, and under its influence, with the participation of controlled factions, the reform government of V. Juschenko was dismissed in 2001 by the Superior Rada (the parliament). A conflict between the president and the opposition has been developing in the background of the negative tendencies, arising with the growth of the shadow economy. The legitimacy of the president is seriously undermined, and the political elite is extremely fragmented. (Attempts to elect a speaker of the new Rada in spring of 2002 provide evidence of this fragmentation.) An unexpected initiative to transform the presidential republic into a parliamentary-presidential republic by the president L. Kutchma in the spring of 2003 allows only one interpretation: the elite reached a deadlock in solving the problem of succession of authority and were looking for a way out through "elite agreement" about its division after Kutchma's departure. Simultaneously, the potential for internal conflicts remains because of the poor living conditions of the population and unfair redistribution of property, including the reallotment of land, and ethnic reasons (the religious and linguistic confrontation between Eastern and Western Ukraine and the problematic national situation in the autonomous republic of the Crimea.)

In spite of the different trajectories in the post-authoritarian transformation, the countries under study have come to similar results at the present moment. The economic reforms have been stopped and have not brought the expected fruits—the creation of an effective market economy. The political regimes in the subregions are democratic in form rather than in content, with the preservation of authoritarian elements or the possibility of a return to authoritarianism. The political parties take marginal positions in these systems and do not carry out the full complex of functions that are characteristic of parties in liberal democracies. The parties are in a period of formation and institutionalization, and they have not yet become influential political actors. In general the situation is characterized by the dying away of the third wave of democratization.[1]

PARTIES IN THE POLITICAL SYSTEMS OF THE SUBREGION

Belarus

In Belarus the first period of the formation of political parties (from the late 1980s to 1994) was characterized by a dominant nationalistic ideology. The main promoter of this ideology was Belaruski Narodny Front (the Belarusian People's Front) (BNF). At first, the Front won with the politics of consistent anticommunism, but when the new national flag and coat of arms were accepted, the Belarusian language was proclaimed to be the state language, the USSR collapsed, and the Communists were deprived of power, the program of the Front was exhausted. From that moment the BNF's influence started to decrease, as did the active formation of political parties representing alternative ideologies. Simultaneously, the communists' activities began to revitalize. By the end of the period the most popular were political parties[2] of the social-democratic trend (nine parties with a total rating of 18.4%); the national-democrats followed them (two parties with a total rating of 12.3%); then the communists with the rating of 9.0%; the rightist conservatives—three parties with a total rating of 4.7%; the Christian democrats—two parties with a total rating of 2.5%; and the liberals with the rating of 2.4%. Thus, the political trends accounted for more than half of the electorate. It was the peak of the political parties' popularity. Later on, at the elections to the Superior Soviet of the XIII convocation in 1995 and the presidential elections of 1994, many of them showed extremely low results, which is connected with the influence of the majority system, as well as with ineffective party tactics and propaganda. The results of the presidential elections of 1994 gave evidence that the majority of the population refused liberal-democratic and nationalistic ideas, whose spread between 1991 and 1993 was accompanied by painful reforms and the weakening of authoritative bodies.

The political parties got a powerful push to development in connection with the elections to the Supreme Soviet of the XIII convocation, elections which were a central event of the second period (from the middle of 1994 to the second half of 1996), accompanied by a kind of socialistic revenge. Sixteen parties managed to win places in the supreme legislative body,[3] permitting one to speak of the Belarusian multiparty system as a developed phenomenon.

Since 1996, a new, third phase in the development of Belarusian political parties has begun. The majority of the parliamentary parties, in spite of their ideological orientation, refused to accept the results of the 1996 referendum and a new version of the Constitution, questioned the legitimacy of the executive power, and intensified work in international organizations with the aim of isolating the Belarusian political regime. Along with the authorities' actions and the opposition's difficulty in accessing mass media, the impossibility of really influencing the political situation in the country by means of a new parliament led to an abrupt decrease of the parties' authority.[4] They have been showing less and less activity of any kind, from work with the population to participation in the elections.[5]

Moldova

In Moldova the political situation was relatively safe, judging by external markers. In comparison with other post-Soviet republics, Moldova presents perhaps the most stable system of political parties in the NIS territory. In 1996 the change of president took place calmly, and relations characterized by little confrontation with separatists were developed. However, political reforms were not used to optimize the political system, but rather to redistribute power among various political groups and individuals. Thus, the period of 1991 to 1994 was characterized by the establishment of the presidential regime, and the consequent concentration of power around president Mircho Snegur. Between 1994 and 1999 a half-parliamentary regime was formed: the new Constitution gave significant powers to the head of the parliament and the prime minister. After the introduction of changes to the Constitution in July 2000 in the conditions of extreme party pluralism, when the stability of the government was contested by various political forces, a parliamentary regime was formed that provided a privileged position to the speaker. In 2000, the Moldavian centrists, having come to an agreement with the communists, changed the state order from a presidential republic to a parliamentary republic but did not manage to use the situation for their benefit.[6] As a result the old centrist parties did not even enter the arena of legislative power.

At present, the entire political system of Moldova, including its ruling party, is controlled by one person—president Vladimir Voronin. In accordance with sociological data,[7] in December 2001 he was trusted by up to 70 per cent of the population, whereas almost the same portion of the population did not trust the parliament or the government. A capable opposition does not really exist in Moldova. Parliament opposition (by the groups Aljans Bragisha and the Christian-democratic people's party) merely plays the role of an appendix for the communist "voting machine." The communists have a constitutional majority in the parliament. The opposition outside of parliament has experienced deep internal contradictions, has not carried on a dialogue with the voters, and appears rarely except at the noisy activities in the center of the capital supporting the national culture. The parties that appeared in Moldova during the first decade of its independence are losing their influence swiftly. None of the parties is able to contest the Party of Communists of the Republic of Moldova from the point of view of the organizational structures. Not a single opposition leader is able to offer a consolidating idea to society—an alternative to the program directives of the communists. It is clear that the old parties will hardly manage to adjust effectively to the change of the regime, and the political system in Moldova will face serious changes, connected also to the possible creation of a federal state if the Pridnjestr conflict is effectively solved.[8]

Ukraine

An extremely unstable party system has developed in Ukraine, characterized by a large number of parties in all parts of the political spectrum, constant fragmenting of the parties on the basis of personal, regional, economic, and other interests, and an unprecedented number of parliamentary factions and deputy groups. A significant variety of parliamentary parties has been generated by a number of factors. First, in 2002 elections to the Superior Rada of Ukraine by mixed electoral system took place for only the second time. Second, a very low, four percent, barrier, is offered at the elections to the Superior Rada. Third, Rada's standing orders make the formation of factions and deputy groups extremely liberal, which promotes fragmentation of the parliament. Fourth, in accordance with the Constitution, the parliament is a strong representative authority with a wide range of powers, which can influence the formation of internal and foreign policy of the state. Along with that, the president of the country also has extremely wide powers, which increases the danger of a political crisis.

It is possible to identify two phases in the history of the modern political system of Ukraine. The first stage (1991–1998) was characterized by the absence of any dominating party after the communists lost their influence. In the course of this phase nonparty governments were formed, and the parliament was elected by the majority system and splintered into a lot of groups and factions that did not have real party structures. The second (contemporary) phase started in 1998, after the first elections by the mixed electoral system. During this period, the contemporary Ukrainian political system started to develop. The main feature of the political system is the formation of the parliament by the parliamentary factions, grouping around three coalition centers. After the elections of 2002 the following centers appeared: the *left* (the Communist party of Ukraine); *propresident* —the Social-Democratic party of Ukraine (united), and an election bloc Za edinuju Ukrainu! (For unified Ukraine!), that formed a parliamentary faction under the same name; and the *right* Nasha Ukraina (Our Ukraine). This is a party system of polarized pluralism. At its *left* wing are the Communist party of Ukraine, Seljanskaja (Rural) party of Ukraine, Socialist party of Ukraine, and some other parties with the social basis in the central and eastern parts of the country; the *right* wing is made up by the Ukrainskij Narodnyi Rukh (Ukrainian People's Movement), Narodnyj Rukh Ukrainy (People's Movement of Ukraine), Congress Ukrainskikh Natsionalistov (Congress of the Ukrainian Nationalists), Ukrainskaja Respublikanskaja Partia (Ukrainian Republic Party), with a social basis in the Western parts of Ukraine, and also the *ultra-right* wing Ukrainskaya Natsional'naja Assambleja (Ukrainian National Assembly) and Schit Batkyvshcini (Shield of Fatherland). In the center are Partia Regionov (Party of Regions), Trudovaja Ukraina (Working Ukraine), Demsojuz (Democratic Union), the Social-Democratic Party of Ukraine (united), as well as the Narodno-Democratichskaja Partia (People's Democratic Party) and Agrarnaja Partia Ukrainy (Agrarian Democratic Party of Ukraine,), which were created under the patronage of the president and his administration.

However, this kind of categorization does not present a complete picture of the specifics of the party system in Ukraine. Thus, it is possible to single out parties with a dominant national ideology and social basis in the western regions of Ukraine: Rukhs, the Congress of the Ukrainian Nationalists, the Ukrainian Republic Party, and so on. There are parties created by financial-economic groups on the basis of regional economic structures. Their social basis is concentrated in one or two regions, and their ideological stance is of secondary importance (Social-Democratic Party of Ukraine [united], Party of Regions, Working Ukraine, Democratic Union, Jabluko, [Apple], etc.). In addition, there are parties created directly under the patronage of the president and his administration. Regional groups of adherents of a particular charismatic politician also form their parties—Progressivnaja politicheskaja partia Ukrainy (Progressive Political Party of Ukraine), Gromada, partly Socialist Party of Ukraine, and so on.

The contemporary system of political parties is in the process of formation; however, it has a visibly larger potential for development in comparison with the political systems in the other countries of the sub-region.

We will try to characterize the main factors that influenced the formation of national party politics in the subregion. However, it is difficult to define stable regularities of political transformation in the countries of the subregion in general, inasmuch as the political systems are themselves in an unstable state, and the situation can change any time under the influence of various factors. During 10 years of transition the rules of the game have changed very often. In Ukraine, a parliamentary republic was replaced by a presidential republic, and the majority election system by the mixed election system. In Belarus, the Constitution was changed (a two-chamber parliament was instituted, and the electoral legislation changed accordingly, although the majority election system was preserved), the post of president was introduced, and an agreement about the creation of a united state made up of Belarus and the Russian Federation was signed. In Moldova, the electoral system was changed from the majority system to a proportional system, the post of the president was introduced, and then as a result of the conflict between the executive and legislative powers, it was transformed into a parliamentary republic, where the president is elected by the parliament.

It is possible nonetheless to define several factors that influence the functioning of the political elite in Belarus, Moldova, and Ukraine. These factors are closely interconnected, so it is impossible to determine the exact degree of each factor's influence. Some are influential at the level of the political system in general (macro level); others at the level of political parties (micro level). At the macro level, depending on the peculiarities of genesis, it is necessary to distinguish the factors representing the heritage of the Soviet period, the factors that emerged during the period of independent development, and the factors of external political context.

THE MACRO-LEVEL FACTORS DETERMINING THE SPECIFICS OF PARTY POLITICS IN THE SUBREGION

The Heritage of the Soviet Period

Economic heritage. The economic heritage of the Soviet period played a significant role in the formation of the contemporary situation in the subregion. Many post-Soviet economic problems are similar for Belarus, Moldova, and Ukraine: lack of proportion in the structure of production, suppression of the private initiative of agricultural producers during the period of the kolkhoz system, undeveloped small and medium-sized business, lack of investments, narrowing of the tax base, growth of the shadow economy, technological backwardness, high social expenditure in the budget, and so forth. Under the influence of these problems in the countries under study, a kind of clan-oligarchy system of public product redistribution, closely connected with the political systems of the state, developed along with an electorate characterized by the predominance of poverty and left-leaning political tendencies.

Political regimes. Political regimes in Belarus, Moldova, and Ukraine are similar in many respects. They are unable to take total control over society, and they do not have a unified national ideology or, as in some Asian republics, religion. Their ideology is based on populism and speculation on the problems important in public opinion (language issues, struggle against corruption and crime, public consensus, and civic peace). Numerous cleavages are deliberately developed by regime leaders in order to create opposition among various groups of the population and to establish themselves as arbiters between them. The formal division of powers, the multiparty system, and the presence of other attributes of democracy are not sufficient to allow us to speak about democracy in these countries as a fully developed phenomenon. However, these regimes cannot be dismissed as dictatorships—they do regularly hold elections, they do not practice mass repression, and they enjoy the support of a significant part of the population. In each of them we see the formation of a quasi-democracy, where the ruling elite manipulates democratic processes in its own interests, using the apparatus of bureaucracy and repression they inherited from the Soviet period, enjoying a monopoly over the means of forming public opinion, and speculating on the peculiarities of post-totalitarian mass consciousness. The political parties serve as an instrument of population mobilization in support of various elite groups that struggle for power and control over economic resources.

Electorate. An electorate with quite a high educational and professional potential that lives in very hard economic conditions is a very important feature of the countries under study. Accustomed to stability and state guarantees under Soviet rule, citizens were encouraged to believe that the transformation to market relations would bring general prosperity. Instead, in the course of liberalization, in the beginning of the 1990s, the majority of citizens lost their savings and were pushed aside from the privatization process. Simultaneously, small groups of new elites became rich rather quickly as a result of half-criminal privatization (in fact, looting) of former state property. All this significantly influenced the formation of political opinion.

Sociocultural factor. Neighboring cultures still contribute to social divisiveness in all three nations and inhibit social consolidation around the main issues of further development of each country—democracy or authoritarian rule, market or planned economy, independence or integration; if integration, then either to the European Union or to the Commonwealth of the Independent States(CIS), and so on. Belarus and Ukraine, either completely or in part, were part of the Polish and Russian empires, and later the USSR, several times during the course of 200 years. It is possible to say the same of Moldova: before inclusion in the USSR it was a part of the Oman empire, the Russian empire, and Romania. Collectivization and industrialization during the Soviet period, the absence of traditions of independence, and the political and economic reforms that took place after 1991 formed a classical set of sociocultural cleavages in Belarus, Moldova, and Ukraine: economic status, religion, ethnic affiliation, level of urbanization, and education. The most significant are the ethnic and economic cleavages.

Until the mid-1990s, the main cleavage can be considered the *ethnic* cleavage in all three countries. It was expressed in the attitude towards the issue of language (the problem of the status of the Russian language), the problem of national revival and self-determination, building a national state, and the problem of how to assess the role of the Russian empire and the USSR in the national history of the republic. From the end of the 1980s to the beginning of 1990s, the ethnic factor was actively used by the national fronts in Belarus, Moldova, and Ukraine and became the main part of their political programs.[9]

In similar fashion, the communist parties, associated in public memory with the stability and social guarantees of the Soviet period, have been able to use economic cleavage (especially the terms of social justice), to achieve victories at elections in every country.[10]

Factors That Formed—or Changed Significantly—during the Period of Independent Development

Economic factor. The economic factor has evolved considerably in the post-Soviet era and is now represented by the following elements: (1) permanent crisis and instability of the economy; (2) powerful shadow sector; (3) unfinished privatization (the possibility of a new redistribution of property—without observing juridical norms or market and free competition laws—is preserved); (4) strong influence of non-market key determinants, such as the possibility of getting significant economic privileges and competitive advantages with the help of state structures. In our opinion, the economic factor dominates at present, and its influence manifests itself in several ways. Firstly, the electorate is disappointed in the economic reforms, and this disappointment contributes to the stable popularity of the communist parties and to a decrease of trust in democratic and market institutions in general. The parties and blocs that did not formerly take part in political reforms now conduct and win the elections, thus reducing the prospects for institutionalizing the parties involved earlier in the formation of the governments and responsible therefore in public opinion for its socioeconomic aftermaths. Secondly, victory in the struggle for power brings high economic dividends, given the conditions of economic crisis and instability. Together, these factors have transformed political contests into struggle for economic profit and do not allow the party system to achieve stability.

Legislation. Every political force that comes into power tries to use legislation to guarantee that their power will be preserved. In Belarus, the crisis in relations between the executive and legislative powers led to significant changes in the Constitution in favor of the executive power,[11] and to new regulations and interpretations of electoral qualification.[12] In Moldova, the requirements on the number of party members necessary for registration or re-registration were significantly changed, the requirements for obligatory representation in the regions were introduced, and voting qualifications were increased. In Ukraine, the permanent confrontation between the president and the parliament is determined to a large extent by a complicated interweaving of political and clan-oligarchy interests.

As the parties were being formed, Constitutions, laws about political parties, and electoral legislation were also being created. Thus, the juridical environment of the political parties' functioning was and is still extremely unstable. Accordingly, large parties either lose a significant number of their members or split apart: the most effective party organization is a small, mobile, technologically advanced structure, oriented at participation in parliamentary elections and accumulating resources from external sources. The communist parties are less likely to split apart over issues of the ineffectiveness of the work of the party bureaucracy than the other party structures: their high electoral potential is more connected with the population's nostalgia for Soviet times An alternative way of adapting to the conditions that have developed is to create so-called parties of power, that actively use administrative resources.

Electoral systems. Electoral systems form the most salient differences in party politics of the countries under study. Practice shows that in the post-Soviet territory, the proportional system appeared to be the most efficient for institutionalizing political parties. A completely proportional system in Moldova contributed to the emergence of political parties and the party system of polarized pluralism. The introduction of proportional representation in Ukraine led to similar results, where a mixed electoral system exists (50% of the deputies are elected on the basis of party lists and 50% by majority electoral districts). The presence of proportional representation in Ukraine also accelerated the process of institutionalizing political parties and transformed the atomized party system into a system of polarized pluralism. In Belarus, a majority electoral system has been preserved. The first democratic parliamentary elections of 1995 showed that this system stimulates the formation of political parties' territorial representations and allows rather large parliamentary fractions to organize. However, both in Belarus and Ukraine significant drawbacks appeared in the application of the majority system as a result of the conflict between the executive and legislative powers during the transformation period. It is much easier to use the administrative resources of the executive power in majority electoral districts for securing the victory of their candidates. That is why majority representation has been preserved in Ukraine, allowing the formation of representations of political-administrative groups in parliament, as well as influential propresidential fractions, that are a kind of insurance policy for the president and his supporters.[13]

Disparity between branches of power. The disparity between branches of power in all the countries of the subregion is constantly reproduced by the political system. It is expressed in conflicts between the executive branch and some of the parliamentary political parties, grouping (and regrouping in case of power change) in opposition. The inherent reason behind this conflict has already been mentioned—it is the unfinished character of property redistribution and the possibility of gaining additional economic advantages in case of winning power. Besides that, in this subregion the president (except for the situation in Moldova after the elections of 2001) never represents any party. Exclusively nonparty candidates win the presidential elections, managing to avoid the limitations of a definite ideology and consolidating a maximal number of adherents around themselves.

This automatically places the president in opposition to the political parties. As a result apparently or latently, a crisis of state governing takes place, created by excessive presidential powers. It is almost impossible for the parliament to influence the president's decisions (taking into account the presence of the propresident fractions, mentioned above). Attempts to centralize power are the usual reaction to a crisis of governing, and, accordingly, a conflict arises between the president and the parliament (or out of parliament opposition).

In Belarus such a conflict developed in 1996 and led to a freezing of the democratization process. In Moldova, the conflict was partly solved in 2000 by means of a change in the form of government, but a potential for its renewal (in case of a confrontation between the communist majority and the rest of the political spectrum) still remains. In Ukraine the conflict between the president and the parliament contributed to the "Orange revolution" in the course of which the opposition has challenged the legitimacy of the victory of the acting president's protégé in the first round of presidential elections, in 2004 and , having mobilized people to mass protest actions, brought to power its candidate. In the background of the conflict between the president and the parliament, the political spectrum in all the countries of the subregion is structured not so much in accordance with a left-right scale, but rather in respect to attitude to the authority in power, that is, following the power-opposition line. In the political market, along with the opposition parties there are political forces, formed with the help of the acting administration and intended for its support. These are the so-called parties of power. As a rule, they position themselves at the political center, and opposition parties are automatically allocated to the left or to the right opposition.

Factors Created by External Political Context

Geopolitical factors. Geopolitical factors are determined by the competition between the world power centers (Russia, the United States, the European Union) for influence in this region. We will not dwell in detail on the peculiarities of geopolitics. Let us just point out that Ukraine is exposed to the largest external influence. Its government is trying to maneuver between the interests of these external actors (above all the United States and Russia) and, at the same time, to carry on an independent foreign policy. Belarus has determined its external priorities and is oriented toward the construction of a united state with the Russian Federation. Moldova happened to be in the sphere of interests of both Russia and the European Union. In addition, Ukraine, which borders the unrecognized Pridnjestr Moldavian Republic, takes an active part in the negotiation process about the reunification of Moldova.[14] A complicated merging of the super-states' interests in the subregion leads to almost every one of the political parties having its own point of view on the foreign policy of its state, and consolidation of the political elite on issues of the dominating vectors of external policy has not yet been achieved.

Russian Federation. The Russian Federation is a key external policy factor in the subregion. After the destruction of the USSR, Belarus, Moldova, and Ukraine automatically fell in the zone of its national interests. In Belarus, the 1996 intervention of Russian politicians in the conflict between the president and the parliament stopped the procedure of impeachment and led to the acceptance of the Constitutional changes initiated by the president. Russia is the country that supports Belarus economically (through technical loans and supplying power carriers at subsidized prices) and politically (by recognizing the directive the parliament formed in 1996, as well as the results of the elections in 1999, 2000, and 2001, which the European Union and the United States consider undemocratic). The intervention of Russia, in particular the "peaceful mission of the 14th army," significantly influenced the situation regarding the Pridnjestr territory. The state of the Moldovian economy—external debt makes up nearly three-quarters of the gross national produce (GNP)—determines to a large extent the general trend of internal political processes in the country and relations between Kishinev and Moscow.

Russia's policy towards Ukraine is influenced mainly by economic levers: Ukraine depends on the Russian gas supply and is in significant debt to Russia. The same mechanism was successfully carried out with Belarus, when its leaders tried to distance themselves from integration models based on the unified state rather than on the Russia-Belarus Confederation, and sought to avoid the privatization of property, which Russia insists on. The dominating role of the Russian Federation in the region, and its scientific, economic, and military-technical superiority above its neighbors put Russia in the range of factors that render a determining influence on the trajectory of transformation in Belarus, Moldova, and Ukraine. Nevertheless, one should not conclude that ambitions to recreate an empire are the exclusive motivation for the political elite of Russia to participate actively in the politics of the subregion. Frequently, in crisis situations, the political elites of the Newly Independent States seek the support, help, or mediation of Moscow. In addition, the increase of Russian political authorities' pragmatism influences positively the process of elite consolidation, compelling them to organize their own forces and leading to a greater emphasis on the notion of national interests in their political vocabulary.

European Union. The European Union (EU) shows a high level of activity in the subregion. It helped settle the political crisis in Moldova and has successfully imposed external political pressure on Kiev and Minsk. It is also necessary to take into account that after 10 new states were invited to join the European Union, Belarus, Moldova, and Ukraine became direct neighbors of the EU, and thus became part of the zone of its geopolitical interests. Undoubtedly, the influence of the EU on the processes taking place in the subregion will increase. Thus, for example, all the states under study are participants in the Central European initiative,[15] a European program that intends to render assistance to countries that border the EU in their efforts to carry on democratic and economic reforms. Thus, local political elites will have a real alternative to cooperation with Russia. The perspective of joining the European Union can stimulate reforms in accordance with the standards accepted in it and with the active financial and consultation support of European structures, thereby intensifying the democratization processes.

MICRO-LEVEL (ORGANIZATIONAL) FACTORS DETERMINING SPECIFICS OF PARTY POLITICS IN THE SUBREGION

The quality of leadership, long-term strategies, internal political dialogue, and ideological discourse help determine the course of party politics in all nations, and Ukraine, Moldova and Belarus are not exceptions.

Charismatic leadership. The political parties in Belarus, Ukraine, and Moldova that are most notable for analysts (and recognizable to the population) were mainly formed from "above," as a team of like-minded supporters around a famous political figure, and then agitation was carried out and a social base was built—for example, BNF (Poznjak) and OGP (Bogdankevich) in Belarus, Batkovschina (Timoshenko) and NRU (Chernovol) in Ukraine, Al'jans Bragisha (Bragish) and PVSM (Snegur) in Moldova; and so on. Accordingly, most of the parties have charismatic leaders. This means that the parties are practically unable to cooperate with each other, and merger takes place very rarely, only, as a rule, under the influence of external factors (re-registration, elections), and not as a result of similar ideological directives. Internal party factions emerge when an alternative candidate for the leader's position appears. That is why party splits are frequent. Small political parties are more inclined to merge, either with similar ones or with stronger competitors, but this rarely affects their electoral perspectives.

Long-term strategies. Long-term strategies of the political parties in Belarus, Moldova, and Ukraine as a rule are absent; the parties are mainly guided by short-term (tactical) interests. In conditions of less-than-ideal legislation, a weak judiciary system, a low level of civil society development, limited freedom in the mass media, and the clans' struggle for political and economic influence, the main aim of the political parties is to achieve power and to keep it.[16]

Political dialogue. Political dialogue is an extremely rare phenomenon, and it appears mainly in the context of international structures' support. As a rule, while the power and opposition are in confrontation, the representatives of the parties in conflict will attempt strategies to undermine one another. Being politically omnivorous and unscrupulous, the political parties discredit themselves in the eyes of the population, and the notions of democracy, freedom, market economy, socialism, communism, and so on are used just as pre-election ideological patterns, devoid of content. Absolutely all political forces appeal to them in order to fight for their own interests. Simultaneously, political parties rarely take the real interests of the population into account.

Ideological orientations. The ideological orientations of the political parties in the majority of cases appear to be vague. The quantity, variety, and depth of cleavages lead to the fact that the political parties that strictly follow a definite ideology are practically unable to win the majority of votes in elections. This is especially visible at presidential elections when party candidates are not effective, and nonparty candidates win, since they are able to attract various categories of the electorate ("to catch all"). At the same time, the presence of a leader who is clearly associated with some achievements or with mistakes in state policy during a definite period of time makes it difficult if not impossible for parties to use flexible electoral strategies.

The fact that constant work with the electorate is not necessary for victory in the elections influences the role and place of parties in a political system. They rarely have a high rating, and the number of parties is high (in Belarus and Moldova there are about 30, in Ukraine more than 100), making it difficult for the population to become oriented in the political spectrum. Except for specific parties (e.g., the Greens, the Unionists), which are not numerous, the majority of parties aspire to reflect some modern ideology (liberalism, socialism, nationalism, and more rarely, conservatism). However, social groups that could become the carriers of these ideologies have not been formed yet in the countries under study, with the exception of socialist (communist) ideology, which is closely held by a large part of the population in the countries under study, since it is associated with a relatively successful period of the Soviet Union.

All in all the political systems in Belarus, Moldova, and Ukraine can be characterized as populist democracies, where staying in power by any means is the main aim of the political forces and is realized in a demagogic form by promising to protect the interests of justice, democracy, and freedom; much more rarely the interests of the population are taken into account (see Table 3.1).

As seen in Table 3.1, the level of trust in political parties in the subregion is very low. It is interesting that in Moldova and Ukraine, where the parties have already actively participated in sociopolitical life and the struggle for power for a long time, the level of trust is lower than in the NIS on average. In total, less than a tenth of the population trusts the political parties, and there are quite a few people who are unsure about this issue. Along with that, in Belarus, where the parties have in fact been excluded from the political process and cannot influence the process of decision making at the state level, trust in parties is one and a half times higher, and

Table 3.1 Do You Trust Political Parties (in %)

Alternatives	*Belarus*	*Moldova*	*Ukraine*	*NIS*
Yes	4.8	1.6	2.5	4.2
Rather yes	11.5	7.5	7.4	11.2
Rather no	28.8	33.5	29.9	31.3
No	28.6	41.0	47.6	39.0
Hard to answer	26.3	16.5	12.1	14.2
Total, in absolute figures	2000	2000	2400	18428

Source: Data of international comparative research in eight NIS countries: "Living conditions, way of life and health" (in 2002, 2400 polled respondents in Ukraine, 2000 polled respondents in Belarus and in Moldova); collection of data was carried on by representative national samples. The data is given by the Center for Sociological and Political Research at the Belarusian State University (program executor in Belarus).

the number of unsure people is twice as high as in the other countries of the subregion. This can be explained by the fact that the political parties have not had enough time to compromise themselves in the eyes of the population with unsuccessful reforms or public political squabbles and still maintain the image of effective democratic institutions.

Thus, we can say that in Belarus, Moldova, and Ukraine "formal democracies" have formed. The political parties carry on a function of articulation and protection of the interests of the electorate on a very limited scale. Such "formal" functioning of the political parties is not accidental, inasmuch as being in power in Belarus, Moldova, and Ukraine is a way to receive economic profits rather than a way to achieve realization of the electorate's interests.

PERSPECTIVES OF DEVELOPMENT FOR THE POLITICAL SYSTEMS IN THE SUBREGION

The process of the formation and institutionalization of political parties in Belarus, Moldova, and Ukraine is inseparable from the political-economic transformation in general. On the one hand, the economic crisis stands in the way of the formation of stable political systems; on the other hand, political forces act separately, and the ineffectiveness of public dialogues makes it impossible to carry on economic reforms consistently. Since the process of reform has slowed down, it is logical to expect that the quasi-democratic systems formed here will exist for some period of time, developing in accordance with their internal logic.

The degree of democracy of the political regimes in the countries under study is characterized not only by the success of democratic reforms, but also by the possibility of recoiling to a command-administrative economy and an authoritarian political system. In Belarus, which started market and political transformations quite intensively at the beginning of the

1990s and was the most likely candidate for entering the EU (in comparison with the majority of the NIS countries), such a recoil has already occurred. An indicator of it is the state of party politics—the process of political parties' marginalization has reached a final stage.

In Moldova, it is very possible that events will unfold according to a similar scenario. The situation after the last parliamentary elections (establishment of executive-power control over the key state positions and the parliament in total, the mass media, and economic resources, etc.) recalls the first years in power of President A. Lukashenko in Belarus. Most political parties have been losing control over the situation in the country swiftly, and sometimes escape from the sphere of political struggle or try to enter into an agreement with the current group in power. It is apparent that the political systems in Belarus and Moldova have practically exhausted their internal potential for democratization.

In Ukraine, the institutionalization of political parties has been taking place extremely slowly. Nevertheless, the parties are gradually changing from appendices to financial-economic groups into structures that depend more and more on their voters. These processes have already started among the parties of leftist and national-democratic trends. Some stabilization of the political spectrum took place and, in fact, there is almost no free electoral field for the creation of a new party structure.

Stable power centers like the president and administration, whose functioning largely determines the political situation, have formed in the countries under study. All the countries came to this condition in different ways, but in the end they have achieved similar results: the institution of the presidency has become an important factor restraining further development of democratic processes, and authoritarian tendencies are clearly visible. That is why a search for optimal ways of cooperation and formation of mutual restraint between the executive and legislative powers will determine the fate of party politics in the subregion in the near future.

CHAPTER 4

Party System Development in Belarus, 1988–2001: Myths and Realities

Elena A. Korosteleva

INTRODUCTION

There has been very little scholarly discussion regarding Belarus's political and economic development, either in the West or in Belarus itself. Nevertheless, it is a very useful example of a highly complex and as yet unsuccessful transition to democracy.

Belarus has accumulated most of the generic problems associated with ex-Soviet states, such as an authoritarian legacy and an ineffective legal environment. It has also experienced privation and the constant fear of impending social and economic decline. The development of institutional and structural settings, such as a majority runoff electoral system, bicameral parliament, state-controlled media, and malfunctioning democratic institutions, seem to resemble those in other post-Soviet states. The surface configuration of political conflicts also shows signs of similarity, being mainly structured along socioeconomic divides and often associated with reformist and national movements on the right, and successor communist activities on the left. There is also an enduring tradition of governance by decree and presidential proxy control over decision making, juxtaposed to legitimate but powerless political parties and interest organizations. Reelected in 2001 by a massive majority vote (75.6%),[1] Belarusian President Alexander Lukashenko provides a generic example of a populist leader thriving in the uncertain and malleable environment of a transitional state.

At the same time, Belarus differs considerably from other post-Soviet states by demonstrating some unique features of its transitional development. In the early years of transition Belarus was deemed to be a well qualified outsider for democratization. Yet its continuously nonreformist and authoritarian style of governance has dragged the country further into isolation from the international community and placed much higher dependence on its relationship with Russia. Belarus has accidentally adopted a form of "third way socialist" policy making, which implies an attempt to reconcile socialist properties with the challenges of a global market. Despite continuing financial and economic decline, state enterprises remain dominant and private business dormant; there is widespread administrative control over production, prices, exchange rates, subsidized credits, and employment. This feeble balance is largely maintained with the help of the Russo-Belarus Union, which, on the one hand, allows substantial loans and hence, the opportunity to patch up the social security system in Belarus, and on the other hand, reserves strategically important grounds for Russia in both military and economical terms in the light of the NATO/EU enlargement.

Politically, Belarus can be described as falling within the best Soviet traditions. Among the most notorious examples are the nationally organized *subbotniki;* bureaucrats' humiliation in public by the president; a well-paid KGB and militia staff; presidential directives that cut wages from one stratum of the population to feed another; collective responsibilities of government officials for harvesting and street sweeping; allegedly rigged elections; obligatory public sport events, and so on.

There are political parties, but since the dissolution of the 1996 parliament the majority have been shunted away from mainstream politics. They boycott parliamentary elections to protest against Lukashenko's "injustice" but have been unable to recover power or influence.[2] In opposition, parties that entered the restructured legislature in 1997 abandoned their feeble ideologies in exchange for various state benefits and presidential bonuses.

It comes as no surprise that Belarus's relations with the European Union (EU) and the United States continue to falter. Belarus's Special Guest status in the Council of Europe was suspended in 1997, and most international dialogue has since stopped. This policy, nevertheless, proved ineffective in promoting human rights and the struggle for democracy in Belarus; instead, it allowed Belarus to focus more on strengthening its relationship with Russia and other CIS members, and to pay little attention to its own growing isolation.

In an attempt to assist the democratization process, the Organization for Security and Cooperation in Europe (OSCE) introduced an Advisory and Monitoring Group (AMG) in February 1998 in Belarus. However, the authorities have subsequently demonized the AMG as scare-mongering and provoking civil unrest between the Belarusian people and their popularly elected president.[3] The 2000 parliamentary elections changed nothing but reinforced the president's control over the decision-making process by electing a nonpartisan legislature, which is loyal to the Batska (Father). On September 9, 2001 Belarus witnessed yet another failure in democracy—the second presidential election since independence saw the reelection of Alexander Lukashenko as President of Belarus for another five-year term. Many people in Belarus had hoped that the result of this election would reverse the trend towards dictatorship, yet despite allegations of fraud the majority apparently did vote in support of Lukashenko.

Parties are the most vital part of the democratization process, and in this chapter we will examine the 1988–2001 path of party system development in Belarus. We will see that although there were legitimate parties with predictable group loyalties, they could not develop into a stabilized party system to counter-balance power relations in society. We must address the question as to why initially successful democratization has reversed since 1996, and whether political parties are failing altogether in Belarus. The argument will be based on the following theoretical assumptions. First, the two juxtaposing frameworks—the structure-oriented and the process-oriented approach[4]—appear to be insufficient to encompass a full picture of democratic transition of the newly established democracies. Rather than assuming that either institutions or political actors individually play a leading part in building and strengthening democracy, this chapter insists that one can learn about transitions only by considering the multilayered framework of such elements as structures, agencies, and agents. Parties, nevertheless, remain the main locus of analysis and will be treated as the principal agents in the process of democratization; successful consolidation into a party system will depend on structural factors (cleavages, legacies, and cultural incentives), on the one hand, and institutional settings (electoral system, constitution making, strong presidency), on the other.

Second, there is no straightforward correlation between existing parties and party system consolidation. Although parties may have well-articulated images and predictable group loyalties, these do not directly lead to the consolidation of the party system. The undercurrent for such a development is that although parties are an important individual factor in the process, the *whole* structure of political choices, institutions, and conflicts determines further system institutionalization. If they do not operate in accord, as recent developments in the third-wave democracies witness,[5] the systems may be sustainable but have little tendency to institutionalize.

The analysis of Belarus's party system development will proceed in three parts. A brief description of parties' political history in Belarus will be given in the first part. The second part will focus on the analysis of parties as organizations. The third part will briefly highlight what "procedural" (structural and electoral) incentives parties in Belarus must have—and presently lack—if they are to combine as an institutionalized party system.

BELARUS'S PARTY SYSTEM: AN OVERVIEW

Belarus formally declared independence from the former Soviet Union on August 25, 1991 and became an independent sovereign state. However, its independent path to democracy appears to have been a long and unsuccessful detour.

It is a common assumption that Belarus's post-communist party politics did not have enough structural, cultural, or institutional incentives for democratic advancement. Some scholars suggest that national motives were subtle and could not therefore unravel into a stable cleavage system and party competition based upon them. They also suggest that due to traditional tolerance, popular conservatism, and leftover legacies, mass political mobilization was minimal, and hence, representation has easily acquired an authoritarian form of leadership.[6] The principal hypothesis here will be that Belarus's political development was subject to a fateful course of events despite the existence of the political/social fabric, the balanced structure of power, and coordinated interests of elites necessary to foster democratization. In other words, at the outset of transition, political conflicts were strong and enduring, and the institutional background was appropriate; the electorate was open to political suggestion, and the proximity of the West was highly inspiring. What Belarus lacked originally was a political initiative, which over time has turned into a democratic deficit. This in turn has resulted in the lack of an adequate institutional framework to pursue further democratization, and a misbalance of power relations between parties and other representative institutions vis-à-vis a strong presidency. The analysis will show that despite existing cleavage structures and legitimate forces, the process of building democracy, including party system formation, has taken an alternative route.

The advent of multiparty politics in post-communist Belarus was associated with several profound conflicts, of which the center–periphery conflict became the most prominent. This struggle was stimulated by a strong sense of political inequality and characterized by calls for freedom and autonomy from Moscow on the national level; and by urban/rural frictions between the regions and the capital, Minsk, on the regional level. It is a conflict that dates as far back as the beginning of the twentieth century.[7]

The second divide emerged with perestroika and signified a traditional showdown[8] between old-guard communism and the necessity of change and economic-cum-political reforms. This constellation of conflicts consequently developed into a left–right linear spectrum of party alternatives in the early days of democratization, with the communists/socialists, who were generally pro-union, on the left, and the nationalists, liberals, and democrats on the right. What is more extraordinary is that this historical conflict configuration had persisted relatively unchanged until 1994, when the presidential period began.

Democratization was initialized in Belarus with the establishment of the Belarusian Popular Front movement (BNF), and other democratic movements.[9] In November 1990 the liberal United Democratic Party (OGP) emerged, based on a parliamentary faction of like-minded deputies, and soon afterwards Alexander Dobrovol'ski, a prominent oppositional politician, became its leader. In 1991 the liberal farmers' party, the Belarusian Peasant Party, was founded, but ceased to exist soon after the 1996–1997 political reshuffles. The existence of the Social Democratic Assembly in the 1990 parliament inspired many smaller right-wing nationalist, democratic, and liberal movements to foment in Belarus. In June and July 1991 the radical National Democratic Party of Belarus was registered; and the Belarusian Christian-Democratic Union held its first congress. At the end of 1991 a group of pro-Russia, market-oriented intellectuals organized a movement called Democratic Belarus and registered accordingly in 1992. Later, some of its supporters would unite with the United Civic Party, and others would launch a sister-branch to the Russian party 'Yabloko.'

Overall, the years 1991 and 1992 were marked by the emergence of many alternatives to the successor movements, influential party and nongovernmental organizations, which thus gave a solid basis to the settlement of today's opposition. Among them should be noted smaller but nonetheless important parties such as the People's Consent (PNS), led by Gennady Karpenko (deceased); pro-Russian patriotic Slavic Union "White Russia," which was established in 1992 with the major goal of achieving a union of Slavic nations; and the People's Movement (NDB), which united both communists and Pan-Slavists (analogous to the red-brown bloc in Russia). Sergei Gaidukevich headed the center-left Liberal Democratic movement (LDPB), which later become a mirror organization of the LDPR in Russia. Communist and LDPB leaders played a significant role in dismissing the moderately progressive speaker of the 1990 parliament, Stanislav Shushkevich. By 1992 the Agrarian Party (AP) registered, led by Semion Sharetski, the speaker of the 1995–1996 parliaments. On the left end of the spectrum there was a successor party, later named The Communist Party Belarusskaya (PCB), which in 1993–1994 was rejoined by a group of some smaller satellite parties of pro-socialist orientation: The Belarusian Labour Party (PT), The Party of Labour and Justice (PTS), The Socialist Party, The Republican Party, and The Party of All-Belarusian Unity and Consensus.

By 1992 the Belarusian political spectrum had a relatively clear linear shape. Theoretically, Belarus had the real potential to develop a stable party system, based on the existence of salient conflicts, an active mass response to them, and emerging party competition. However, the democratic endeavor ceased with the introduction of the presidency, when a non-democratic quality was introduced to avoid "hazardous" political pluralism. Fragile, but democratically reliable, semi-parliamentarism has been rapidly succeeded by super-presidentialism, bringing fear and repression back into society.

With Lukashenko's rise to power, the 1995 parliament eventually lost its authority, some of its seats, and, more important, public confidence in a long battle of interests and wills with the government.[10] In 1997 it was replaced by a bicameral legislature designed by the president. The House of Representatives—the Lower Chamber—was composed of 110 members, 70 percent of whom were members of the pro-presidential faction "Zgoda" of the prior parliament; and about 30 percent communists and agrarians. Anatol Malofeev, who was the first secretary of the Communist Party of Belarus during 1990–1991, was appointed chairman of the new parliament. There were debilitating consequences for many parties, including the PCB, which split as those supporting Lukashenko's formed the Communist Party of Belarus (CPB) headed by Victor Chikin, while others remained in opposition led by Sergei Kaliakin. The PCB lost about 50 percent of its membership and the Agrarian Party ceased to exist as such, but the pro-regime core of the party was revamped by presidential endorsement in the spring of 1999. There was also a breakdown in the fall of 1999, as disagreements regarding leadership style and party strategies led the party's radical and liberal wings to separate, the latter forming a new party, eager to collaborate with the government, under the leadership of Vintsug Vyachorka. Furthermore, many smaller political organizations, that is, parties, NGOs, and new-wave trade unions, quietly disappeared from the Belarusian political scene after alterations to the 1994 constitution. Traditional trade unions presently eke out a humble existence, being successfully "nailed down" by the president.[11] Belarus's political community has split in half: a propresidential part that steadily receives support of about 40 per cent of voters; and an opposition protesting and resisting the injustice of authorities.

The 1997–1998 political years were characterized by continuing party decline and their further disintegration. The new propresidential parliament proved to be compliant and non-initiative, obeying Lukashenko's orders in exchange for his promises of support for the parliamentary elections in the autumn of 2000.[12] The opposition had begun the politics of coalition but, lacking trust in each other, failed spectacularly in April 1999 during their campaign for an alternative presidential election, and again two years later—at the time of the presidential election. Petty disputes, internal disagreements between the members of the opposition, and profiteering individualism let them down again. As Silitski notes:

> [T]he November 1996 referendum looked like a fair and civilised process compared to the opposition elections in 1999. A well-known leader, Pozniak, who ran as BNF's candidate against Michael Chigir,[13] withdrew from the race in the last days before the vote in order to prevent Chigir's rising to political prominence.[14]

A third set of parliamentary elections took place in 2000 and were erroneously boycotted by the opposition parties in protest against the authorities' violations of the law. As a result, opposition parties have remained outsiders to the policy-making arena, and the president enjoys a steady support of around 40 percent of the population.[15] In 2001 Lukashenko was reelected with an absolute majority, by the free will of Belarusian people, but in unfair circumstances. Belarusians were given the opportunity to ratify the institutional, structural, and cultural circumstances dictated to them—but not to elect an alternative.

Continuing relapse into nondemocratic politics cannot be explained solely by the weakness of existing cleavages, the parties' incapacity to mobilize the masses, or Lukashenko's remarkable political skills. As stated before, other factors—structures reinforcing the nomenklatura's power control, especially in the regions; cultural adherence to a strong leadership; subsequent institutional and constitutional reinforcement of nondemocratic decisions; and the lack of organizational unity among political organizations have all been equally important.

The powerful influence of structures can be seen in the eventual organizational failure of the 1990–1996 Belarus parliaments. The parties in public office had an opportunity for institutionalization and successful survival. Belarus's two parliaments (1990–1994, and 1995–1996) developed into structured bodies with well-defined cleavages and organized competitive forces. There was a certain degree of polarization of interests in the parliament, which under a moderate number of parties with relative proportionality of forces had the potential for further institutionalization. Moreover, contrary to a general opinion that Belarus had no incentives to generate oppositional politics and thereby to condition a democratic breakthrough, our study has confirmed that Belarus's parliament in 1990–1996 was better structured before its dismissal than that of Russia. Over the years two salient divides, associated with conservative-reformist and power distribution conflicts, had developed. They included such traditional issues as populism and moderation on the left and marketization and liberalization on the right. Issues of sovereignty were also at stake, as opposed to the communists' idea of a happy return to union with Russia. Power arrangements, as a second conflict line for party competition, came to the fore in 1992 and gradually reached their apex in 1996 (see Figure 4.1).

Within a few years the Belarusian legislature had developed well-organized and legitimate factions and seemed to have moved away from the politics of personalism to the politics of factional coalitions. If in 1990 there was a moderate democratic minority, opposed by the overwhelming majority of the communist nomenclature, by 1996 the situation was radically different. There was a formal division of the entire parliament into party factions, and full engagement of members of parliament could be observed. Even nonpartisan deputies acted as if they belonged to a single group having many parameters in common.

However, system potential does not in itself provide the motivation for irreversible democratic changes and party settlement. Since the introduction of the presidency and the occupation of that post by Lukashenko, the prospects of creating a democratic state have drastically declined.

Figure 4.1 Positions of the Members of the 1996 Belarusian Parliament

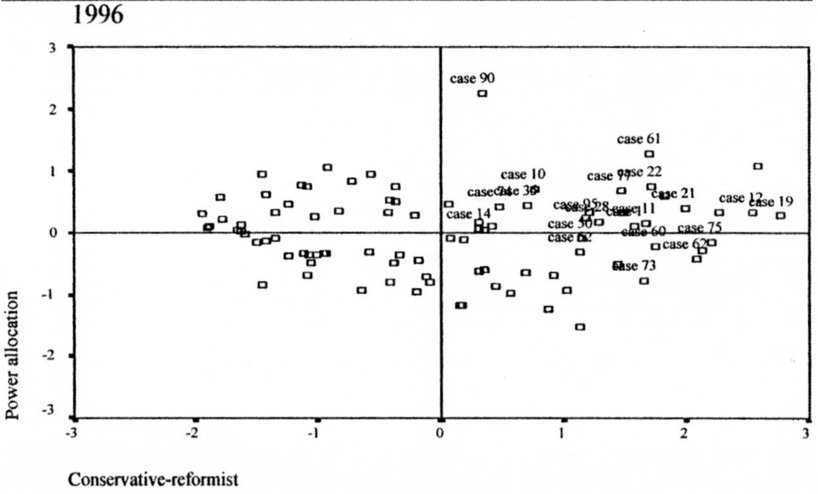

Note: One can see a relatively linear distribution of parliament's political forces. Named cases signify the democratic bloc. Full description of the methodology and results can be found in E. Korosteleva, *Explaining Party System Development in Post-Communist Belarus*, unpublished Ph.D. thesis. University of Bath, 2001. The method of Multiple Scaling (SPSS) was applied.
Source: Parliamentary Bulletins 1996, Minsk. Author's calculations.

Belarus's political spectrum has taken on a new shape, and the direction of party competition has changed to a battlefield between parties vis-à-vis the president. Legacies of the past, among which are public adherence to a strong leadership, the nomenklatura's unlimited access to state resources, state-controlled mass media, a highly centralized system of governance, and an undeveloped civil society, have noticeably weakened the chances of the political opposition to sustain public confidence. In addition, parties as organizations have been quite ineffective from the outset, caring less about social linkage with the electorate, and more about personal profiteering politics.

PARTIES AS ORGANIZATIONS

Party organization is often cited as a key independent element in explaining party effectiveness. As an aggregate of individuals forming constellations of rival groups,[16] party organization functions as a three-level political institution. We have briefly touched upon parties in public office and their failure to sustain power, and we now move on to the analysis of parties' activities in the central office and on the ground.

Parties differ from each other not only ideologically but also in their organizational modes, as well as in their degree of loyalty to the incumbent president. The latter presently determines parties' position in parliament and their welfare. Parties on the left are mainly mass-type organizations with the PCB in the fore. The BNF and the LDPB also join their ranks, in opposition to the majority of right-wing parties representing a new trend in party politics. They are highly centralized, candidate-centered, with minimal paid staff in the central office, an ephemeral regional network, great flexibility in membership policies, and capital-intensive election campaigns.

Findings presented below are based on interviews with major political actors (both governmental and in opposition) conducted by the author in 1996 and 1999—one of the most controversial times in the political development of Belarus, as well as other available documentary sources of information. In 1996 the president overruled parliament and dismissed it as ineffective and disloyal. The start of 1999 was marked by a new conflict between parties and the president. Lukashenko signed Decree Number 2, which required compulsory registration of parties and other organizations, thereby imposing a political audit on existing parties. Interestingly, this happened on the eve of the local elections, which were scheduled on March 4, and obviously put not only the parties' participation in elections, but also their legitimate existence, under threat of official closure. Another signal of the developing conflict was the forthcoming "anti-presidential" election, which was legitimately declared by the underground opposition on May 16 on the basis of the 1994 Constitution. These two facts together spurred new political debates and opposition.

Close examination has demonstrated that the "mass" parties are organizations only on paper, and they significantly deviate from Duverger's[17] original definition of the type. They are relatively weak, and many depend on the state for material and financial resources. Only central decision-making structures enjoy some degree of financial independence. Formally some parties have extensive regional structures, but these are not fully functional. In reality only the BNF and PCB can truly be considered as mass parties, with modern survival policies. The BNF and PCB assist their local branches in developing organizational infrastructure and by that reduce their dependency on other financial sources. For the most part, anti-Lukashenko parties do not support policies of coalition and hence cannot organize themselves into a coherent opposition. Thus, they find it impossible to resist the increasing power of the president. They do not trust each other and often pursue ineffective strategies against the current regime.

The new parties are, as a rule, right-wing reformist organizations, organized from the top down with weak linkage in society and a low membership base. They are generally located in urban areas and assign a low priority to building up local structures. Their campaigns are usually capital-intensive, and they tend to be highly dependent on the state for material resources. The United Civic party (OGP), The Belarusian Social-Democratic Party People's Assembly (BSDP NG), and the Party of People's Consent (PNS) exemplify the new type of parties in Belarus. These parties' finances are largely based on sponsorship and grants from the international community, as well as voluntary membership fees. They also seem to be better organized in their technical, publishing, and human resources. With the President's Decree Number 8 (12.03.01), "On Some Measures Concerning the Rules of Receipt and Utilization of Foreign Gratuitous Aid," parties that rely on Western sponsorship will find it more difficult to survive in a highly state-centralized political environment.

In summary, Belarus's parties are factional, have ephemeral membership, and lack party discipline. Internal conflict largely emanates from within the party leadership and is based on personal ambitions rather than policy implementation, causing even further disintegration of the parties. Even the most organized parties, such as BNF and PCB, have failed to provide adequate leadership and save the party from internal feuding. BNF has resisted this tendency longer than others and has only recently split. PCB faced party division in 1996 and was devastated by it. This was a tangible conflict for the party as it related not only to personalities but also to the policy agenda and redefinition of its ideological standpoints. Those who joined the splinter party CPB and supported the president were hard-line communists, believing in "third-way" socialist economy, social security, and public proprietorial rights. The Agrarian Party ceased to exist due to the conflict between the leadership and the party members: farmers refrained from supporting an anti-system leader. OGP, BSDP NG, BSDG, and LDPB are dominated by the leadership and are essentially candidate-centered. What has appeared in interviews and content analysis is that these parties at large have feckless memberships, which on paper represent a wide network of more than 2000 supporters on average, but in reality are very limited. Only 17 out of 28 parties have survived the 1999 political audit—a forcible party reregistration declared by the president.

Given the parties' inability to act cohesively in central office, it is believed to be essential for them to develop governmental links. However, if they collaborate with the incumbent government they will lose the financial comfort they receive from the West by way of grants and partnership aid and certainly receive no welcoming reception from the authorities. Therefore, they have decided to pursue their anti-system policies, which seems to be a long-term vocation. In the situation of an increasing possibility of dictatorship, they logically should mobilize their scarce resources in order to oppose the president and fulfill their mission. However, they failed to unite in order to successfully run an anti-presidential election campaign in the 1999 or 2000 parliamentary elections. The majority of oppositional parties boycotted elections as their gesture of protest against the authorities. They have refused to believe in the old Russian saying, "poor peace is better than a good quarrel." As a result, their present policies seem to be heard, rather than seen.

From interviews with party leaders one can find further discrepancies between party rhetoric and action. In their interviews party leaders keep naming each other as political partners, for example: OGP referred to BSDP NG as their primary associate, and BNF, trade unions, PT, and PCB as already established contacts. BSDP NG, however, found itself closer to BNF, and PT did not enthusiastically confirm this linkage. The BNF in turn affirms that as long as parties continue pursuing their personal ambitions, it will not form any alliance with them. The Labour party (PT) remains independent and hopes to collaborate with the communists if they tone down their orthodoxy. The communists in turn assume that they already have a potential partner in the trade unions and are unwilling to support any collaboration with the liberals and democrats. Parties have recently tried to overcome their ideological differences in order to resist the move towards dictatorship together. They attempted to organize a united movement with a single coordinating body and to rally uniformly for the presidential election in 1999, 2000, and 2001. They spectacularly failed to do so on any occasion.[18]

Another issue relates to parties' collective boycotting of regional and national level elections in 2000. The opposition parties refused to participate in any of them, as their way of demonstrating against gross violations of the law by the authorities. This, nevertheless, was a strategic mistake, as by not having representatives at any levels within the government they are unable to negotiate with the authorities who are presently in the position to dictate the rules of the political game. Huntington[19] notes that elections are not only the life of democracy; they are also the death of dictatorship. The opposition in Belarus has yet to learn this lesson.

The analysis above shows how dramatically dissipated parties are at present in Belarus. Ambitious party leaders are unable to overcome personal feuds when attempting to campaign together against the president. They are limited by formal and informal institutional (high threshold for turnout, majority voting, single-member district) and legal (alterations in the Constitution, new law requirements for party candidates, etc.) rules. Moreover, they lack a distinct ideological profile and doctrine and have limited power resources and organizational cohesiveness. Parties therefore attempt to mobilize support from a population that does not see them as likely ever to be able to equal the power of a single man, the president. This issue will be thoroughly analyzed in the next section.

Nevertheless, parties still survive and are gaining skills. One can say that in Belarus contemporary parties, as is perhaps true of many transitional parties, are seeking "accommodating" opportunities to adapt. They are more candidate-centered due to their volatile electoral currency; policy making has become the sole prerogative of party leadership rather than party membership; therefore, circumstances, rather than existing programs or ideologies, dictate decision making. Organizational structures are thus flexible and low-maintenance. Even the parties that closely resemble true mass parties, BNF and PCB, in fact only look like mass parties with regular members, press, congresses, branches, and so on. In practice they tolerate independent leadership taking dictatorial forms at times, and they emphasize the predominance of parliamentary activities over party policies. Belarusian liberals and democrats never did have strong relations on the ground and now prefer to develop modern strategies (online publishing, Internet discussion clubs, youth conferences, public seminars) to capture free and uncommitted voters.

Party policy at present seems to be to make enough efforts to be visible, rather than compromise and win office. Nevertheless, there are ways for parties to reestablish their authority. One is to survive by capitalizing on uncommitted voters in the regions, and another is to negotiate with the state. Hunting for votes can be quite fulfilling provided that the power cleavage is highly divisive. Thus mass party organizations may still be able to regain vitality and mobilize voters' support. Negotiation with the state is also necessary, as institutional, structural, and cultural environments are becoming increasingly unfavorable for parties in exile. Opposition parties may also attempt to form a wide anti-presidential coalition, as this is the only realistic means for them to survive while in opposition.[20] Otherwise, by not fighting the battle today, they may lose the war tomorrow. The issue of whether electoral mobilization can be foreseen and what chances parties may have with their alienated voters will be raised in the following section.

THE INSTITUTIONAL EFFECT OF A STRONG PRESIDENCY IN WINNING THE ELECTORATE

The effect of the presidency in a new democracy is such that voters are encouraged to focus on individuals and place their trust in nonpartisan candidates—political entrepreneurs—rather than party members. Lukashenko was elected as a populist and he continues to act as an anti-party man, violating the rules of the game that was thought to be becoming the only game in town—semi-parliamentary democracy. The psychological effect is such that since the presidency can be occupied only by a single individual, voters tend to refrain from supporting marginal candidates out of fear of wasting their vote and will support more popular candidates who are capable of winning the office and governing with better effect, even if they are not the voters' first choice. Lukashenko was and still is seen as the better of the two evils, as parties are increasingly regarded by the electorate as not capable of winning office and retaining power. Voters may cherish their beliefs and remain faithful to parties' ideas; however, this does not prevent them from responding rationally to the opportunities provided by the existing institutional order.

The situation of dual legitimacy makes effective decision making ever more difficult. Lukashenko's personality has played an overwhelming role in the politics that brought him popular support in a system of weakening parties and a nonproductive, conservative, and confrontational legislature. The further aggrandizement of the president's power has been achieved not only due to Lukashenko's efforts, but also due to the nature of Belarusian institutions and to collective electoral choice. Lukashenko proved that it is quite possible to outplay institutional limits and to tailor the constitution to the tailor's needs, if personal ambitions and available resources permit. In order to achieve such stunning results, one must play the game as forcefully as Lukashenko does, under the principle of winner-take-all or all or nothing, and have a relatively malleable parliament and all-permissive electorate. This is to say that cultural and structural incentives should be such that they will allow high levels of political volition and demagoguery, permit public faith in the antipartisan leader rather than the parties, and tolerate their own transformation into a system of legalized autocracy. Thus it was that Lukashenko managed to avoid a showdown with the parliament such as Yeltsin had faced with the Russian Congress of People's Deputies in the autumn of 1993, in fact achieving a similar result relatively peacefully, with little bloodshed: a "pocket" legislature, oppositional parties that have voluntarily gone underground, and a whole range of new powers at his disposal.

Both parties and voters tend to act rationally in an attempt to optimize their benefits in the situation of uncertainty and pending crisis in Belarus. Their rationale, nevertheless, appears to be different. Parties have scarce electoral support and remain out of power. Instead of channeling the governed to their governors, parties often act out of the instinct of self-preservation. They cannot afford to mobilize the mass of uncommitted voters, so they either ally with the state to access the unlimited pool of resources, or seek funding elsewhere to acquire votes for the purpose of winning office. Electors, in turn, make their own preference for political investment and seem to choose to support the president as the more realistic source for social change. In other words, parties act by themselves and for themselves, and so do voters. "Participatory linkage," as described by Kay Lawson,[21] appears nonexistent.

The principal question, nevertheless, remains as to why the discrepancy between public expectations and people's real choice persists even when parties go beyond their self-seeking motives and try to reestablish linkage with their voters. It is puzzling why people theoretically believe in a party's mission but stake little hope on their capacity to govern; or conversely, why people steadily support Lukashenko knowing that the concentration of power may lead to dictatorship. This raises the question as to what extent the existing presidential divide between the parties and the incumbent can damage voters' choice and the prospect for democratization.

According to Oleg Manaev,[22] in 1994, 48.7 percent of the population believed that President Lukashenko could solve the economic and political crisis of the country. This level of electoral endorsement steadily continued over the next six years and decreased by four percent between 1995 and 1999. Conversely, public expectations that parties are capable of governing the country out of the economic-cum-political crisis have significantly declined. In 1991, 79.9 percent of the population believed that parties were an essential element for building a democratic future. However, by 1998 only 3.9 percent of the electorate still adhered to this premise, with the main decline occurring between 1996 and 1998 when many parties failed to remain in public office. Paradoxically, the public's belief that parties are fundamental for balancing power in society did not change very much and remained on average at 29.6 percent between 1996 and 1999.[23] These calculations suggest that the dilemma of choice for the Belarusians has been whether to support the president or the parties, which would be the better political investment for saving democracy. The high-level volatility of the people's choice is evidence of the painful process of the formation of public opinion, which has increasingly leaned towards the presidential-led administration during recent years. The situation can be likened to a tug-of-war between the president and the remaining parties. This occurs because both blocs recruit their human capital from a largely overlapping and rationally oriented pool of electors.

When one analyses the level of trust of various political and social institutions, three profiles of the Belarusian electorate can be observed (see Table 4.1).

As one can see from the table, public opinion (middle column) in general is very divided and ready for political mobilization. Three groups of the population can be clearly observed—progovernmental, oppositional, and undecided voters. It may be noted that the propresidential part of the Belarusian electorate seems to be more consolidated and coherent in its judgment; whereas the protest electorate seems to be more skeptical and less enthusiastic in its support of nonpresidential institutions, such as the former parliament.

The Belarusian electorate judge by what they see, not by what they have been promised in grandiloquent terms. After more than 10 years of transition with no sound achievements, the electorate has become more conservative and wary of political and economic experiments and pledges. This seems to be one of the main reasons for such a large proportion of the hesitant electorate, and the challenge for parties is therefore to mobilize these undecided voters. As Rotman[24] notes, at present 53.7[25] percent of the population are undecided about their attitudes towards contemporary political players. This figure remained unaltered between 1997 and 2001. This pool of undecided voters appeared to have constituted a principal source of Lukashenko's victory in the presidential election of 2001.

Table 4.1 Public Trust in Political and Social Institutions in Belarus, 1998

Political values *Public attitudes to social institutions:*	*Presidents supporters (26.0%)*	*All respondents (100%)*	*Presidents opponents (20.8%)*
Government:			
Trust	61.6	26.2	2.6
Do not trust	5.9	25.9	76.2
New Parliament:			
Trust	36.1	15.8	2.6
Do not trust	10.2	24.7	67.1
Constitutional Court:			
Trust	35.8	20.1	9.0
Do not trust	19.2	33.3	70.4
Army:			
Trust	52.2	30.5	12.9
Do not trust	9.0	21.2	53.7
Local Authorities:			
Trust	41.8	21.2	5.8
Do not trust	22.8	35.1	70.4
Traditional Trade Unions:			
Trust	12.0	7.2	3.9
Do not trust	18.2	27.3	56.3
Independent Trade Unions:			
Trust	5.4	9.5	18.6
Do not trust	23.8	22.4	36.7
13th Supreme Soviet:			
Trust	16.9	8.5	9.0
Do not trust	19.5	26.5	53.9
Church:			
Trust	65.0	48.3	39.5
Do not trust	7.4	11.8	25.1
Official Mass Media:			
Trust	75.1	43.7	15.8
Do not trust	5.1	21.0	60.1
Independent Mass Media:			
Trust	13.8	25.4	33.9
Do not trust	33.8	24.1	21.9

Source: Retrieved from O. Manaev, (1998) "Belorusskii Electorat: Za i Protiv Presidenta" [Belarusian Electorate: For and Against the President], NISAPI News (Independent Institute for Social, Economic, and Political Research), Minsk, 1:27.

CONCLUSION

It has been demonstrated in this chapter that the regime in Belarus had the potential to build democracy incrementally, utilizing such prerequisites as a relatively stable economy and social-political conflicts, but that this did not take place due to incongruous interactions of structure and agency. Legacies and inherited structures, reinforced by institutional developments, created an unfavorable environment for further party system consolidation in Belarus. At the other extreme, parties' low ideological profile, their inability to capitalize on voters' preferences, their limited organizational and financial capacities, and the alteration of the competition mode—which focused political parties' attention on the unequal struggle against the president—explains why they remain legitimate but increasingly powerless players of the political game. This has been reflected in their declining membership and partisan support, and their low impact on policy-making in the country.

The public's noninclusion in the decision-making process, through the failure of parties and other interest organizations, has facilitated a formal process of power delegation to an individual leader. This has had a great impact on the mode of democratization in the country. Parties have become increasingly second-rated by the population, which favors the immediate achievements of the president. The formal contribution of trade unions and nongovernmental organizations remains unsound, as there are only limited structural and media mechanisms to articulate their mission. In addition, since 1997 the essential function of parliament as an interest-accommodating arena is no longer fulfilled, due to the total unanimity of opinions among the propresidential forces in the legislature. Today's Belarus is highly divided: many favor the incumbent president and oppose democracy, as they favor the policy of integration with Russia and the CIS in opposition to those who favor democracy and closer union with the EU. As the recent presidential election demonstrated, the former prevail.

To recapitulate, Belarus is metaphorically like a building site within the new Europe. Historically it has some foundations on which to construct a legitimate democratic state. However, it needs to be strengthened institutionally and by consensual decision making of political workers, capable of identifying future prospects for democratic national development and a role of parties in the political arena.

CHAPTER 5

Parties and Party System in Moldova, 1990–2002

Valeriu Mosneaga

Political parties are one of the key components of modern democracy. They play the important role of intermediary between civil society and state bodies in all modern democracies. They form the political culture of a society and at the same time are both a consequence and a condition of the democratic development of a country.[1]

HISTORICAL AND SOCIOCULTURAL CONTEXT

Background of Party Development in Moldova

Moldova declared its independence from the Soviet Union in 1991, following the collapse of the August coup d'état. In its contemporary territorial setting and ethnic composition the Republic of Moldova did not experience either national statehood or national party politics.[2] As a part of the Russian Empire, it did have a rudimentary multiparty system during the first Russian revolution of 1905–1907. Basarabia—the right-bank part of the contemporary Republic of Moldova—was a part of Romania from 1918, and as such accepted the party and electoral system of that regime and participated in elections and in its party politics. In the left-bank part of Moldova—Transdniestrian—all political parties were liquidated in the 1920–1930s, and their supporters were subjected to repression.

After the Soviet annexation of Basarabia in 1940, all political parties were forbidden. Any attempt to create illegal anti-Soviet political organizations[3] in the post-war period was quickly thwarted. The members of these organizations were subjected to repression and were frequently executed.

As a part of the Soviet Union from 1940, Moldova therefore had only a single party—the Moldavian republican branch of the Communist Party of the Soviet Union. The Communist Party of Moldova (CPM) was not a genuine political party. It was a well-defined state structure with all the appropriate functions and mechanisms of decision making, strictly preserving its monopoly of authority.

The withdrawal from bilingualism that started in the beginning of the 1960s provoked an ethnic issue and stimulated protest on the part of representatives of the Moldavian intellectual elite. As a result, in the second half of the 1960s, prominent representatives of the intellectual elite were subjected to reprisals and accused of nationalism. Among them were N. Testimitanu, N. Korlatianu, S. Radautan G. Gimpu, and M. Morosanu, all of whom were condemned for organizing a demonstration in Chisinau, the capital of Moldova.

In the late 1960s to early 1970s, Moldavian students created an illegal anti-Soviet political organization. The purpose of the organization was to penetrate into the leadership of CPM and the supreme state structures of Moldova, and to reorient gradually the political course of the republic. However, the head of the organization, A. Soltoianu, was arrested and had to serve time for more than 19 years in correction camps and in exile. After that, obvious displays of protest in the republic stopped and civil society structures ceased to exist altogether.

The liberalization of the communist regime under Gorbachev created a climate of more openness and led to the beginning of a grassroots civil society as various public groupings, concerned first and foremost with problems of national language, began to emerge.

The first democratic elections of the People's Deputies of the USSR in 1989 and the elections to the Moldavian SSR's Supreme Soviet in 1990 contributed to this process. When, during the 1991 August coup d'état in Moscow, the Soviet military in Moldova tried to impose a state of emergency in the country, the public supported the legitimate government. Nevertheless, Moldova was the first country in Europe that reestablished a Communist party after having achieved national sovereignty.

A Portrait of Political Parties in Independent Moldova

The proclamation of independence (August 27, 1991) and the adoption soon after that of the "Law on Parties and Other Socio-Political Organizations" of the Republic of Moldova (September 17, 1991) created the base for the development of a multiparty system.[4]

In general, the political formations that appeared in Moldova were weak and were searching for their own agendas. They were completely new organizations, which lacked traditions, organizational history, and standard norms of operation. Their field of activity was limited to capital and concentrated around the media. Despite loud claims to speak on behalf of the people, political parties in the parliament of Moldova, as well as the parliament as a whole lacked real political power. The hypertrophied role of leaders in emerging political groupings led to frequent internal splits caused by the personal conflicts among the leaders, on one hand, and to the spreading of formations of a clientelistic type, on the other. At the same time, the divergences between the parties' political programs and their real political practice were significant and persistent.

However, under the influence of the elections and new legal regulations governing the process of party formation, their internal organization, and their political activities, parties began gradually to come forward from their embryonic stage and acquire real structures and influence on the population of the country.

By adoption of the "Law on Parties and Other Socio-Political Organizations" (September 17, 1991) 14 political formations were registered. Most of them passed reregistration after the law was enacted. The number of parties and political formations increased by September 1998 up to 55 and then dropped to 30 after the next reregistration. The growth of the number of parties was most noticeable on the eve of the parliamentary elections of 1994 and 1998, even though optimization of the legislative base aimed to constrain this process.

Under the effect of the new legislation, the tendency to develop new parties by means of internal splits gave way to the tendency to unification.[5] (See Table 5.1.)

However, the institutionalization of political parties is connected first of all with their participation in elections. R. Rose and T. M. Mackie claim that it is possible to speak about the institutionalization of a political party when it has taken part in at least three elections.[6] In the time span under discussion there are 15 parties that meet this criterion. Seven of them participated in elections only as part of electoral blocs and/or gained less than one percent of the vote. Thus, it can be said that only eight political parties have been institutionalized.

As Table 5.2 indicates, most political parties have originated outside the legislature, in keeping with M. Duverger's theory regarding the internal and external origin of parties.[7]

Table 5.1 Dynamics of Splitting/Mergers of Political Parties (According to Registration)

	Until September 17, 1991	*September 17, 1991 to September 30, 1998*	*After September 30, 1998*
Number of parties	14	55	30
Number of splits	8	22	—
Number of mergers	—	16	8

Table 5.2 Types of Political Parties in Moldova by Origin

	Quantity		
Type of origin	*Till Sept. 17, 1991*	*From Sept. 17, 1991 until Sept. 30, 1998*	*After Sept. 30, 1998*
External	11	45	23
%	78.57%	81.82%	76.67%
Internal	3	10	7
%	21.43%	18.18%	23.33%
In total	14	55	30

The rise and alignment of political parties has been significantly influenced by cleavages presented in the society.[8] In particular the center–periphery cleavage played an important role. Having clearly emerged in the late 1980s, the center–periphery cleavage dominated the Moldavian society up to the mid-1990s, and to a smaller degree it still persists today. Despite the traditional view of the center–periphery opposition, in our understanding, the concepts of center and periphery are ambiguous. They simultaneously include the national-cultural dimension, noted by A. Lijphart, the foreign policy dimension, and "the support of existing order"[9] dimension. Undoubtedly, this ambiguity is connected with the lack of experience of independent statehood and, consequently, a similar lack of understanding of this question among the Moldavian political elite.

This cleavage is reflected in the opposition of various political forces. Three general groups of political formations, with their state and foreign orientations precisely defined, appeared in the political spectrum of the country. On the right were unionist political formations, which supported the connection of Moldova to Romania and viewed independence as a short, intermediate stage in its development. On the left were pro-Russian political formations oriented towards supporting the reconstruction of the Soviet state in any possible form. All of these formations were opposed to independent Moldavian statehood. In addition to these political groups, in the center of the political spectrum were the political formations that stood for the independence of the Republic of Moldova. Each of these three groups has had its own center—Bucharest, Moscow, Chisinau—and, correspondingly, its own periphery—Chisinau, Gagauzia, and/or Transnistria. A national survey, "Counsel with People," conducted before the 1994 parliamentary elections, found that the majority of the population preferred that the center be Chisinau.

The church–state cleavage has been of lesser importance, yet it is still reflected in the activity of political formations in Moldova. This cleavage develops around the question of the legitimacy of the Basarabian metropolia of the Romanian Orthodox Church. The Moldavian state consistently refused to register the Basarabian metropolia, thus favoring the Russian Orthodox Church, which monopolized the Moldovan parish under Soviet regime, and has agreed to register it only under pressure of the Parliamentary Assembly of the Council of Europe in July, 2002.

From the second half of the 1990s the owners–workers cleavage began to gather force. However, in the conditions of social and economic crisis, this cleavage is better shown on the rich–poor line, where the poor make up more than 80 percent of the population. This cleavage is also reflected in the activity and policy statements of political parties. Above all, it concerns the left-wing parties, as the communists have significant social support.

THE CONSTITUTIONAL AND LEGAL CONTEXT

Legal Regulation of Political Parties, 1988–1991

During the Soviet period in Moldova, as well as in the entire USSR, the political system was characterized by the presence of one communist party, the role of which was fixed in the Constitution. Although the numerous nongovernmental organizations were formally free, in practice they could not be created without the appropriate decision of party bodies, which led and supervised their daily activity.

With the advent of perestroika, new unofficial arrangements gradually began to emerge and make political demands. Under pressure from public opinion, the Presidium of the Supreme Soviet of Moldavian SSR adopted, in August 1989, the decree "On the Provisional Procedure of Registration of Public Associations of Citizens in Moldavian SSR," and on October 26, 1989 the first four new formations were registered.

Thus, an important step was made on the way to the promoting of a multiparty system in the republic. However, even if the decree accepted the right of these organizations to participate in the political life and to nominate the candidates, it avoided recognizing them as political organizations, fearing evidently a negative reaction from Moscow. Nevertheless, by the time of the elections of the deputies of Supreme Soviet MSSR (February–March 1990) the new public formations had found extensive social support. The Popular Front of Moldova took the lead in parliament and succeeded in generating a noncommunist government.

In May of 1990, the Supreme Soviet of Moldova introduced modifications in articles 6, 7, and 49 of the Constitution of MSSR. The de jure managing role of the CPSU (CPM) in MSSR was liquidated. For the first time a multiparty system was recognized at the constitutional level, even if political parties were mentioned along with other public associations, as peers. At the same time the Constitution prohibited the activity of parties, political movements, and organizations whose purpose was "the violent change of a social order and integrity of the state" (Art. 7).

In addition, real steps were taken to deprive the CPSU of its exclusive position in the Moldavian society. In July of 1990, the government adopted the Decree "On State Power," which banned the formation of party organizations at enterprises and clearly stipulated which state posts were henceforth incompatible with membership in a party. Although this latter requirement applied to all parties and other social and political organizations existing in the republic, it was directed first of all against the CPM whose members dominated in governmental bodies

Moreover, the Provisional Regulations of the Parliament of Moldova, adopted in June of 1991, manifested antiparty feelings, particularly against the Communist Party, in that this legal act did not even mention political parties, party factions, or MP groups based on common political views and beliefs.

The struggle against the monopoly of the Communist Party culminated in August of 1991. The putsch in Moscow showed that although the CPSU had lost its dominant position granted by the Constitution, it had nevertheless kept enough influence in state structures to make it possible for its leadership to engage in nonconstitutional actions in order to regain or maintain power. In Moldova, as well as in other regions of the former USSR, the struggle against the Communist Party ended with the interdiction of the CPM and confiscation of its property. The disappearance of the monopoly of Communist Party on the government was "a part of an initial impulse to constitutional changes."[10]

Formation of the Legal Base of a Multiparty System (1991–1994)

The independence achieved by the Republic of Moldova gave a new powerful push to the formation of a multiparty system in the country. In September 1991 the parliament passed the "Law of the Republic of Moldova on Parties and Other Socio-Political Organizations."[11] Under the rubric "Other Socio-Political Organizations" the law meant "leagues, fronts, unions, political mass movements, *etc.*"

The law was an important positive document, which assisted in the political articulation of interests, raised the social activity of the Moldavian population, and aided in the legal institutionalization of political formations in Moldova. In the law, the place and role of parties in the political system of the country, the basic ways of their formation, functioning, financing, and interaction with other institutions of the political system were precisely stipulated. The law declared that only Moldavian citizens who were at least of 18 years of age could be members of a party. Political parties could operate only in the territory of the country. At the same time, the activity of foreign parties in the territory of the Republic of Moldova was forbidden. For the registration of a political formation, its statute (charter), program, and a minimum membership of 300 people were required (Art. 5). The law demanded political neutrality of the educational system (Art. 9) and forbade the financing of political parties on the part of the state with the single exception of the financing of election campaigns (Art. 10). The state was to supervise and control the financing and activities of political parties and other sociopolitical organizations by means of financial and legal measures. The law outlined a procedure for the suspension of the activities of a party or other sociopolitical organization, and for ceasing the activities in case the party or sociopolitical organization were to dissolve itself or be dissolved by the decision of the Supreme Court of Justice.

Besides the adoption of the "Law on Parties and Other Socio-Political Organizations," the parliament also initiated other laws in which the rules of interaction of political formations with other political institutions were regulated indirectly, as, for instance, in the "Law on the Election of the President of the Republic of Moldova" (October, 1991), in which the rules regarding the participation of political parties in the presidential elections were stipulated.

However, in the presidential elections of 1991 many provisions of the law regulating the activities of political parties and of candidates remained largely theoretical because only one candidate took part in the elections and political formations were too weak to play any significant role in the electoral campaign.

Further steps in the institutionalization of parties in the political system were carried out at the end of 1993. For the formation of an effective mechanism for the functioning of a multiparty system in Moldova, the adoption of the "Law on Elections to Parliament"[12] was particularly important. In contrast to the Law "On the Elections of the People's Deputies in the Moldavian SSR" (1989), this law defined parties, sociopolitical organizations, and electoral blocs as the main actors of the electoral campaign with the right to nominate candidates for election to the parliament.

Instead of the former majority system, "Elections to parliament shall be conducted—after the new law—in multiple-seat electoral districts based on voting according to lists from parties, socio-political organizations, electoral blocs and independent candidates, according to the principle of proportional representation" (Art. 6). The Central Election Commission makes public the names and boundaries of electoral districts and establishes the number of seats for each electoral district through dividing the number of voters in the district by the norm of representation. To avoid excessive political-party fragmentation of the future parliament, the law established an elective threshold of four percent of the valid votes in the country as a whole for political formations and one percent for independent candidates, who also may be nominated. However, while for political formations, registering with the Ministry of Justice was enough in order to participate in the elections, independent candidates had to present the signatures of at least 1,000 voters to the Central Election Commission to qualify.

The law provided for the formation of a smaller and, accordingly, more efficient parliament. Instead of 380 deputy mandates (following the 1989 Law), their number was reduced to 104 members (one deputy for 28,000 voters). Also, while earlier the deputy term was defined as five years, the Law on Elections to Parliament reduced the term to four years.

While the new law created a real basis for elections to the supreme legislature of the country on a multiparty basis, the decision of the Presidium of Parliament to cancel the interdiction of the Communist Party of Moldova as a nonconstitutional political formation created a real basis for the establishment of uniform democratic rules of the game for all political actors of Moldova, irrespective of their orientations. The prohibition of the activity of a political party was from now on possible only according to the law.

Having enacted the law "On Parliamentary Elections" and created equal opportunities to all political parties to compete for seats, Moldavian legislators began to improve the "Law on Parties and Other Socio-Political Organizations."

Thus, article 12 (10), which regulates political party financing, prohibits financing of parties by:

- foreign states, foreign individuals, and legal entities, and individuals without citizenship
- state organs, state enterprises, organizations, and institutions with the exception of financing in accordance with the present legislation of elections for the representative organs of state power
- joint ventures in which more than 20 percent of the capital is foreign or owned by a foreign state or founder
- all unregistered civic associations
- any anonymous persons

At the same time, where earlier the law affirmed that the financial assets of a political formation be comprised of registration and membership fees, the updated version allows parties and other sociopolitical organizations to accept voluntary contributions; donations by physical and legal entities, except for the cases indicated in the first part of Article 12 (10); profits received from the activity of mass media; and funding from many other sources.

The parliamentary elections of February 1994 marked the consolidation of the multiparty system in the Republic of Moldova. Political parties had become a necessary component of the political process. The representation of political parties in the parliament was legitimated and realized in practice. This development was constituted by the new "Rule of Parliament" (March of 1994), which stipulated the activity of parliamentary factions, their roles in the formation of working bodies of the parliament (bureau and committees) and in the functioning of the supreme legislative body of the country.

Relapses into the authoritative regulation of the activity of political formations have failed. There were attempts to forbid the activity of CPFM (PFM), Socio-political Republican Movement "Ravnopravie" (Equality), and the National-Christian Party of Moldova for their opposition to government, but judicial bodies did not find legal ground for their interdiction.

The institutionalization of political parties in the political system of the country proceeded. A special clause, "Freedom of Political Association" (Art. 41), entered into the new Constitution of the Republic of Moldova in July of 1994, declared that "The State shall ensure the protection of the rights and legitimate interests of parties and other social/political organizations."[13]

The new constitution, the law on the elections of local authorities from December 1994, and the law "On the Special Status of Gagauzia (Gagauz-Eri)" that called for elections to the National Assembly of this autonomous republic in March, 1995, the first in its history, finalized the creation of the legal base for institutionalization of parties at all levels of the political system.

In April of 1996, a new modification of the "Law about Adoption of the Parliamentary Rules" governing the legislative process was accepted. As before, legislators were anxious to prevent the excessive fragmentation of parliament. The political-party configuration based on the results of parliamentary elections was preserved. According to the 1994 and 1996 Parliamentary Rules, parliamentary factions could be created only by the political formations that won more than four percent of the vote and had at least five seats. The presence of new factions created inside the parliament due to a regrouping of political forces between existing factions was not allowed, but the creation of parliamentary groups was expected. The right to propose nominees for key posts in the parliament was given only to established factions.

The acceptance of the "Law on the Election of the President of the Republic of Moldova" (May 1996) and the competitive presidential elections in November–December 1996 demonstrated that the process of the institutionalization of political parties and the multiparty system at all levels and in all structures of the government had actually been completed.

At the same time, the "Law on Parties and Other Socio-Political Organizations" needed further development. After an amendment made in September 1998, the law not only defined a political party, but also accented the fact that political parties promoted the realization of the political will of the population of the country through gaining control over the government by legal means. Changes were made to the requirements for registration. Now, to be registered a political formation has to submit to the Ministry of Justice the charter and the program, and the signatures of 5,000 persons living in half of the administrative and territorial units of the second level, including at least 150 signatures from each of the administrative and territorial units. Besides that, the law required the reregistration of political formations every three months and stated that "the political formations that do not pass re-registration will be considered self-dismissed."

Next came administrative-territorial reform of the country. As of May 21, 1999, 12 administrative districts replaced the 40 "areas" at the second level of government, and further changes were made to article 5, raising to 600 (as compared to 150) the number of signatures necessary to gather from each administrative and territorial unit in order to register a new political formation.

The next modification of the law on political parties was dated February 3, 2000. While earlier the legislature modified the external conditions of the existence of political parties, now it paid attention to the regulation of their internal conditions and organization. Henceforth the charter and the program of a party was to be authorized at a congress or at a conference (Art. 5.1). The legal address of a political party could be the address of an individual. The payment amount for the registration of a charter of a political formation was set at 10 times the minimum hourly wage. The law demanded that the supreme body of a party—the congress—be convoked at least once in four years. A political formation should have territorial organizations. Procedures for liquidating a political formation were set for the first time (closely resembling the procedures for liquidating an economic entity.

The various amendments added to the "Law on Parties and Other Socio-Political Organizations" throughout a period of almost 10 years have reflected not only the process of the maturity of the supreme legislature of the country, but also a quantum leap in the development of parties in the political system of Moldova. By May 4, 2000, the updated law contained 35 articles regulating the activity of political formations.

Electoral Law

While the law on political parties reflects the creation, internal organization, and liquidation of political formations, electoral law reflects the dynamic interactions of political parties with civil society and with the institutions of the political system of the country.

In November of 1997, the "Election Code" was accepted, standardizing electoral procedures and the interaction of political parties with the authorities on all levels of the Moldavian electoral system.

The administrative-territorial reform that was begun in November of 1998 with the transition to large administrative districts brought modifications to this law in 1999, including new stipulations regarding how to fill a parliamentary vacancy. A presidential decree of June 24, 2000, aimed to overcome some legal deficiencies that had become evident during May to June 1999. It brought further changes, including changes in thresholds: for political parties, electoral blocs, and alliances, the elective threshold was raised from four to six percent; for independent candidates it went down from four to three percent. Art. 41 (2a) was added, stating that political formations wishing to participate in elections must be registered for at least two years prior to the beginning of the election campaign.

The transformation of Moldova from a parliamentary-presidential to a parliamentary republic (July 5, 2000) prompted further alterations in the Election Code. The president of the country was to be elected by the parliament, which consequently led to a substantial increase in the role and responsibility of political parties in this process. They became direct intermediaries between society and the president.

The next modification in the Election Code of January 25, 2000, was the declaration that a party independently participating in elections now had to collect at least six percent of the vote in order to pass into parliament; an electoral bloc consisting of two political parties had to collect at least nine percent; and a bloc consisting of three or more parties had to collect twelve percent of the vote.

Further changes dated February 14, 2002 required that private mass-media structures give air time on equal terms to all political parties during election campaigns (Art. 46). Given that it was the practice of the Communist Party to limit the access of other political formations to a bare minimum on state TV channels, as well as to practice heavy-handed censorship, the development of the Election Code can be understood as the desire to keep the private structures of the mass-media under control and to ensure complete supervision of the forthcoming election campaign at the time the changes were made.

THE PARTY SYSTEM IN MOLDOVA TODAY

A modern party system requires not only the presence of two or more parties but also competition for the posts of power.[14] In Moldova, rejecting single-party government has meant the introduction of different political visions for the development of the independent nation. In the process, the different formations have frequently shown intolerance and animosity toward one another to the point where the system may be described as one of extreme political pluralism.[15] The aptness of this label can best be shown by reviewing the nation's parliamentary elections since independence.

Elections to the Moldavian parliament in the 1990s took place in unique circumstances. First, Moldova was one of the post-Soviet republics. Second, the elections were carried out in the conditions of ethnic mobilization, aggravation of interethnic relations, and growth of nationalism. Third, these elections were the first in which the Communist Party was not the single political choice. The new public formations registered by the autumn of 1989 acquired significant social support and nominated candidates, but unlike the communists did not propose programs calling for specific reforms to bring about perestroika, economic *uskorenie* (acceleration), advancement of the nation's interests, or moderation of interethnic relations and the protection of the interests of all ethnic groups. Fourth, the elections took place in 380 single-member districts.

As a result, a formally communist parliament was elected (83 percent of the deputies were members of Communist Party of Moldova (CPSU). The Moldavian Popular Front (PFM) won 133 seats, and the Unity movement got 32.

In practice, however, the influence of PFM in the parliament was dominant, especially during the first one and a half years. Representatives of the Popular Front headed all the parliamentary factions, led the presidium of parliament, and dominated the cabinet. The PFM established itself as the party that was ready to act in the interests of Moldavians, while other deputies, especially representatives of the rural elite, many of whom were directors of collective farms and state farms, feared losing their management posts and refused to take leading positions in the permanent bodies of parliament.

Using the oratorical skills of their deputies and their command of parliamentary and inner-parliamentary activity, the PFM managed to realize its program de jure. By using national-state symbols canceling the monopoly of the Communist Party, and expanding the powers of the republic in relation to the allied center, the PFM created a base for noncommunistic and confederative development of Moldova within the structure of the USSR.

This, however, was only the first step, which permitted it to attain the support of moderate nationalists prior to pursuing its strategic purpose, the entrance of the new republic into the structure of Romania and the rejection of Moldavian autonomy. Toward that end, the PFM stimulated the growth of party structures and the fragmentation of parliament. Numerous political formations actively began to divide MPs into different groups. By the end of the activity of the parliament in autumn of 1993, it consisted of eight deputy groups.

At this point, however, the Moldavian population began to turn away from the PFM, especially in the southern areas of the republic, occupied basically by the Gagauzian population, and in the eastern region where the Russian-speaking population prevailed. Attempts to control these separatists by military force in the south and in Transdniestria were undertaken, but soon afterwards the PFM prime minister, Mircea Druc and the chairman of parliament, Mircea Snegur, were released from their duties, and the new prime minister, Valeriu Muravschi (May 1991–August 1992) took a softer line.

The opposition in Chisinau after the Moscow putsch, the interdiction of the Communist Party, and the acceptance of the "Declaration of Independence" (August 27, 1991) united the radicals from PFM and the noncommunistic bureaucracy of Moldova for a short time. However, the resolution of the Great National Assembly, which was carried out by

PFM on August 23, 1991, showed that the leaders of this political formation had not abandoned their unionist purposes and still considered the independence of the country as a short transitional period on the way to association with Romania. The consolidation of supporters of the independent Moldavian state in the parliament resulted in the acceptance of the "Law on the Election of the President of the Republic of Moldova," which favored M. Snegur. The Agrarian-Democratic Party of Moldova was created and eventually provided his victory in the December 1991 presidential elections.

The Popular Front responded with an appeal to boycott the presidential elections, as well as with attempts to consolidate all the political formations of the democratic right orientation into the Alliance (December 16, 1991). Realizing that its influence was decreasing, the PFM agreed to provide its partners equal representation in directing bodies of the Alliance.

The armed confrontation in the eastern areas of the country that began in the spring of 1992 united the supporters of independence and the supporters of the association with Romania to oppose separatism. However, it was not possible to win over separatism and to restore the constitutional authority in the eastern areas of the country.

The Popular Front made new attempts to achieve its goal, particularly by using the religious factor. Its policy aimed to create a deliberate split of Orthodox parishioners of Moldova between the Russian Orthodox Church and Romanian Orthodox Church, which, in spite of the official position of the secular authorities of Romania, openly supported dissenters and created a (restored) Basarabian metropolis (old style) in December 1992.

Unionists among the top politicians called for the celebration of Romanian national holidays, for a scientific conference to work out how to achieve the economic integration of the two countries, and so on. Finally, however, the president, supporting the actual parliamentary majority, called for a national referendum on the issue of Moldavian independence. As a result, the unionist leaders in the parliament resigned and their places were taken by supporters of an independent Moldova. In October of 1993, the parliament made the decision to hold early parliamentary elections.

Nine political parties, 4 electoral blocs, and 20 independent candidates took part in the parliamentary elections of 1994 under the new system of proportional representation. Multi-seat electoral districts were formed corresponding to the second-level administrative-territorial units of the republic. Nearly 80 percent of the registered voters turned out to vote.

The main issue that divided society during the electoral campaign was the question of whether Moldova should be independent or not (see Table 5.3).

Four contestants (the four top contestants listed in Table 5.3) won the elections. The Agrarian-Democratic Party of Moldova (ADPM) came to be seen as the strongest supporter of an independent state and as such received 43.18 percent of votes that brought 56 of 104 seats in parliament.

Table 5.3 Results of 1994 Parliamentary Elections

Electoral Contestants	*Abbreviation*	*Number of votes*	*%*	*Number of mandates*
Democratic Agrarian Party	DAP	766,589	43.18	56
Socialist Party and "Unitate-Edinstvo" Movement Bloc (Socialist Party of Moldova, "Unitate-Edinstvo" Movement)	SPUEMB	39 ,584	22.	28
Peasants and Intellectuals Bloc (Intellectuals Congress) (Alliance of the Free Peasants, Women's Christian-Democratic League, Democratic Christian Party, National Liberal Party)	PIB	163,513	9.21	11
Alliance of the Popular Christian Democratic Front (Christian-Democratic Peoples Front, Council of the Voluntary Combatants of Moldova, Christian-Democrat Youth Organization)	APCDF	133,6 6	7.53	9
Social Democratic Bloc (Social-Democratic Party of Moldova, National Youth League of Moldova)	SDB	65, 28	3.66	
Association of Women	AW	5 ,243	2.83	
Democratic Party of Labour	DPL	49,21	2.77	
Party of Reform	PR	41,98	2.36	
Democratic Party	DP	23,368	1.32	
Association of Victims of Totalitarian Regime	AVTR	16,672	.94	
Republican Party	RP	16,529	.93	
Ecological Party Alianta Verde (Green Alliance)	EP	7, 25	.4	
National Christian Party	NCP	5,878	.33	
Independent Candidates	IC	45,152	2.54	

Source: Association for Participatory Democracy. http://www.parties.e-democracy.md/en/

In total, 11 political parties were able to attain representation in the parliament. The parameter of the effective number of political parties (the Laakso-Taagepera index)[16] was equal to 3.96.

The dominant ADPM, possessing the majority parliamentary faction and enjoying the support of President Mircea Snegur, gained control over the government and began to advance democratic reforms in all spheres of public life. On many issues ADPM was supported by the bloc of Socialist Party and Unitate-Edinstvo, which was interested in the defeat of the political forces impelling association with Romania. Due to this support the Constitution of independent Moldova was accepted. The victory of the political forces advocating independent statehood was confirmed by the results of the survey "Council with the People" and changed the components of the center–periphery cleavage. Moldova became the center, and its regions became the periphery. Thanks to a similar transformation within the party in power, it was possible to change the constitutional field of the Republic of Moldova and to solve the Gagauzian conflict.

The democratic transformation of the political system was, however, accompanied by a sharp fall in the standard of living, huge social stratification, and the impoverishment of the overwhelming majority of the population. The issues discussed during the parliamentary elections of 1998 represented rather the rich–poor than owners–workers cleavage. In the center of discussion was the ability of authorities to lead the country out of social and economic crisis.

Nine political parties contested elections as independent players, 27 parties participated as members of parties, movements and associations composed seven electoral blocs, and 60 persons were independent candidates. Turnout was 69.12 percent of the registered voters. (See Table 5.4.)

Once again four competitors surpassed the four-percent threshold and succeeded in entering parliament. The Laakso-Taagepera index was 5.7.

Table 5.4 Results of 1998 Parliamentary Elections

Electoral Contestants	*Abbreviation*	*Number of votes*	*%*	*Number of mandates*
Party of Communists	PC	487,002	30.01	40
"Democratic Convention" Electoral Bloc	DC	315,206	19.42	26
(Party of Rebirth and Reconciliation of Moldova, Christian-Democratic Peoples' Party, "Green Alliance" Environmental Party of Moldova, Women's Christian-Democratic League of Moldova, Christian-Democratic Peasants' Party)				
"For a Democratic and Prosperous Moldova" Electoral Bloc	FDPM	294,691	18.16	24
("For a Democratic and Prosperous Moldova" Movement, Civic Party of Moldova, "Forta Noua (New Force)" Socio-political Movement, Peoples' Democratic Party of Moldova)				
Party of Democratic Forces	PDF	143,428	8.84	11

Table 5.4 (Continued) Results of 1998 Parliamentary Elections

Electoral Contestants	*Abbreviation*	*Number of votes*	*%*	*Number of mandates*
Democratic Agrarian Party (Agrarian Democratic Party of Moldova, "Femeia Moldovei [Moldovan Woman]" Socio-political Movement, Democratic Youth Alliance of Moldova)	DAP	58,874	3.63	0
"Furnica" (Ant) Civic Alliance Electoral Bloc ("Civic Alliance for Reforms" Socio-political Movement, Party of Progressive Forces of Moldova, "Civic Unity" Movement, Youth Union of Moldova, Centrist Democratic Party of Rebirth of the Republic of Moldova)	FCA	53,338	3.29	0
"Alliance of Democratic Forces" Electoral Bloc (National Peasants' Party of Moldova, Liberal Party of Moldova, National Liberal Party)	ADF	36,344	2.24	0
Party of Economic and Social Justice	PESJ	31,663	1.95	0
Social Democratic Party	SDP	30,169	1.86	0
"Socialist Unity" Electoral Bloc (Socialist Party of Moldova, "Unitate-Edinstvo (Unity)" Republican Movement for Equal Rights, Communist Union of Moldova, "VATAN" Peoples' Party)	SU	29,647	1.83	0
"Speranta" (Hope) Social Democratic Electoral Bloc (United Social-Democratic Party of Moldova, "Speranta-Nadejda [Hope]" Professionals' Movement, Women's Association of Moldova)	SSD	21,282	1.31	0
Party of Socialists	PS	9,514	0.59	0
Party of Reform	PR	8,844	0.54	0
Christian Democratic Union	CDU	8,342	0.51	0
United Party of Labour	UPL	90,997	5.60	0
Independent candidates		17,736	1.09	0

Source: Association for Participatory Democracy. http://www.parties.e-democracy.md/en/

Having won the elections and having generated the largest faction, the Communist Party nevertheless appeared in opposition. The propresidential bloc "For a Democratic and Prosperous Moldova," the electorate of which was to a great degree left-centrist, was able to form a right-centrist majority "Democratic Alliance for Reforms" (DAR) to take over the government. Prime Minister Ion Sturza's government began to emphasize the pro-Western orientation of the country, refusing opportunities offered in the eastern market by Russia and the CIS. This policy led to a growth of discontent, and after the Christian Democrat Popular Front withdrew from the Democratic Convention and the DAR, the latter lost parliamentary majority. Sturza had to resign, and the DAR passed into opposition.

By the end of 1999, joint efforts of the communists and independents formed a technocratic government under Dumitru Bragis, and in July of 2000, all parliamentary factions voted for the transition to a parliamentary republic. However, after three consecutive attempts in December of that year to elect the president by the parliament failed, the parliament was dissolved and new elections were called for 2001.

This time 27 competitors took part in the elections: 12 political parties and movements participating independently, and another 15 parties, movements, and associations—in five electoral blocs. Ten persons fought for seats as independent candidates. 67.52 percent of registered voters cast ballots to elect the parliament.

Once again the most sensitive issue for the public was the low standard of living and increasing impoverishment of the population. These conditions benefited the Party of Communists, a party that had not been in power since Moldova's independence and was seen by many as the last chance of moving out of the present social and economic crisis. The communists received 50.07 percent of the vote, and 70.30 percent of deputy mandates (71 of 101 seats).

Only two other competitors surmounted the six percent barrier and succeeded in entering the parliament: the left-centrist electoral Bloc "Braghis Alliance" with 13.36 percent of votes and 19 seats, and Christian Democratic People's Party (CDPP) with 8.24 percent of votes and 11 seats. In total, eight political parties appeared in parliament. The Laakso-Taagepera index was 3.45.

The Communist Party now had the opportunity to try to put its electoral program into effect, and even to exact a measure of revenge for its years in exile. However, the party now lacked staff and had no experience in running government under the conditions of democracy. Nevertheless, the realization of the "small open economic" model, initiated by Bragis's government, allowed Vasile Tarlev's government to achieve some positive results in the economic sphere.

Attempts to realize pre-election promises in the national-language sphere caused numerous student protests, initiated and controlled by the

Table 5.5 Results of 2001 Parliamentary Elections

Electoral Contestants	*Number of votes*	*%*	*Number of mandates*
Christian Democratic People's Party (CDPP)	130,810	8.24%	11
Electoral Bloc "Faith and Justice" (BECD) (Party of Reform, National Romanian Party)	10,686	0.67%	0
Communist Party (CP)	794,808	50.07%	71
National Liberal Party (NLP)	44,548	2.81%	0
Social-political Movement "For Order and Justice" (SPMFOJ)	23,099	1.46%	0
Party for Rebirth and Conciliation (PRC)	91,894	5.79%	0
Democratic Party (DP)	79,757	5.02%	0
Peasants' Christian Democratic Party (PCDP)	4,288	0.27%	0
Electoral Bloc "Lawyers and Economists' Alliance" (AJE) (New National Moldovan Party, Party of Civic Dignity)	14,810	0.93%	0
Electoral Bloc "Edinstvo" (BEE) (Republican Party of Moldova, Party of Socialists of the Republic of Moldova, Party of Progressive Forces of Moldova)	7,277	0.46%	0
"RAVNOPRAVIE" Republican Socio-Political Movement (RRSPM)	7,023	0.44%	0
National Peasants Christian Democratic Party (NPCDP)	27,575	1.74%	0
Party for Democratic Forces (PDF)	19,405	1.22%	0
Agrarian Democratic Party (ADP)	18,473	1.16%	0
Electoral Bloc "Braghis Alliance" (BEAB) ("New Force" Socio-political Movement, "Speranta-Nadejda [Hope]" Professionals' Movement, Socialist Party of Moldova, Labor Union, Centrist Union of Moldova, "Furnica" [Ant] Party of Social Democracy)	212,071	13.36%	19
Electoral Bloc "Plai Natal" (BEPN) ("Plai Natal" Socio-political Movement, National Youth League of Moldova)	25,009	1.58%	0
Social Democratic Party of Moldova (SDPM)	39,247	2.47%	0
Independent candidates	36,477	2.31%	0

Source: Association for Participatory Democracy. http://www.parties.e-democracy.md/en/

CDPP. Attempts to introduce censorship on national television caused a strike among media employees.

The new alignment of parties in the parliament brought about the easing of political centrism in the life of the country. The communists attempt to pursue a policy of minimizing the political center, since they have subordinated the left-centrist branch in parliament. The CDPP, likewise, aspires to suppress right-centrist forces in the country, engaging in dialogue with the right-centrist branch provided it fully accepts the CDPP's leadership.

Perspectives for the Consolidation of the Moldavian Party System

Parliamentary elections in the first decade of independence have confirmed the validity of the conclusion that in Moldova there is a party system of extreme pluralism characterized by the presence of a dominant party as well as the absence of a stable party system.

At the same time, the effective number of political parties testifies that there is a basis for the evolution of the party system. The index of Laakso-Taagepera for the 1994 and 2001 parliamentary elections—3.96 and 3.45—testifies to the possibility of an evolution to a party system of limited pluralism. However, the same index for the 1998 parliamentary elections—5.7—testifies to an opportunity for the consolidation of a party system of extreme pluralism.

It seems that the 1998 parameter is more adequate for evaluating the present party system of the Republic of Moldova than the 1994 (and 2001) parameter for the effective number of political parties. The 1994 (and 2001) parameter reflects the moment of *actualization and extreme delimitation* of public opinion about the problem caused by the influence of a certain cleavage. The decrease in the acuteness of a topic (for example, in the 1998 elections) shows a change in the situation and in the parameter of the effective number of political parties.

The methodology of "problematic measurements"[17] confirms our conclusion and, based on the cleavages allocated by S.M. Lipset and S. Rokkan, reveals the correlation between this parameter and the parameter of effective number of political parties. For Moldova, this parameter is equal to 5.5.

In reality, there is a struggle between the tendency to be drawn to one of two extremes, fluctuating between the pluralistic party system and the moderate pluralistic party system.

CONCLUSION

The multiparty system of Moldova is still far from stabilized. Since December 1, 2002, five more parties have ceased their activity. At present there are 21 political parties, movements, and associations in Moldova, and party elections are a routine attribute of politics.

Competing in the recent regular parliamentary elections of March 6, 2005, were the two winners of the preceding elections, Party of Communists and the CDPP, plus 12 other parties and sociopolitical organizations (seven of them as independent players and five as members of two electoral blocs), and 12 independent candidates.

As a result only 3 out of the 23 contestants passed the threshold of representation—Party of Communists (45.98% votes, 56 mandates), Moldova Democrata Bloc composed of Democratic Party of Moldova, "Moldova Noastra (Our Moldova)" Alliance and Social Liberal Party (28.53% votes, 34 mandates), and CDPP (9.07% votes, 11 mandates). The remaining votes, 16.42 percent of the total, were cast for the 20 contestants who failed to pass the threshold. These votes were redistributed to the three winners according to the d'Hondt formula. Voter turnout was 64.84 percent of the total number of voters included in the voter rolls.

The International Election Observation Mission found that the elections were generally in compliance with international election standards. However, during the electoral campaign some observers pointed to the use of administrative resources and biased election coverage by media, especially the state-owned media.

The Party of Communists, having 56 out of the 101 seats in Parliament, is able to elect parliament governing bodies and appoint the government on its own. Still, communists are no longer able either to change the Constitution single-handedly (for which they would need 68 mandates—two-thirds of the deputies), or to elect the president (61 mandates needed—three-fifths of the deputies). So, they are forced to negotiate and to cooperate with other parliamentary factions. The Christian-Democratic Peoples' Party (CDPP) got 10,000 more mandates and confirmed the tendency of slow but steady increase in their rating. Eighteen of the 101 MPs have not joined any party faction.

The Republic of Moldova had no prior experiences either with independent statehood or with democracy and the multiparty system. During the last 10 years, however, constitutional and legal bases for a multiparty system have been created; democratic, free, and competitive elections have been carried out; and the process of the institutionalization of political parties is well under way.

Political parties accumulate experience of participation in parliamentary, presidential, and local elections, become accustomed to competition, to democratic rules of the political game, and to the need to search for compromises and allies, and so forth. Accrued experience is the reflection of the process of maturity of political formations, their transition from political romanticism to political realism, and the real formation and functioning of the multiparty system in the Republic of Moldova.

CHAPTER 6

Influence of the Electoral System on the Role of Political Parties in the Development of Democracy in Ukraine

Volodymyr Fesenko

DEMOCRATIC THEORY ON THE ROLE OF POLITICAL PARTIES IN THE DEVELOPMENT OF DEMOCRACY

Contemporary democracy is impossible to imagine without political parties. The genesis of liberal democracy is inseparably connected with the appearance of political parties. According to Austin Ranney, "The political parties have created democracy," and "the present democracy is unthinkable other than in party expression."[1]

Political party scholars single out different functions of parties. We tackle only those of particular significance for the functioning of democratic systems. Political parties not only represent the interests of different groups, but also express and substantiate them ideologically—in the form of systematized program demands addressing the authorities and the state policy. Convincing comparative substantiation of the parties' role as expressing social cleavage was made by S.M. Lipset and S. Rokkan.[2]

Political parties do not restrict themselves to expressing different social interests; they organize and represent them in the political process—fighting in election campaigns for the right to participate in the development and implementation of a state policy. As electoral mechanisms, parties promote citizens' involvement in policy making, as well as the organization and structuring of the political process in democratic systems. Interacting with each other in the bodies of state power and local government, political parties reconcile different, frequently adverse, social interests, thus easing social controversies and overcoming public tension by the way of compromise, without aggression and violence.

The main purpose of any party is the conquest of political power by getting seats in representative bodies performing legislative functions and key positions in the executive branch. Therefore, to participate in power, parties must carry out a personnel function: the formation, selection, and promotion of political leaders. These functions characterize political parties as an indispensable institution of a democratic society. Even disputes about the crisis of contemporary political parties failed to reveal a possible alternative capable of replacing them completely in the functioning of democratic systems.

TRANSFORMATION OF THE ELECTORAL SYSTEM IN UKRAINE

The March 1994 election of the People's Deputies of Ukraine was the first election in the contemporary history of the Ukrainian state in which political parties became a full-fledged subject of the electoral process. They were conducted on the basis of the majority electoral system, with winners being determined by the results of two rounds.

The law provided for a more complex procedure for candidate nomination by parties and affected the outcome of the nomination process. Out of 6,488 nominees for the 1994 elections to the Verkhovna Rada of Ukraine (parliament), 1,679 persons were members of political parties (25.9 percent of the total number of the candidates), and only 694 candidates were nominated by regional branches of political parties.[3] Furthermore, as will be shown below, political parties' representatives gained almost half of the seats in the highest legislative body of the country.

An important result of the increase of party representation in the Ukrainian parliament was a change of the electoral system. On September 25, 1997 the Verkhovna Rada of Ukraine adopted the new Law on Elections of the People's Deputies of Ukraine, based on a mixed (majority-proportional) electoral system. According to the law, one half of the composition of the Verkhovna Rada of Ukraine (225 deputies) was to be elected in single-district constituencies in one round of voting based on a relative majority, and the other half in accordance with candidate lists presented by political parties and/or party blocs in a multi-mandate nationwide constituency based on proportional representation, with seats awarded only to parties gaining four percent or more of the vote.[4]

As to the presidential election and election to local councils, despite changes in the legislation, terms for party participation in those election campaigns did not change significantly. The elections to local councils both in 1994 and in 1998 were based on a majority electoral system.

There was a tradition in Ukraine that every new election is conducted under a new law (true for all elections: presidential, parliamentary, and elections to local bodies of power). Though parliamentary elections in March 2002 were the second based on a mixed (majority-proportional) electoral system, yet in 2003 the Verkhovna Rada was working on draft laws envisioning the transition to a proportional system of election of the People's Deputies. The all-Ukrainian referendum supported the proposal to create a second chamber of parliament, to represent the interests of the regions and to simultaneously reduce the total number of deputies of the highest legislative body of the country to 300.

POLITICAL PARTY REPRESENTATION IN THE LEGISLATURE UNDER DIFFERENT ELECTORAL SYSTEMS

Our guiding hypothesis is that substitution of a majority electoral system with a mixed electoral system has enhanced the role of political parties in the development of a democratic political system in Ukraine.

Changing the electoral system directly affects the process of formation of the highest legislative body of a country. To see how this has been true in Ukraine, we compare the number of deputies who were members of political parties within the Verkhovna Rada during its thirteenth session, when deputies had been elected according to the majority system, to the composition of the fourteenth session, elected under the mixed electoral system. In addition, the influence of political parties on structuring the Verkhovna Rada after both the thirteenth and the fourteenth sessions is analyzed.

Despite the complicated procedure of candidates' nomination to the Verkhovna Rada during the 1994 election, political parties managed to achieve significant representation quotas in the highest legislative body of the country. From 394 People's Deputies of Ukraine elected by October 1994, 182 Deputies (46 percent) were members of political parties.

According to the experts of the Ukrainian Perspective foundation, the electoral success of the candidates who were party members in the election to the Verkhovna Rada of Ukraine in the spring and summer of 1994 was more than twice as high as that of nonparty candidates (see Table 6.1).

Table 6.1 Ballot Efficacy As a Function of Party Affiliation

	Nonparty members		*Party members*		*Total*
		in %		*in %*	—
Nominees	4,809	74.1	1,679	25.9	6,488
The People's Deputies of Ukraine	212	53.8	182	46.7	394
Percent winning office	4.4		10.9		6.1

Source: Verkhovna Rada of Ukraine: Paradigms and Paradox, Issue 1. Kyiv: Ukrainian Perspective, 1995, p. 7 [In Ukrainian].

In this case, the index of ballot efficacy indicates the percentage of deputies elected compared to the total number of candidates.

According to Sergey Odarich, the head of the Ukrainian Perspective foundation, these data demonstrate that a party affiliation did not prevent a candidate from being elected, and even fostered his election.[5] One could have agreed with this conclusion, if it were not for one important circumstance. Over half of the deputies—party members, elected to the Verkhovna Rada in 1994, belonged to one party—the CPU (Communist Party of Ukraine). If we view electoral success in party terms (see Table 6.2), we will see that the political effectiveness of individual parties differed significantly. Only the communists and the agrarians demonstrated high efficiency in the elections. Three parties achieved higher effectiveness compared to nonparty candidates, while the remaining 23 parties' participants on average stayed less effective in comparison to the nonparty candidates.

The activities of the Verkhovna Rada of Ukraine during its thirteenth session took place in an atmosphere of steadily growing party power. Aleksandr Moroz, the leader of the Socialist party of Ukraine, was elected head of the highest legislative body with the support of deputies from left-wing parties. The number of parties and party-members in the Ukrainian parliament increased throughout the session. As of December 1994, representatives of 14 political parties had been elected to the Verkhovna Rada of Ukraine and 46.2 percent of the deputies were party members; by the end of the session (early 1998), the parliament comprised 19 political parties, and 57 percent of the deputies were party members.[6]

The increase in the number of party members in the composition of the legislature resulted not from by-elections, but by two other means: existing parties attracted nonparty deputies to join them and new political par-

Table 6.2 Ballot Results in Verkhovna Rada of Ukraine Election of Spring 1994 by Candidates from Separate Parties

	Candidates number (in brackets—of total number of the candidates)	*Number of elected deputies (in brackets—% of total number of the deputies)*	*Efficacy of ballot*
Communist Party	388 (6.7%)	86 (25.4%)	22.2%
National Rukh	241 (4.1%)	20 (5.9%)	8.3%
Socialist Party	180 (3%)	14 (4.1%)	7.8%
Republic Party (RPU)	137 (2.3%)	8 (2.4%)	5.8%
Peasant Party	65 (1.1%)	18 (5.3%)	27.7%
Remaining parties	557 (9.5%)	22 (6.5%)	3.9%

Sources: The Central Electoral Committee of Ukraine, Voice of Ukraine, 1994, March 24 [In Ukrainian]; Election to Verkhovna Rada of Ukraine: Experience and Examples, Kyiv: NISD, 1994, p. 41; V. Litvin, Political Arena of Ukraine: Persons and Doers, Kyiv: Abris, 1994, pp. 415, 418.

ties were created. Sometimes this process took on rather bizarre forms. For instance, the Liberal Party of Ukraine, which failed in 1994 to get even a single deputy in the Verkhovna Rada of Ukraine, in 1995–1996 created first a deputy group in parliament and then a faction. The Agrarian Party of Ukraine and Party of Regional Revival of Ukraine managed to register with the Ministry of Justice and set up their factions after the election. The reason for this phenomenon lies in the strengthening of the clan-and-corporate tendencies both in society and the legislature, which meant an ability to use hidden financial and administrative-political levers. For example, the Agrarian Party of Ukraine and its parliament faction were formed on the presidential administration's initiative, aimed at creation of a counterbalance to the socialist-oriented Peasant Party. It was, of course, cheaper to create a post-election party faction within Verkhovna Rada than to develop the infrastructure of a party in the regions and to conduct election campaigns in dozens of districts.

It should be noted that the factions of political parties and deputy groups, the core of which was formed by members of political parties, constituted nearly two-thirds of the legislature, thus promoting its political structuring. Nevertheless, it proved impossible at this time to achieve stable structuring of the Verkhovna Rada, and the identity of the factions changed during each session of parliament (see Table 6.3).

The data analysis presented in Table 6.3 demonstrates that the most stable factions were those created by political parties, those competing for the highest number of seats, those with clear ideological platforms (such as the Communist Party, National Rukh of Ukraine, and the Socialist Party). The Peasant Party created a broader party faction, known as Agrarians of Ukraine, but it ultimately dissolved, and on the eve of parliamentary elections of 1998 the peasants united with the socialists into a single faction and electoral bloc. The change in faction structure of the Verkhovna Rada of Ukraine on the eve of the March election of 1998 mirrored a regrouping of political forces caused by the preparation for the election. It should also be noted that the strongest efforts to rearrange factions and deputy groups were made by nonparty deputies and representatives of nonparty deputy groups. For example, the declaration of the creation of a faction Social-Market Choice in February, 1996 was signed by 29 deputies, 25 of whom were nonparty members, although 9 had earlier belonged to Inter-Regional Deputy Group (IRDG), 8 to the group Unity, and 3 to the group Center.[7]

From 446 People's Deputies selected to the Verkhovna Rada of Ukraine in 1998, 306 (69 percent) were members of political parties. Representation of political parties in the legislature had increased 1.5 times. However, this impressive breakthrough was reached mainly due to voting by party lists. Two-thirds of the deputies who were members of a party (198 out of 306) were elected within the framework of the proportional system of representation established for the nationwide constituency.[8]

Table 6.3 Change in Structure of Factions in the Verkhovna Rada of Ukraine (1994–1998)

	Number				
The title of a faction (deputy group)	*August 1994*	*January 1995*	*January 1996*	*February 1997*	*February 1998*
Faction of the CPU	91	90	89	86	80
Faction of the Socialist Party	25	27	26	25	—
Faction of the Socialist Party and Peasant Party	—	—	—	—	40
Faction of the NRU	27	27	28	27	25
Group Agrarians of Ukraine	34	48	27	38	—
Group Agrarians for reforms					
Faction Agrarian Party of	—	—	25	—	—
Ukraine	—	—	—	—	27
The inter-regional deputy Group (IRDG)					
Faction of a Party of regional	27	31	31	28	—
revival of Ukraine	—	—	—	—	32
Group Social—market choice	—	—	31	25	25
Group Statehood	26	30	29	—	—
Group Center	38	33	31	—	—
Group Constitutional Center	—	—	—	56	50
Group of Reform	27	36	30	29	—
Group Unity	26	31	33	37	32
Group Forward, Ukraine!	—	—	—	—	30
Group Independent	—	29	27	25	25
The non-faction deputies	23	19	25	16	45

Sources: A. Tkachuk, Deputy Factions and Groups in Ukrainian Parliament. Political Orientation. Change Dynamics, Citizen Voice, 1997, no. 4, p. 24 [In Ukrainian]; Verkhovna Rada of Ukraine: Informational Reference, Kyiv, 1998, p. 24.

If we compare the electoral success of the party and nonparty candidates in the People's Deputies of Ukraine in single-district winner-take-all districts, we can see that political party nominees appeared less successful than their nonparty colleagues (see Table 6.4). At the same time, the difference in success rate is not that significant. Furthermore, a number of crucial circumstances should be taken into account. In the election campaign of 1998, parties had much wider participation than in 1994. Over half of the candidates represented political parties (whereas in 1994 it had been only a quarter). The competition in single-member majoritarian districts increased considerably as the number of such districts had been reduced by half. The success of the candidates running in these districts was determined, first of all, by two main conditions: the amount of funds allocated to finance the election campaign and to resolve pressing problems in a region, and the support of the local authorities (permitting the use of

Table 6.4 The Relationship of Ballot Efficiency in Majority Districts to the Party Affiliation of the Candidate (Verkhovna Rada of Ukraine of the Fourteenth Convocation, 1998)

	Nonparty members		*Party members*		*Total*
		in %		*in %*	
The deputy candidates	2,039	47.7%	2,237	52.3%	4,276
Seats won in parliament	113	51%	108	49%	221
Effectiveness of ballot, %	5.5		4.8		5.2

Source: Calculated from the data provided in the collection: Election 98. As Ukraine Voted, Kyiv, 1998 [In Ukrainian].

administrative resources to influence the electoral process). A majority of the nonparty deputies elected in single-member districts were entrepreneurs and publicly acknowledged, in a post-election meeting with the nation's president, having spent an average of one million dollars each on their election campaigns.[9] Political parties, on the other hand, had to reserve financial resources for conducting the election campaign by party lists in the national constituency. In conditions of increasing competition (made clear by the decrease of the index of ballot efficiency from 6.1 in 1994 to 5.2 in 1998), the parties received slightly less than half the seats in single-member districts, the same as in 1994.

Compared to 1994, a greater number of political parties managed to obtain seats in the parliament (14 in 1994, 21 in 1998); of these, 20 won some of their seats in single-member districts.

The strengthening of party influence in the fourteenth session of parliament had significant and often controversial results. The structuring of parliament became clearer. A decision was adopted, according to which the exclusive right to create factions was granted only to the parties that crossed the four-percentage barrier. As a result, the representatives of the eight party factions that, victorious in the election in national constituency, comprised 90 percent of all the deputies. On the other hand, the ideological opposition increased. Strife between leftist factions, supported by Hromada deputies, and centrist propresidential factions led to a two-month legislative deadlock before a compromise could be reached and the parliamentary leadership could be formed on a parity basis. The speaker, his deputies, and chairpersons of all committees of the Verkhovna Rada represented party factions. The majority were members of political parties.

However, on December 9, 1998, the Constitutional Court annulled the Verkhovna Rada decision to give parties the exclusive right to form factions and this led to a significant change and fragmentation of the faction structure of the Ukrainian parliament (see Table 6.5). Kuchma's victory in the presidential election in 1999, the formation of a new government, and the parliament crisis resulted in a new faction reallocation in the legisla-

Table 6.5 Change in Structure of Factions in the Verkhovna Rada of Ukraine (1998–2000)

	Number of members			
Faction	*June 24, 1998*	*July 6, 1999*	*December 22, 1999*	*July 12, 2000*
CPU	120	122	115	115
UNR	47 (before split)	30	27	—
Ukrainian national Rukh	—	—	—	21
UNR (first)	—	15	16	—
Ukrainian national Rukh	—	—	—	19
Leftist center (SPU and PPU)	33	—	—	18
Socialist party of Ukraine	—	24	23	—
Peasant party of Ukraine	—	15	15	—
Green Party of Ukraine	2	23	17	17
National-democratic	89	29	28	23
Hromada	45	17	14	—
Progressive Socialist Party of Ukraine	14	14	4	—
Social-democratic party of Ukraine (united)	25	2	36	34
Faction Motherland	—	26	32	35
Reforms and order	—	24	15	15
Reforms-center				
Reforms-congress				
Revival of regions	—	28	33	35
Working Ukraine	—	17	28	44
Independent	26	20	13	—
Solidarity	—	—	—	24
Nonfaction deputies	15	16	19	46

Sources: Political calendar. 1999, no. 12, p. 26 [In Ukrainian]; V. Yablonsky and Ya Latko, Modern Political Parties of Ukraine, Kyiv, 1999, p. 7 [In Ukrainian]; Regular Rotations in Parliament Majority, Day, July 13, 2000 [In Russian].

ture,[10] with the result that faction instability abruptly increased in comparison to the previous session, and the Communist Party remained the only stable deputy formation.

The main reason for the instability of the party structure in the highest legislative body of the country lies in the increased influence of the executive power in the hands of the president. At the beginning of the fourteenth session, the party in power was the National Democratic Party (NDP), whose leader, V. Pustovoytenko, was head of the government. The National Democrats had managed to create the second largest faction (28 party members were elected to the parliament, and 89 other deputies, for the most part nonparty members, joined the faction). However, the deterioration in the relations of some of the NDP leaders with the president, and the steady weakening in the position of Pustovoytenko, culminating in his resignation at the end of 1999, naturally affected the number of members in this party faction. In its turn, the Social-Democratic Party (United) faction, drawing on good relations with the nation's president and the fact that the party leader, V. Medvedchuk, was the vice-speaker of the parliament, grew and prospered. One of the president's favorites, A. Volkov, created an influential deputy group, Revival of the Regions.

The defeat in the presidential election of A. Moroz, the leader of the socialists, and that of N. Vitrenko, the leader of the Progressive-Socialist party, resulted in the split of the Socialist Party and a considerable decrease in the size of its faction, while the Progressive-Socialist Party faction ceased to exist altogether. After A. Tkachenko, the Peasant Party representative, was elected the speaker of Verkhovna Rada (not without the consent of the presidential administration), the Peasant Party set up its own faction, having separated from the socialists. The displacement of A. Tkachenko from the post of the speaker, caused by his opposition to Kuchma during the presidential election, and the formation of a propresidential majority in Verkhovna Rada, led to the dissolution of the peasant faction. The formation of a propresidential majority in the parliament took place under the immediate influence of the presidential election results and the threat of a possible dissolution of parliament. These are only some of the many examples confirming the influence of the executive power over the changes in the political structure of the legislature.

The second important factor increasing the fragmentation of the faction structure of the Ukrainian parliament was the strengthening of economic groups based on clientelistic relationships and the rise of their influence in the development and transformation of political blocs. Now many of the factions—for example, the Social-Democratic Party (United), Revival of Regions, Working Ukraine, Motherland, partly the Green party of Ukraine and the National-Democratic Party—were based on common political and economic corporate interests, rather than on ideological features.

Thus, the transition from a majority to a mixed electoral system resulted first of all in an increase of party representation in the legislature, but at the same time it failed to provide stable structuring of the parliament's political structure. An increase in the influence of the executive power (primarily of the presidential administration) over the activity of the Verkhovna Rada weakened the significance of parties and their ability to guide the development of a faction structure of the legislature. Despite the changes in the electoral system and enhanced representation in the highest legislative body, political parties failed to control the formation of their own factions within parliament.

On the eve of the 2002 parliamentary elections the new division of party factions in Verkhovna Rada became dominant: propresidential versus antipresidential. This division became more important than ideological distinctions declared before. Former opponents from right- and left-wing parties united in an antipresidential camp. On March 31, 2002, 33 lists of candidates (11 from blocs and 22 from parties) participated in elections by proportional system. Only three blocs and three parties received more than four percent of votes and entered the Verkhovna Rada. See Table 6.6.

At the same time political parties competed with each other in majority constituencies for the second part of the seats in Verkhovna Rada (225). Due to the single-member majority system the seats were distributed between deputies who had collected only 36 percent of the votes. The largest two blocs—For a United Ukraine and Our Ukraine—together received 48 percent of mandates. Nonparty candidates also won a considerable share of the mandates—42 percent. After elections the structure of the Ukrainian parliament greatly changed. See Table 6.7.

New factions appeared in Verkhovna Rada. Our Ukraine, led by the former prime minister V. Yushchenko, and the propresidential For a United Ukraine, together with SDPU, were expected to form a majority coalition. Furthermore, it was even supposed that Our Ukraine and For a United Ukraine could unite in a single party. The populist bloc of Y. Tymoshenko (also former minister) was now represented for the first time and became a new element of the opposition different from the left , that is the CPU and the SPU.

Table 6.6 Ballot Results in Verkhovna Rada, Spring 2002 (Proportional system ballot)

Our Ukraine (bloc)	23.57% votes	70 seats
CPU	19.98% votes	59 seats
For united Ukraine (bloc)	11.77% votes	35 seats
Y. Timoshenko (bloc)	7.26% votes	22 seats
SPU	6.87% votes	20 seats
SDPU (U)	6.27% votes	19 seats
Total	75.72% votes	225 seats

Source: www.cvk.ukrpack.ua

Table 6.7 The Structure of Factions in the Verkhovna Rada after the 2002 Elections

Our Ukraine	112 mandates	24.9%
For a United Ukraine	101 mandates	22.4%
CPU	65 mandates	14.4%
SDPU (United)	24 mandates	5.3%
SPU	23 mandates	5.2%
Y. Timoshenko bloc	22 mandates	4.9%
Other parties	9 mandates	2%
Nonparty	94 mandates	20.9%
Total	450 mandates	100%

Source: www.cvk.ukrpack.ua

However, on the eve of the presidential elections in 2004 the composition of parties' alliances and coalitions greatly changed and began to reflect regional cleavages combined with clannish interests rather than any others. Our Ukraine and the bloc of Y. Tymoshenko united under the head of V. Yushchenko became the main oppositional force that countervailed against the Regions of Ukraine party supported by president L. Kuchma and headed by prime minister V. Yanukovych.

THE INFLUENCE OF POLITICAL PARTIES ON THE PROCESS OF FORMATION OF THE GOVERNMENT AND MANAGEMENT OF EXECUTIVE AUTHORITY UNDER DIFFERENT ELECTORAL SYSTEMS

The second hypothesis tested in our study was based on the assumption that the influence of the political parties of Ukraine over the formation and activity of the executive power was limited by the presidential-parliamentary form of government and the accompanying constitutional process for formation of the government and other executive bodies. The presidency was established in 1991, and the presidential-parliamentary form of government was reflected in the new Constitution of 1996. Within the framework of this system, the government was responsible to both the president and to parliament. The prime minister's candidacy was nominated by the president and approved by the Verkhovna Rada. The president also decides whether or not to accept the recommendations of the Cabinet of Ministers in the selection of the heads of the local state administrations, and in their eventual dismissal. The elections to Verkhovna Rada do not lead to an automatic change of government, unlike the presidential election. Verkhovna Rada can influence the formation and activity of the government only by refusing to approve the prime minister nominee, or by a vote of no-confidence in the government.[11]

The relationship between the strength of the parties and the powers of the chief executive can be analyzed by examining the results of the presidential elections of 1991, 1994, and 1999 from the party perspective (participation and results by party candidates), as well as by considering the representation of political parties within different cabinets of ministers.

At the time of the first Ukrainian national presidential election (December 1, 1991), 15 political parties had announced their formation, but the Ministry of Justice registered only eight of them. Seven candidates registered as presidential candidates. Of these, two (the chairman of the Verkhovna Rada, Leonid Kravchuk, and the minister of agriculture Alexandr Tkachenko) represented the former Ukrainian nomenclature, the majority of which, after the CPSU collapse, abandoned party affiliation, refused to defend communist ideas, and came to support the state sovereignty and independence of Ukraine.

The other five candidates actually represented embryonic political parties in opposition to the ex-nomenclature. The national-democrats were represented by other candidates (the leader of National Rukh of Ukraine V. Chernovol, the leader of the Republican Party L. Lukianenko, and the candidate from the Party of Democratic Revival of Ukraine (PDRU), formally a nonparty member, I. Yukhnovsky). A member of PDRU, V. Grinyov, not supported by his party, ran for the presidency independently. One more candidate, L. Taburianskiy, represented the People Party, the core of which consisted of the employees and clients of his commercial structures.

The ex-nomenclature consolidated around Kravchuk (A. Tkachenko withdrew his candidacy in his favor), who received 61.59 percent of the votes. His main opponent, V. Chernovol, received 23.37 percent of the votes. In total, the party opposition collected 34.24 percent of the votes.[12]

By the presidential election of 1994, 32 political parties were registered, but almost all of them simply ignored the presidential elections. Of the seven registered candidates, only one—the chairman of Verkhovna Rada A. Moroz—represented his political party (the Socialist Party of Ukraine). However, in the election campaign, even he made use not of the party resource, but of the organizational potential of Verkhovna Rada and his connections with local bodies. In the presidential election of 1994, political programs were presented not by political parties, but by political leaders, and the personality factor was decisive. Except for the socialists, political parties were unable to put forward competitive candidates capable of waging effective battles for the post of head of state. Even the largest and most organized parties (CPU and NRU) found it extremely difficult to sustain two major election campaigns in a row within half a year. Their resources had been exhausted during the parliamentary elections in the spring of 1994 and without an actual possibility of success they did not want to take chances during the presidential election.

It cannot be said, however, that political parties were completely passive during the presidential election. Some of them directly (or indirectly) supported particular candidates. The national-democrats grouped together, especially in the second round, to support acting president Kravchuk. The interregional bloc of reforms (IRB) actively supported former premier Kuchma. The communists, having sharply criticized the political course of Kravchuk, indirectly encouraged their supporters to vote for Kuchma in the second round.

In the presidential election of 1999, political parties again actively declared their existence. Out of the 15 presidential candidates registered by the Central Electing Committee, 12 represented political parties. Out of the 13 candidates participating in the election (two withdrew their nominations), 11 were representatives of political parties. This time parties' active participation in the struggle for the highest post in the state was obviously linked to their strengthened role in the parliament. Out of the 15 registered candidates, 12 were deputies, including the chairman of

Verkhovna Rada; six candidates were the leaders of political parties that crossed the four-percent threshold in the parliamentary elections of 1998.

Furthermore, the two nonparty candidates (the acting president of Ukraine Kuchma and the ex-premier, people's deputy of Ukraine, E. Marchuk) enjoyed strong political party support. A bloc of 21 parties, Our choice—Kuchma, supported Kuchma, while E. Marchuk was supported by a number of national-democratic parties and the Social-Democratic Union, a party that emerged in the midst of the election campaign.

However, victory went once more to a nonparty candidate, Kuchma. His victory was brought about not so much by the support of the centrist parties (and in the second round also of the national-democratic and right-wing parties), but by the massive use of the informative and financial resources of the state. The decisive reason for Kuchma's victory was his management not of an ideological, but of an administrative resource.

The leaders of political parties participating in the presidential marathon received 49.63 percent of the votes in the first round of voting.[13] For comparison, in the election to Verkhovna Rada 45.4 percent of the total number of votes were cast for the members of political parties. This figure is fairly consistent and most likely reflects the level of actual party-mindedness of the Ukrainian society.

A major factor reducing the chances of political party candidates in the presidential election lies in the particular features of the Ukrainian society. Ukraine is rather diverse in ethnic, sociocultural, and social and economic dimensions. All the presidential and parliamentary elections held in independent Ukraine have demonstrated considerable differences in the political and ideological preferences of the electorate of eastern, central, and western regions of the country. The party system of Ukraine has two clearly distinctive ideological poles: the left-wing parties and the national-democrats. The electoral basis of each of these poles is limited.

A presidential candidate leaning to one of these poles is incapable of getting the absolute majority of votes (even if he succeeds in forming a coalition of political parties). And a candidate without a clear party and ideological placement on this axis is actually able to form and manipulate a wide electoral basis.

Although no political party could conquer the highest post in the country, it remains possible that the political weight of separate parties within the Verkhovna Rada or party support during the presidential campaign influenced the formation of executive bodies. To consider this possibility we examine how the outcome of the presidential and parliamentary elections influenced the changes in the party representation within the Cabinet of Ministers.

For the first time, elements of the coalition approach were applied in the formation of the government at the end of October 1992, when Kuchma was appointed the prime minister. The Verkhovna Rada dismissed the previous government, and the relations between the parliament and the president were aggravated, while the economic crisis in the country was deepening. Under these circumstances, the decision to include three prominent representatives of national-democratic opposition in the Cabinet of Ministers was a demonstrative political gesture. I. Yukhnovsky, formally a nonparty member of the opposition faction National Rada, an ex-rival of Kuchma in the presidential elections, was appointed the first vice-premier, while NRU members, People's Deputies of Ukraine V. Pinzenyk and Yu. Kostenko, became the vice-premier on economic reform issues and the minister of environmental protection respectively. I. Yukhnovsky held the post for less than half a year, V. Pinzenyk for almost one year, and Yu. Kostenko retained the post of the minister throughout a number of the subsequent compositions of the Cabinet of Ministers. In the spring of 1994 the newly formed Ministry of Nationalities and Migration was headed by one of the leaders of the Party of Democratic Revival of Ukraine, A. Emets. The party-mindedness of the government also manifested itself in another manner. The president of the joint-stock company Nord, V. Landuk, appointed the vice-premier in June of 1993, created the Labor Party before the end of that year.

After Kuchma was replaced by Ye. Zvyagil'sky as the chief of the Cabinet of Ministers, the principle of the presence of some party members in the government continued to be enforced. However, the parties had very little power over the government, which was formed not on the basis of political party coalitions, but by the president's and prime minister's own requirements for the professional qualities of each minister.

This tendency continued. The party and political approach to the formation of the government remained secondary and subordinate to the professional one. The inclusion of separate party members into the Cabinet of Ministers demonstrates formal participation of political parties in the execution of power but does not mean actual influence of parties on the development of government policy.

The second essential point is that the election of a new legislature and certain changes in the party structure of the highest legislative authority of the country did not in any way change the Cabinet of Ministers or bring about any essential rotation of its composition. Rather, the case is the opposite: high-ranking officials left the government (and other highest bodies of executive power) when elected to parliament.

In 1994 all party ministers resigned from the government of E. Zviagilskiy when they were elected as deputies to parliament. In the course of the presidential election campaign, V. Masol was appointed to the post of the prime minister. He retained his post with the government after the election of President Kuchma. In the government formed by V. Masol, there was not a single member of a political party.

In 1998 the government of V. Pustovoytenko was abandoned by Yu. Kostenko (NRU), the minister of Environmental Protection, Yu. Yekhanurov (NDP), chairman of the State Committee on Issues of Development of Business, V. Suslov (a nonparty member, but elected by the list of the electoral bloc of Socialist Party of Ukraine—Agrarian Party of Ukraine), the Minister of Economics, and G. Udovenko (nonparty member, elected by the list of NRU). All of them were elected people's deputies. V. Kremen left the presidential administration when he was elected to the Verkhovna Rada as a member of the Social-Democratic Party of Ukraine (United). Similarly, newly elected deputies V. Matvienko (one of the NDP leaders), B. Boiko (NRU), and G. Filipchuk (NRU) left their posts as heads of Vinnitsa, Ternopol, and Chernovtsy regional administrations, respectively.

On the other hand, members of the National-Democratic Party, elected to the parliament—prime minister V. Pustovoytenko, minister of the Cabinet of Ministers A. Tolstoukhov, and Head of Kharkov regional state administration O. Demin—all preferred to decline their deputy mandates and to retain their posts within the executive branch.

Political practice also demonstrates that a political party's support of the winner in the presidential election did not increase that party's influence on the executive power. V. Grinyov, the leader of the interregional bloc of reforms (IBR), one of the pillars in the Kuchma election campaign in 1994, became the president's only advisor, after Kuchma's victory, but no other political prizes were awarded to IBR for the help it gave Kuchma in the presidential election.

During the presidential election campaign of 1999, the NDP leaders V. Pustovoytenko and Ye. Kushnaryev created the political bloc Our Choice—Leonid Kuchma! The administrative resources of the government headed by V. Pustovoytenko were put to work on behalf of the acting president. Nonetheless, after Kuchma's reelection, the government of V. Pustovoytenko was made to resign (with the assistance of parliament).

The NDP exemplifies the destiny of a party of power. It was set up in 1996 by a number of high-ranking government officials and well-known politicians affiliated with several centrist parties and public and political organizations. It was intended to become a political core of the consolidation of centrist forces, thereby overcoming the ideological bipolarity of the Ukrainian party system. In its organizational development, NDP relied not on party resources or lower-level party leaders, but rather on the administrative potential of the executive power it controlled. After the NDP members Ye. Kushnaryev and V. Pustovoytenko headed the Administration of the President of Ukraine and the Cabinet of Ministers respectively, the party membership started to grow.

Characteristically, the Cabinet of Ministers headed by V. Pustovoytenko from July 1997 until December 1999 was not a party government either. During its formation, the prime minister clearly stated that "the government will be formed only on professional basis."[14]

The relative failure of NDP in the parliamentary elections of 1998 (the party managed to get only five per cent of the votes in the national constituency), the president's gradually cooling attitude toward the national-democrats, the internal party crisis caused by this, and, finally, the resignation of V. Pustovoytenko from the post of the head of the government resulted in the party's acute decline.

The NDP example clearly demonstrates that the strategy of party development that heavily relies on the executive power can be efficient only when good connections with the highest power in that branch (the president) are maintained. Without this support the political influence of a party is undermined.

The subsequent Cabinet of Ministers led by V. Yushchenko was unlike any other in the contemporary history of Ukraine with respect to the number of political parties (eight) and their members (nine) represented in the government. But at the same time this government was not a coalition for the activity of which political parties could be held responsible.

The parliamentary majority built in Verkhovna Rada under the pressure of the presidential administration was propresident, and not progovernment. In fact, the Cabinet of Ministers was the only executive body of power whose formation could be influenced by political parties.

Furthermore, during Kuchma's presidency, the political significance of the government in the executive authority structure declined due to the increase in the influence of two other bodies of executive power—the Administration of the President of Ukraine and the National Security and Defense Council. The head of state directly formed both without the participation of parliament. This circumstance did not promote an increase in the influence of political parties on the executive power.

Thus, the influence of the party factor on the formation and activity of the executive bodies of power was realized in a dual way. On the one hand, separate political parties regularly delegated their representatives to the Cabinet of Ministers. On the other, some high-ranking officials of the executive power became members of political parties or participated actively in the creation of new parties.

The second scenario led to the strengthening of the lobbying influence of parties, the members of which became high government officials, but it did not imply the formation of a system of mutual political responsibility of parties and executive authority for the execution of state policy. The introduction of a mixed electoral system and the considerable strengthening of party representation in the legislature did not qualitatively change this situation, since it was caused by specific features of the presidential and parliamentary form of government.

THE INFLUENCE OF THE ELECTORAL SYSTEM ON THE INSTITUTIONALIZATION OF POLITICAL PARTIES AND DEVELOPMENT OF THE PARTY SYSTEM

The peculiarities of an electoral system influence not only the level and quality of political parties' representation in government bodies, but also the development of a party system as a means of interaction between different parties struggling for power. Maurice Duverger has formulated three laws regarding the relationship between electoral and party systems:

1. The proportionate election system leads to a party system comprising numerous, inflexible, independent, and stable parties.
2. The majority system of voting in two rounds stimulates the appearance of a party system consisting of numerous, independent, and relatively stable parties that hold flexible positions and strive for mutual contacts and compromises.
3. The majority system of voting in one round in one-mandated districts generates a party system characterized by the rivalry of two main parties, not prone to form unions.

Duverger himself noted that a long historical process underlies the laws he discovered. The psychological effect gradually gains momentum upon the mechanical effect of an electoral system.[15] Not all political scientists share Duverger's conclusions, claiming that the laws he formulated can be viewed as hypotheses that require verification.

In this regard, let us examine to what extent the change of the electoral system in Ukraine has influenced the transformation of a party system, as well

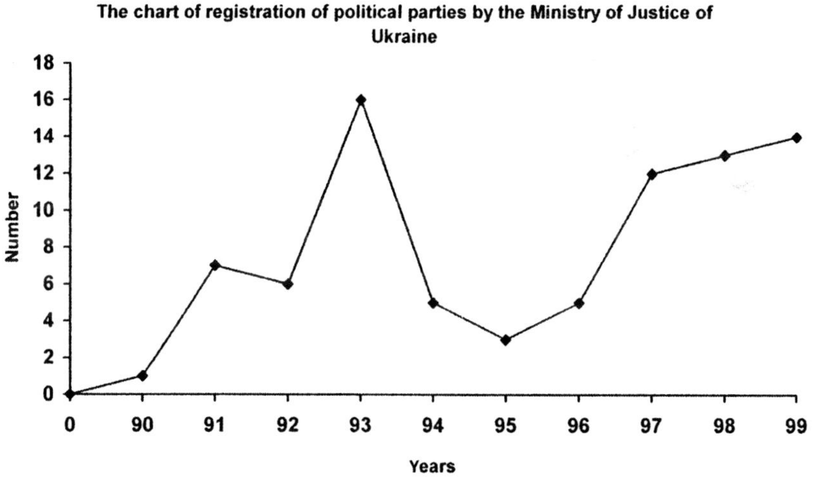

The data in the chart show the number of political parties registered during a given year. Some of the political parties registered in earlier years ceased to exist. 1999 data show not only the number of parties registered, but also those that held their founding conventions.

Source: L. Yablonskiy, and Y. Latko, Modern Political Parties of Ukraine, Kyiv, 1999 [In Ukrainian]; Political calendar: information-analytical review. 1999. No. 1–12 [In Ukrainian].

as the quantitative and qualitative parameters of development of political parties. Does Ukrainian political practice confirm the laws of Duverger?

Ukraine, as well as many other post-communist countries, has confronted the phenomenon of avalanche-like growth of political parties, when each year yielded several new political organizations. Currently, according to observers' estimates, about 100 political parties have declared their existence in Ukraine. In the process certain patterns can be traced. (See The chart of registration of political parties by the Ministry of Justice of Ukraine.)

The data presented in the chart demonstrate that a change of the electoral system and approach of each parliamentary election fosters the appearance of new political parties. After the parliamentary elections of 1998, there was no decline in the formation of new political parties for the following reasons.

First, political parties were gripped by another epidemic of splits. In 1998–2000 over 10 political parties faced this problem, including 6 parties that gained victory in the parliamentary elections of 1998, in the national constituency.

Second, the growth in the number of political parties boosted the planned transition to a proportional electoral system and the expectation of pre-term parliamentary elections. The changes in the configurations of political space after parliamentary and, especially, presidential election, are supported institutionally. Thus, the leaders of a number of electoral blocks that participated in the parliamentary elections of 1998, the leaders of new deputy blocs within Verkhovna Rada, and some participants in the presidential election of 1999 set up their own political parties. The leaders of small political parties attempted to use their organizations as tools in political disputes in order to create new interparty coalitions.

Ten years of democratic development in Ukraine is a relatively short historical term to make unequivocal conclusions. But during this period the laws of Duverger were substantiated when applied to Ukrainian practices, albeit with some peculiarities.

The single-member district majoritarian system, followed by a mixed electoral system with proportional representation as one of its components, promoted the appearance of numerous political parties, most of which were not inclined to enter electoral unions.

It should be noted that when we speak about a large number of political parties, we are not referring to the formal number of registered parties, but to the quantity of parties actually influencing the political process. The quantity indicator that describes this aspect of party system development is called "an efficient number of parties." Markku Laakso and Rhine Taagapera proposed the following formula for its computation:

$$N \qquad \frac{1}{p_i^2}$$

(*N* is the efficient number of parties; *p* is percent of votes received by a party in the election, or percent of the deputy mandates in a legislature divided by 100.)[16]

According to our calculations "the efficient number of electoral parties " for Ukraine (from the results of the March 1998 election to the Verkhovna Rada of Ukraine by national constituency) constitutes 10.6. For comparison, in the majority of liberal democracies this index ranges from 2 to 6.[17]

Apart from the influence of an electoral system, there is another explanation of the large number of political parties in Ukraine. The American political scientist Arend Lijphart has shown that, based on comparative research of 21 democracies, the development of a party system is significantly influenced by the quantity and degree of pressing problems that create significant political discord in the given society. As the main types of public discord, which A. Lijphart labeled "issue dimensions," the following were singled out: social and economic, religious, cultural-ethnic, "city–village," regime support, foreign policy, and post-materialistic. The most crucial issues were marked by A. Lijphart with 1, less crucial ones with 0.5. This allowed him to compute a quantitative indicator of issue dimensions for different countries. For example, for Ireland, the United States, and New Zealand this parameter equals 1; for France, Norway, and Finland it is 3.5. Lijphart's research also revealed the correlation between the quantity indicator of issue dimensions and "the number of efficient parties." It appears that on the average "the number of efficient parties" equals the "quantity of issue dimensions" plus one.[18] According to our estimates, "the quantity of issue dimensions " for Ukraine constitutes 5.5 (social and economic discords—1, religious—1, cultural-ethnic—1, city–village—0.5, regime support—1, foreign policy—1, post-materialistic—0). Thus, "the number of efficient parties " for Ukraine hardly will be lower than 6–7.

In view of the high index of the issue dimensions for Ukraine, the large number of efficient electoral parties promotes the implementation of parties as representation of different social interests and ideological orientations.

The use of a majority system of relative majority during the election to Verkhovna Rada of Ukraine in single-member districts in 1998 also has confirmed Duverger's theory, but in a particular form. The two-party phenomenon (the duality of political process) was manifested in the form of a competition between the nonparty candidate and the candidate who represented the strongest party in the district. Out of 225 majority districts this very situation was observed in 120. The regionalization of the Ukrainian party system manifested in the elections of 1994 was confirmed in 1998. In eastern Ukraine the main struggle was between the CPU members and nonparty candidates; in western areas the national-democratic parties dominated; in the agrarian areas of central Ukraine the main competition between the nonparty candidates and the communists was supplemented by participation of the representatives of APU, NDP, SPU, and Peasant Party. In Dnepropetrovsk, Hromada and communists struggled together against nonparty candidates.

The difficulty of establishing a stable party system in Ukraine follows a pattern typical for many post-communist countries. The institutionalization of political parties implies a process, by means of which some parties are strengthened and acquire importance as well as stability.[19] The institutionalization of parties is not only a process, but also a property or a state. As a property, institutionalization can be defined as the extent of the public's familiarity with a party, as a result of which it exists independently of its leaders since it is regularly involved in significant models of conduct.[20] From this viewpoint, there are only two parties in Ukraine that can be considered institutionalized: CPU and NRU (before the split). To measure institutionalization, different indicators are used: the lifetime of a party and its stability (involvement in splits and mergers), electoral stability, stability of representation in the bodies of legislation, and so forth.[21] R. Rose and T. Mackie, for example, assert that "we can speak of an institutionalization of a party if it participated in more than three nationwide elections."[22] If we take into consideration both the parliamentary and presidential elections, only five parties meet this criterion in Ukraine: CPU, NRU, SPU, UWP, and the Peasant Party.

The introduction of a mixed electoral system has affected the institutionalization of political parties and the development of the party system in a rather controversial way. On the one hand, the sufficiently high level of institutionalization of such parties as CPU, NRU, SPU, and the Peasant Party has been confirmed in the voting by party lists. On the other hand, there were many paradoxical discrepancies in voting in majority districts and by party lists.

The green party (PGU)—one of the first parties to register in Ukraine—was able, thanks to an efficient television advertisement campaign, to get 5.4 percent of votes in voting by party lists, which yielded it 19 deputy mandates. However, none of the 97 PGU candidates competing in majoritarian districts won a seat in parliament..

It was discovered that in many regions there was no link between the ratings of certain parties in a region and the votes for its candidates in single-member majority districts. For example, in the Chernigov region two-thirds of voters when voting by party lists supported left-wing parties, but no candidate from these parties was elected the deputy in the districts of the region. In the opinion of Ukrainian political scientist M. Tomenko, one of the main reasons for such a situation is that voters frequently have an irrational motive for the selection of a party and a more pragmatic one for voting for a specific candidate in a majority district.[23]

One of the most serious problems in the introduction of the proportional representation mechanism within the mixed electoral system was the tendency of parties that were to prove successful in the national constituency to choose weak candidates as their nominees in single-member districts. Combined, the parties that gained more than four percent of the vote put up 111 candidates in majoritarian districts—of these 43 won, 29 came in second or third, 27 were fourth to tenth, and 12 placed eleventh to twenty-fourth (gaining not more than 500 votes in districts averaging 180,000 voters). This poor showing situation testifies to both a weak personnel potential of the parties that won the election and to low standards for leadership qualities of the nominees. Typically enough, the most responsible approach to the nomination of deputy candidates was shown by the more institutionalized parties (CPU, NRU, SPU, and the Peasant Party of Ukraine).

The elections of 1998 and 2002 also made clear that the system of proportional representation was helpful to political parties and electoral blocs that did not have a developed organizational infrastructure or a wide network of local organizations, but had a solid financial base for conducting a powerful advertising campaign in the mass media and/or were able to lean on administrative-political and economic influence in separate regions.

The introduction of a proportional electoral system can thus lead to purely parliamentary parties that have no broad political support in the regions. The introduction of a mixed electoral system in the election of Verkhovna Rada of Ukraine created a deeper gap between the level of party influence in the legislature and in local government bodies. As already noted, more than two-thirds of the deputies of the Ukrainian parliament were party members, while in local bodies formed on the basis of a single-member district majority electoral system, the members of political parties constituted only 7.6 percent.

In its development the party system of Ukraine has reached the crossroads: either artificial "partization" of the legislature, not reinforced with actual growth of party influence in society, or gradual institutionalization of parties, stabilization of the party system, and gradual buildup of electoral muscle through a struggle with the nonparty candidates in majority districts. The selection of a further route will be defined largely by the electoral system under which the next parliamentary elections will be held.

CONCLUSION

Although changing the electoral system has increased party representation in parliament, the nature of Ukraine's presidential-parliamentary form of government and the way executive bodies are formed under the Constitution prevents relaying party influence in the Verkhovna Rada over to the executive authority.

Moreover, the stability of political parties and their factions in parliament largely depends on the attitude of the executive authority, first of all on that of the presidential administration. In these conditions, political parties appear to be a subordinated, auxiliary element of a political system, at best playing the role of political opposition or of lobbying structures—a tool of political influence used by certain politician-businessmen.

A greater role for political parties in the political system of Ukraine is possible only when legislative influence over the process of the formation of the government is strengthened and the government is held responsible to the coalition majority in parliament.

At the same time, the strengthening of political parties' influence in the Ukrainian society also depends on their institutionalization and stabilization of the party system. The frequent change of an electoral system does not facilitate these processes.

In transforming an electoral system, it is necessary to consider not only the need for the artificial enhancement of party influence, but also the conformity of an electoral system to the form of government. According to many researchers the least successful (weak, unstable, and inefficient) is the Latin American model of combining the presidential form of government and the proportionate electoral system.[24] Yet this kind of system, with a strong president, an irresponsible Rada, and a helpless government, existed in the Ukraine until the 2004 presidential election and provoked the Orange Revolution. The functioning of the system was characterized by ineffectiveness and was accompanied by the flourishing of corruption. Under these conditions the struggle in Ukrainian politics assumed a clanship character. Long-standing differences between eastern highly industrialized regions closely connected with Russia and western European-oriented parts of the country divided the electorate between two poles. At the same time several economic clans based in different regions of the Ukraine intensively used these historically rooted distinctions in their fight with each other. The combination of these two factors created a very dangerous political situation fraught with the disintegration of the country.

The struggle flamed up between two blocs led by two prime ministers: the former and the actual. Both worked with one and the same president—L. Kuchma. After the 2002 parliamentary election they were considered as potential allies and supporters of the president in the Verkhovna Rada. However, by the 2004 election the political forces in parliament had regrouped and potential allies now found themselves on opposite sides of the barricade. The electoral blocs were formed over ideological distinctions and based on pragmatic reasons of leaders and their sponsors. Nevertheless, V. Yanukovych united people from eastern regions interested in closer cooperation with Russia, and V. Yushchenko attracted people from western parts of Ukraine as well as opponents of the actual authorities who were seen as wallowing in corruption and clannish intrigues. The two blocs collected an almost equal quantity of votes in the first round on October 31, 2004 (41% versus 42%).

By the second round the situation changed noticeably. Thousands of ordinary people were indignant with the wide range of frauds and machinations, as well as of use of public resources (especially mass media) in favor of one candidate—V. Yanukovych. Particular indignation was caused by active participation in the presidential election of representatives of the former metropolis: several famous Russian political technologists worked for Yanukovych's electoral campaign. From that point the multitude in the streets of the Ukrainian capital mobilized by some youth organizations joined the fight between political cliques, and the whole struggle acquired the character of the Orange Revolution. A Yushchenko presidency as the result of this popular movement gives an object-lesson of what is apt to befall political technologies when political apathy is superseded by mass activity.

The institutional innovations adopted in the course of the conflict (amplification of the parliament's powers, curtailment of the power of the president, transition to a proportional electoral system, and decentralization) may, given certain conditions, rule out the probability of power being monopolized again. The Ukraine has clearly taken a step away from post-Soviet autocracy toward parliamentarianism. Whether it will continue to move in that direction remains to be seen.

PART III

The Baltics

CHAPTER 7

Political Parties and Multiparty Systems in the Baltic Countries, 1990–2001

Algis Krupavičius

Political parties and multiparty systems are constituent elements of contemporary representative democracy. Moreover, political parties create the linkage between political leadership and voters, political elite and civil society, the rulers and the ruled, in all representative democracies. Contemporary transitions from authoritarian rule to democracy in many ways represent institutionalization and consolidation of parties and multiparty systems in new democracies.

From a comparative perspective, the Baltic countries represent successful cases of transition to democracy after 1989 in Eastern Europe. This fact becomes even more important when put in the larger context:

> the transition from communism in Europe and the former Soviet Union has only sometimes produced a transition to democracy. Since the crumbling of the Berlin Wall in 1989 and the collapse of the Soviet Union in 1991, twenty-eight states—most of them new states—have abandoned communism. But only eight—the Czech Republic, Estonia, Hungary, Latvia, Lithuania, Poland, Slovenia, and just last year, Croatia—have entered the ranks of liberal democracies as assessed by Freedom House. The remaining majority of new post-communist states are various shades of dictatorships or unconsolidated "transitional regimes."[1]

Successful democratization in the Baltic States provides a fundamental reason to explore more deeply the processes of institutionalization and stabilization of parties and party systems in this region.

Moreover, if in the late 1980s the Baltic States started to reenter the international community as countries with the "same face" and similar historical destiny, throughout the next decade the world acknowledged that the similarities between Estonia, Latvia, and Lithuania were sometimes overstated and overemphasized for different reasons. Another exaggerated view was that the Baltic countries were completely different and that during the post-independence decade these differences increased even more. How does this dichotomy of similarity and difference work in the case of the emerging multiparty systems in the Baltic States? This question requires serious investigation, presented here.

This introductory chapter is organized in four parts. The first part discusses briefly the conditions of transition to democracy in each Baltic country by focusing on the main political actors, exploring their similarities and differences from a cross-national perspective. The second part explains the structural characteristics of the Baltic party systems. Organizational elements and basic ideological configurations of party systems are discussed in the third part. Finally, broader issues of party system stability and consolidation are addressed in the fourth part.

TRANSITIONAL POLITICS, POLITICAL PARTIES, AND SOCIAL CLEAVAGES

Claus Offe has pointed out that post-communist Europe is in fact undergoing a triple transition, a process involving not just democratization, but also marketization and wholesale economic transformation as well as state-building itself. Moreover, what Western Europe "mastered over a centuries-long sequence (from the nation state to capitalism, and then to democracy), post-communist nations must endeavor to accomplish simultaneously, and within the shortest possible time."[2] The multidimensionality of the post-communist transition was a factor in all Eastern European countries. However, the strength and timing of different transitional causes and issues varied from country to country.

The Baltic States differed considerably from the rest of the former Soviet Union countries in at least two ways. First, Estonia, Latvia, and Lithuania succeeded in establishing democratic order during the first long wave of democratization, that is, in the early 1920s, according to S. Huntington's classification of democratization phases. This democratic experience did not disappear in the ashes of history, but rather was a strong element of the democratic revival in the Baltics in the late 1980s. Second, the history of independence in the inter-war period in the Baltic States was a source of "a strong legacy for statehood."[3]

Not accidentally, the transitional agenda in the Baltic States was marked by two major issues: the reestablishment of statehood and the development of democratic institutions. Many observers of transitional politics in Estonia, Latvia, and Lithuania admitted that these two processes were almost inseparable.[4] Moreover, the Baltic States were leading actors in the collapse of the Soviet Union inasmuch their massive democratization began as early as 1988. On the other hand, transitional politics in the Baltics were characterized as consensual, because major political groups accepted and followed two major goals—national independence and democratization—without substantial disagreements.

The political transition stage in every country was dominated by three types of political actors: hard-liners, soft-liners, and national radicals, who actually reintroduced competitive politics into the Baltic countries. However, in regard to the variables of composition, size, and influence of these three political camps, there are reasons to distinguish two models here. On the one hand, Lithuania represents a case where hard-liners were pushed into the position of insignificant minority, which, since 1988, was losing social and political influence in the country. The few national radicals were also unable to compete with major political groups, that is, the national front—Sąjūdis and the independent Communist Party—that converged in the early phases of transition to a more or less coherent bloc of soft-liners. On the other hand, Estonia and Latvia definitely represented the second model, where the camp of hard-liners was strong (mainly because of substantial support by non-Estonians and non-Latvians), yet the political stage was nonetheless dominated by soft-liners consisting of national fronts and a significant number of the communist parties. National radicals, who emerged as Citizens' Committees in Estonia and as National Independence Movement in Latvia, represented the third substantial component of transitional politics here.

The transitional framework of political competition was a short-lived phenomenon and, since 1992–1993, there have been substantial grounds for speaking about institutionalization of more permanent and more stable parties and party systems in Estonia, Latvia, and Lithuania.

However, the first task is to put the institutionalization of parties and party systems in a certain theoretical framework. In general, the development of parties and party systems might be explored from various theoretical perspectives in new democracies. In the case of the Baltic States, the concepts of Lipset and Rokkan remain useful, in particular their argument that when an emerging party system is coupled to a nation's cleavage structure it can become frozen: the "freezing hypothesis."[5]

S. Beglund, T. Hellen, and F. Aarebrot, following the Lipset-Rokkan logic, have recently noted that social cleavages "structure the behavior of voters and parties alike and they determine the number of parties and the nature of partisan conflict; they are thus of obvious importance for the way democracy works. Indeed, the cleavage concept is crucial to the study of parties, party systems and regime change."[6]

Moreover, these authors have argued and described the importance of social cleavages, stating that

> cleavages go beyond issues, conflicts and interests of a purely economic or social nature. They are in a sense more fundamental, as they are founded on culture,

value orientations and ideological insulation; they constitute deep-seated socio-structural conflicts with political significance. A cleavage is rooted in a persistent social division, which enables one to identify certain groups in society: members of an ethnic minority, believers of a particular denomination, residents of a particular region. A cleavage also engages some set of values common to members of the group; group members share the same value orientation. And finally, cleavages are institutionalized in the form of political parties and other associational groups.[7]

Because the Baltics, as most of Eastern European societies, can be described as a "flattened society," social class identities played a marginal role in the development of party loyalties in the initial phases of the post-communist transition. Here class identities were substituted by sociocultural identities. Moreover, "political parties which operated in the period immediately following the political transition may have articulated only theoretical interests of social groups that did not exist at the time. Class certainly was a weak predictor of electoral behavior, far behind age, education, union membership and, in particular, religion."[8] Initial stimuli of political competition and formation of party preferences, that is, issues of high or macropolotical independence and democratization, lost their mobilizing potential immediately after the international recognition of the independence of Baltic states and the adoption of new constitutions, which established a more or less permanent framework of institutional democracy in each country. From this moment on, issues of medium- and short-range, or low politics dominated the political agenda of the Newly Independent States. In this new situation, social cleavages started to play more important, if not crucial, roles in the development of party preferences.

Looking at the cleavage structure in Estonia, Latvia, and Lithuania in the immediate post-independence period, we can clearly see that ethnicity, ideology, the urban-rural division, and religion constituted the emerging political and party preferences (see Table 7.1).

Historically, ethnicity was the determining cleavage, to which other cleavages, including left–right, were subordinated in the Baltic States.

Table 7.1 Cleavage Structure in the Baltic States after 1992–1993

	Major cleavages	*Minor cleavages*
Estonia	Left-right socioeconomic cleavage Cultural-ethnic Urban-rural	Post-materialist
Latvia	Left-right socioeconomic cleavage Cultural-ethnic	Urban-rural Religious
Lithuania	Left-right socioeconomic cleavage Urban-rural Religious	Cultural-ethnic

Table 7.2 Relevant Parties and Their Main Ethnic Bases in the Inter-War Period

	Social Democratic	*Agrarian*	*Liberal*	*Conservative*	*Nationalist/ Ethnic Defense*
Estonia					
Estonian	x	x	x	x	x
Russian					x
German					x
Swedish		x		x	x
Latvia					
Latvian unitary	x	x	x	x	
Latgalian	x	x	x	x	x
Semgalian		x			x
Russian	x	x		x	x
German					x
Jewish	x				x
Polish	x				x
Lithuania					
Lithuanian	x	x	x	x	x
Polish	x	x			x
German	x				x
Jewish	x				x

Source: Adapted from: Hellen Tomas, Berglund Sten, Aarebrot Frank, The Challenge of History in Eastern Europe, in *The Handbook of Political Change in Eastern Europe,* ed. Berglund Sten, Hellen Tomas, and Aarebrot Frank (London: Edward Elgar, 1998), p.21. Note: The matrix depicts the party systems classified according to ethnicity and party families. The parties included in the matrix may have operated for only a short period in time or only as voting lists or parliamentary clubs (ibid, p.22).

As Berglund, Hellen, and Aarebrot noted, "typical in inter-war Eastern Europe was the existence of parallel party systems for each ethnic group, a tendency which was reinforced by constitutional arrangements which paved the way for extreme multi-partyism particularly in the northern half of the region."[9] (See Table 7.2).

To what extent were historical cleavages able to survive during the Soviet occupation and how much did they shape the emerging party system as a kind of historical legacy in the Baltic States? These questions have no straightforward answers, and researchers seem to be divided into two groups. There are the views that historical cleavages played no (or almost no) role in shaping the new multiparty systems in contemporary Estonia, Latvia, and Lithuania. For example, as Darius Žėruolis points out:

It is tempting to draw parallels between the inter-war and the current party systems, but there is in fact hardly any meaningful continuity between the two. The non-democratic interlude between 1926 and 1990 was too long and the social

Figure 7.1 Three Dimensions of Continuity and Their Impact on the Cleavage Structure

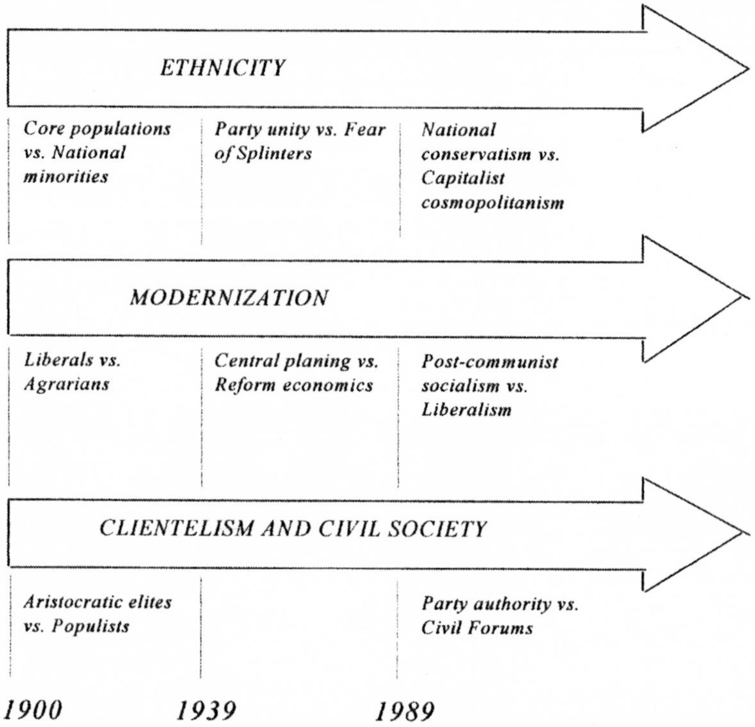

Source: Hellen Tomas, Berglund Sten, and Aarebrot Frank, "The Challenge of History in Eastern Europe," in *The Handbook of Political Change in Eastern Europe*. ed. Berglund Sten, Hellen Tomas, and Aarebrot Frank (London: Edward Elgar, 1998), p. 52.

impact of Soviet rule—through urbanization and secularization—too tremendous for pre-war party historical profiles to have an impact on the electorate. Thus, the history of current party competition dates back only to the national rebirth in Lithuania in the 1980s.[10]

Other researchers, such as Hellen, Berglund, and Aarebrot, and I myself, take an interim position, trying to identify an indirect continuity of certain cleavages that made a serious impact on party structuring in contemporary Estonia, Latvia, and Lithuania, as presented in Figure 7.1.

Certainly, the precise impact of historical cleavages is hard to identify and almost impossible to measure, particularly because cleavages have played different roles in different countries. For instance, although some historical parties based on religious, ethnic, urban-rural, or even ideological cleavages reentered the post-transitional political stage in Latvia and Lithuania, such was not the case in Estonia.

INSTITUTIONAL AND STRUCTURAL DIMENSIONS OF BALTIC PARTY SYSTEMS: DISTINCT RULES WITH SIMILAR OUTCOMES

The choice of the electoral system is one of the most crucial actions of post-transitional politics in all new democracies of Eastern Europe, because it has an impact on many other political institutions. Since the formulation of Duverger's law on the interaction between electoral and party systems, the conventional wisdom is that party constellation is one of the areas most affected by electoral rules.

The standard inherited majority rule in single-member electoral districts was used in most cases in the founding elections for the newly independent nations emerging from the defunct Soviet Union, including Latvia and Lithuania. However, Estonia was an exception, having introduced the Single Transferable Vote by proposal of the Popular Front before the 1990 parliamentary elections. Despite differences in electoral formulas, the founding elections' results in the Baltic States were similar in the sense that proindependence forces received an absolute or relative majority of seats in all three constituent parliaments (48.5 percent in Estonia, 65.2 percent in Latvia, and 70.2 percent in Lithuania). However, there is room to speculate that different electoral rules had an impact on the results of the founding elections inasmuch as the STV system produced more proportional outcomes in Estonia, and the two-round systems in Latvia and Lithuania tended to concentrate votes on the winner's side.

The change of electoral system was part of the constitutional reforms that took place in 1992 and 1993 in the Baltic States. Two circumstances have a crucial influence on the choice of new electoral systems in new democracies. One is the new political elite's knowledge of the effect of different electoral systems on political institutions, and the second is what efforts are made to promote the electoral designs that will prove most profitable to the mainstream political actors.

As a result of constitutional reforms, all three Baltic countries introduced unicameral parliaments in line with the cube root law of assembly sizes and adopted distinct electoral systems.

Estonia introduced proportional representation (PR), which Rein Taagepera has described as a mixture of "a Finnish-type quasi-list" PR (where voters must vote for an individual candidate) with an Israeli-type closed national list for votes left over when full simple quota seats have been allocated in districts. These remainders were allocated so as to restore nationwide near-PR, using unique quasi-d'Hondt divisors (1, 2.9, 3.9, 4.9...), restricted by a German-like five percent threshold."

In 1993 Latvia also introduced proportional representation by dividing the country into five multimember electoral districts and allocating seats to the parties along the Sainte-Lague formula with a threshold of five percent of the national vote since 1995.

Since 1992 Lithuania has had the mixed system, where 71 members of Seimas were elected by majority runoff and another 70 MPs were chosen in a multimember nationwide constituency in which seats were allocated on the basis of party lists using the Largest Remainder-Hare formula with a threshold of five percent of the national vote since 1996.

Did different electoral formulas produce very different election results in the Baltic States? If we are looking only at a few major structural indicators, that is, the number of parliamentary parties, effective party number, and strength of the largest parliamentary party, we can observe a more or less general trend towards party fragmentation since the first multiparty elections in 1992–1993. The actual figures of parliamentary parties were very close to each other in Estonia and Latvia after each new set of multiparty elections. Lithuania has had higher numbers of parliamentary parties because the majority electoral system encouraged party factionalization. These differing trends might be attributed to the effects of distinct electoral norms (see Table 7.3).

On the other hand, until the 2000 Seimas elections, many researchers of Lithuanian party politics, looking at the effective party number and the shares of the largest parliamentary parties, have come to a different conclusion. Žėruolis Darius, for example, finds that

> the Lithuanian party system is not characterized by the kind of fragmentation typical of Latvia and Estonia; the underlying structure of the Lithuanian party system is rather reminiscent of that of Poland. Party labels, at least those of mainstream parties, sound familiar to students of West European politics. In fact, Lithuanian political parties have a tendency to imitate West European, particularly Scandina-

Table 7.3 Number of Parliamentary Parties, 1989–2000

	Estonia	*Latvia*	*Lithuania*	*Average*
Founding elections	1990	1990	1990	
	3	2	2	2.3
First multiparty elections	1992	1993	1992	
	9	8	13	10.0
Second multiparty elections	1995	1995	1996	
	7	9	14	10.0
Third multiparty elections	1999	1998	2000	
	7	6	13	8.7

Source: R. Rose, N. Munro, and T. Mackie, Elections in Central and Eastern Europe since 1990, (University of Strathclyde, 1998); PARLINE Database, Inter-Parliamentary Union, http://www.ipu.org

vian, parties. This may result in programmatic and social profiles not conducive to converting existing divisions into lasting cleavages. Yet the simple structure of the Lithuanian party system has proven a major source of political stability. In the Lithuanian context of low-density civil society, political parties may even serve as vehicles of political modernization.[11]

See Table 7.4.

After the 2000 Seimas elections, however, a wave of party fragmentation has shaken the "perfect and stable" Lithuanian party system as two new political parties—the Liberals and the Social Liberals—suddenly entered the stage of parliamentary politics. In regard to all three above-mentioned indicators—the number of parliamentary parties, effective party number, and strength of largest parliamentary party—the structural characteristics of all Baltic party systems thus became much more similar (see Table 7.5).

Looking at the structural characteristics of Baltic party systems after the third cycle of multiparty elections, we can see that the multiparty system without a dominant party or the single model of party system was in place in all three countries. However, we cannot draw far-reaching conclusions from this fact, given the continuing fluidity of party systems even in the consolidating democracies (see Table 7.6).

Table 7.4 Number of Effective Parties, 1989–2000 (Along the Number of Seats)

	Estonia	*Latvia*	*Lithuania*	*Average*
Founding elections	3	1.9	1.87	2.3
First multiparty elections	5.9	5.1	3	4.7
Second multiparty elections	4.15	6.1	3.3	4.5
Third multiparty elections	5.2	5.5	4.2	5.1
Standard deviation[1]	0.91	0.50	1.0	1.3
Mean	4.56	4.65	3.1	4.1

[1]Standard deviation calculated only since the first multiparty elections in each country.

Table 7.5 Strength of Largest Parliamentary Party, 1989–2000 (Percentage of Seats)

	Estonia	*Latvia*	*Lithuania*	*Average*
Founding elections	46.6	65.2	70.2	60.7
First multiparty elections	28.7	36	51.7	38.8
Second multiparty elections	40.6	18	51.1	36.6
Third multiparty elections	27.7	24	36.2	29.3
Mean	35.9	35.80	52.3	41.3

Source: PARLINE Database, Inter-Parliamentary Union, http://www.ipu.org ; R. Rose, N. Munro, and T. Mackie, Elections in Central and Eastern Europe since 1990 (University of Strathclyde, 1998).

Table 7.6 Structural Dynamics of Party Systems in the Baltic States, 1992–2000

	Estonia	*Latvia*	*Lithuania*
First multiparty elections	4	3.5	3
Second multiparty elections	3.5	4	3.5
Third multiparty elections	4	4	4
Average	3.83	3.83	3.5
Average number of effective parties*	5.18	5.5	4.2

Note: 2 two-party system; 2.5 two-and-a-half party system; 3 multiparty system with two dominant parties; 3.5 multiparty system with one dominant party; 4 multiparty system without a dominant party.
*After the last parliamentary elections in every country.

Table 7.7 Typologies of Party Systems in the Baltic States Using Blondel's Criteria

Party system	*First multiparty elections*	*Second multiparty elections*	*Third multiparty elections*
Multiparty system with a dominant party	Latvia (1993) Lithuania (1992)	Estonia (1995) Lithuania (1996)	
Multiparty system without a dominant party	Estonia (1992)	Latvia (1995)	Latvia (1998) Estonia (1999) Lithuania (2000)

Estonia, Latvia, and Lithuania have changed their structural characteristics several times since 1992–1993 as is reflected in Tables 7.6 and 7.7. Meanwhile, the range of change was rather narrow because all moves were restricted within the pure multiparty framework (according to Blondel's typology), and only two choices were available, that is, a system either with or without a dominant party.

Why do the structural effects of electoral systems seem to be limited in Estonia, Latvia, and Lithuania? The answer might be found in certain similarities of the electorate. The lists of social cleavages in all three Baltic States is quite similar. Although, as mentioned above, the saliency of different cleavages was distinct in each country, in all three the citizenship issue has had the most influence in reshaping national electorates by determining the political roles of non-Baltic minorities. While Lithuania adopted a zero-option on the issue by granting citizenship to all residents in 1989, Latvia and Estonia, after intense debates in the early 1990s, restored citizenship automatically only to the pre-1940 citizens. Despite these differences, the representatives of the titular nation made up approximately 81 percent of all eligible voters in Lithuania, and 78 and 90 percent in Latvia and Estonia respectively. In short, the result was that electorates in all Baltic States became fairly homogenous in ethnic terms.

Socially and demographically, the Baltic peoples have had many similarities during the late Soviet period, and we can assume that transitional politics moving in the same direction towards a market economy did not significantly increase these differences. This means that structural and social characteristics were slightly more favorable for establishing similar party systems in the Baltics.

ORGANIZATIONAL AND IDEOLOGICAL DIMENSIONS, OR THE DIFFERENCES IN ESTONIAN, LATVIAN, AND LITHUANIAN PARTY SYSTEMS

Nevertheless, there are several factors that certainly were driving parties and party systems in Estonia, Latvia, and Lithuania apart.

If we look at the organizational features of Baltic parties, we can see very clearly that party size and patterns of organizations were quite different in each country. The starting points here, of course, are legal regulations on minimum party size. All three countries introduced such regulations in the respective party laws, but the thresholds for parties' founding memberships were established on very different levels. The minimal party membership threshold was the highest in Estonia, reaching as many as 1,000 individual members, a moderate one in Lithuania, equal to 400 members, and a low one in Latvia, equal to only 200 members. As a result of differing party membership thresholds, we have high variations in average party size: 1,678 individual members in Estonia (1999), only 931 members in Latvia (1995), and 4,838 members in Lithuania (1999). The data on party size do not go back as far for Estonia and Lithuania as for Latvia, but appear to reflect post-independence trends quite well given that since the mid-1990s party membership in Estonia and Lithuania has been increasing rather slowly.

The size of the electorate only partially explains the existing differences. Party membership was equal to 5.0 percent, taking into account all parliamentary parties, or to 2.4 percent of the total electorate, if we exclude the Union of Political Prisoners and Deportees, which in many ways was acting as an interest group rather than a political party, in Lithuania in 1999. Average party membership was 3.5 percent of the total electorate in Estonia (1999) and only 0.84 percent in Latvia.

The size of a party seems to be related to more general party organization patterns. If in Lithuania at least a few parties, such as Homeland Union/Lithuanian Conservatives, Social Democratic, and Christian Democratic parties, successfully developed into large parties, Estonian and Latvian parties were based on a more elitist model. Two outcomes of these differences are of utmost importance to the predictability of party politics in the Baltic States. The first is the high dependency of parties on personal leadership, which led to frequent conflicts on the party leadership level in Latvia and Estonia. Recently, because of the high degree of personalization in party politics, Hans Petter Svege and Christer D. Daatland have noted that Estonian parties "seem more like vehicles for political ambition and power-seeking than advocates of specific social groups and ideologies."[12] The same pattern was also present in Latvia where "parties are top-down establishments."[13] Moreover, parties founded within respective parliaments dominated the political scene of Estonia and Latvia. Weak extra-parliamentary organizations were common in Estonian and Latvian parties. The second crucial outcome of the difference in party organization is the high opportunity of new political parties in Estonia and Latvia to participate in politics. The increase in the number of new parties in the parliament after each new election illustrates the general instability of party systems in these countries (see Table 7.8.).

In contrast, party organization has much more importance in Lithuania. Even outside observers of Lithuanian party development conclude that in Lithuania there "is apparently some correlation between membership numbers and the parties' success in the elections."[14] Certainly, nobody can ignore the role of personalities in Lithuanian politics: until now the Homeland Union has been strongly associated with the name of Vytautas Landsbergis; LSDP is very much still Brazauskas' party; and the success of New Union/Social Liberals in local and parliamentary elections of 2000 would have been hard to imagine without the party's association with A. Paulauskas, who was a strong contender of Adamkus during the 1997 presidential elections. Continuity of personalities is a strong factor of stability for individual parties in Lithuania as well as in Estonia and Latvia.

The average shares of new parties since the early 1990s have been lower in Lithuania than in Estonia and Latvia. Initially, this was caused by the successful transformation of the Independent Communist Party into the Lithuanian Democratic Labor Party. Later, the relative organizational strength and political competitiveness of established parties prevented new parties from entering into the political scene. The only successful challenge to mainstream parties was in the case of New Union in the 2000 elections, when an entirely new party, founded only in 1998, entered parliament as the third-strongest party.

Table 7.8 Share of New Parties in the Baltic Parliaments, 1989–2000

	Estonia	*Latvia*	*Lithuania*	*Average*
Founding elections	67%	50%	50%	55.67%
First multiparty elections	100%	100%	54%	84.67%
Second multiparty elections	43%	44%	21%	36.00%
Third multiparty elections	0%	50%	21%	23.66%
Mean	53%	61%	37%	

Sources: Calculated from: R. Rose, N. Munro, and T. Mackie, Elections in Central and Eastern Europe since 1990, (University of Strathclyde, 1998); PARLINE Database, Inter-Parliamentary Union, http://www.ipu.org

Baltic party systems are also different with respect to ideological distribution. Whereas there is more or less bipolar competition on the socioeconomic left-right axis in Lithuania, a unipolar center and center-right dominance are found in Estonia and Latvia. These differences are well illustrated by data on the ideological complexion of parliaments and governments in the respective countries since the first multiparty elections in 1992 or 1993.

The center-right and centrist party secured the parliamentary majority after the elections of 1992, 1995, and 1999 in Estonia. Here five out of six Cabinets of Ministers were described as center-right governments in 1992–2001. Only one Cabinet has had a centrist orientation during this period. Mikko Lagerspetz and Henri Vogt have noted that since the 1992 elections all governments have resigned only as a result of highly personal conflicts and all "incoming governments have made a point of continuing the policies pursued by their predecessors."[15]

Ideological homogeneity of Latvian governments is even more striking because all five Cabinets in a period between 1993 and 1999 have had an identical centrist orientation, and parliaments have been dominated by liberal and center-right parties since 1993.

Consensual centrist and/or center-right policies with the emphasis on radical pro-market positions were common in both Estonia and Latvia.

Lithuania followed a different pattern. In two parliaments out of three, mainstream left- and right-wing parties secured stable parliamentary majorities, that is, the Lithuanian Democratic Labor Party in 1992 and Homeland Union/Lithuanian Conservatives in 1996. After the 2000 elections, the Seimas was dominated by a center-left majority, which failed to form a government immediately after the election. However, among eight governments, as many as four were center-left, three center-right, and one was centrist during the period of 1992–2001. Bipolar fluctuation is a structural feature of Lithuanian party politics.

BALTIC PARTY SYSTEMS: STABILITY OR INSTABILITY?

Frequently, post-communist polities are characterized as taking an antiparty stance, political parties as lacking responsiveness and accountability, and party systems as fluctuating and unconsolidated.

However, political parties themselves play a crucial role in the consolidation of fragile new democracies. As Leonardo Morlino points out, "Party organizations and elites are in a position to most powerfully facilitate consolidation or, conversely, to bring about a regime crisis. They are the social actors most capable of forming, maintaining, expressing, and deepening attitudes relating to regime legitimacy or illegitimacy."[16]

What are the variables of party system stability? Extensive literature on political parties provides many possible answers. Nevertheless, there is an unspoken agreement that some variables indicate more about the stability or instability of party systems than others. In the list of such variables are: electoral behavior with special emphasis on stable voter turnout and low voting volatility scores; patterns of party competition including the number of effective parties; ideological spaces within the party system; the ratio and influence of pro-regime and anti-regime parties; some features of the electoral system such as the stability of electoral rules and proportionality of vote translation to seats; and last but not least, the general quality of the political class.

In regard to electoral behavior in the Baltic States, we can emphasize several trends. First, voter turnout is stabilizing at a comparatively low level in Estonia and Lithuania (around 60 percent of eligible voters) and at medium level in Latvia (about 70 percent). Despite differing absolute figures of voter participation, general patterns of voter activity seem to be established (see Table 7.9). Figures of voter volatility are still much higher than in Western democracies, which is a major source of concern for mainstream parties in Estonia, Latvia, and Lithuania.

Another troublesome issue for political parties in regard to the voters' behavior is a general skepticism or lack of popular trust in democratic institutions. Moreover, political parties are usually among the most distrusted institutions across Baltic countries. This can be partially explained by the fact that democratic institutions, including political parties, are still a new phenomenon in the Baltic countries. Another more plausible explanation is based on the high expectations of transforming societies versus macroeconomic and social performance of democratic institutions. Recent studies show that popular trust in democratic institutions strongly correlates with the quality of life, as indicated by the consumer price index, inflation, index of income inequality, and the social security index in Eastern and Central Europe.[17] However, there is some good news even in this context. As long as voter turnout is stabilizing, it is an indication that vot-

Table 7.9 Voter Turnout in the Baltic Countries, 1989–2000

	Estonia	*Latvia*	*Lithuania*	*Standard deviation*	*Median*	*Average*
Founding elections	1990	1990	1990			
	78	81.3	71.7	4.9	78.0	77.0
First multiparty elections	1992	1993	1992			
	66.8	89.9	75.3	11.7	75.3	77.3
Second multiparty elections	1995	1995	1996			
	68.9	71.9	52.9	10.2	68.9	64.6
Third multiparty elections	1999	1998	2000			
	57.4	71.8	58.6	8.0	58.6	62.6
Average	67.78	78.73	66.63	6.7	67.8	71.0

Sources: R. Rose, N. Munro, and T. Mackie, Elections in Central and Eastern Europe since 1990 (University of Strathclyde, 1998); PARLINE Database, Inter-Parliamentary Union, http://www.ipu.org

ers are accepting and becoming accustomed to political parties as political actors that formulate and present policy alternatives to society. Paradoxically, on the attitudinal level political parties are in many ways evaluated negatively, but on the behavioral level parties are accepted as an unavoidable evil of democracy.

From the viewpoint of party competition patterns, there are two distinct models in the Baltic States: a bipolar model in Lithuania and a unipolar model with dominant center- and center-right parties in Estonia and Latvia. More importantly, anti-system parties play very marginal roles in the party system of every country. A certain stability in the number of effective parties also allows us to speak about trends of freezing of party systems in the Baltic States.

Stable electoral rules are a complementary source of party system stability, and this is the case in Estonia, Latvia, and Lithuania. Moreover, proportional representation in Estonia and Latvia, as well as the mixed electoral system in Lithuania are perceived as fair enough rules to translate votes to seats. The decreasing numbers of electoral exclusion, or the number of voters not taking part in the distribution of seats in the legislature, show that voters are becoming more familiar with electoral rules and starting to vote strategically (see Table 7.10).

The instability of party leadership, numerous political scandals, closed rules of party recruitment, low rates of incumbents' reelection, and factional splits indicate a low quality of political performance as well as low chances of stability and consolidation of the party system. Regarding each listed indicator, there are negative and positive examples in the Baltic States. Nevertheless, the increasing stability and professionalism of political practices seems to be a general trend in Estonia, Latvia, and Lithuania.

Summing up the different trends within party systems in the Baltic States, we can say with certainty that centripetal tendencies leading to party stability and party system consolidation prevail against centrifugal trends. This balance, however, is still quite fragile.

Table 7.10 Index of Electoral Exclusion in the Baltic States, 1990–2000

	Estonia	*Latvia*	*Lithuania**	*Standard deviation*	*Average*
First multiparty elections	1992	1993	1992		
	14.6	10.9	14.1	2.0	13.2
Second multiparty elections	1995	1995	1996		
	12.7	12.2	32.7	11.7	19.2
Third multiparty elections	1999	1998	2000		
	8.4	11.9	23.4	7.8	14.6
Mean	11.9	11.6	23.4	6.7	15.6

Source: R. Rose, N. Munro, and T. Mackie, Elections in Central and Eastern Europe since 1990 (University of Strathclyde, 1998); PARLINE Database, Inter-Parliamentary Union, http://www.ipu.org

CHAPTER 8

Political Parties in Estonia

Rein Toomla

WHAT IS A POLITICAL PARTY IN ESTONIA? A PROFILE OF POLITICAL PARTIES IN THE ESTONIAN REPUBLIC

The activities of parties in today's Estonian Republic are regulated, on the one hand, by the Constitution,[1] where it is stated rather vaguely and indefinitely that "Everybody has the right to assemble into non-profit associations and unions" and, on the other hand, by the Party Law adopted in May 1994. According to the latter, Estonian parties are characterized by the following:

1. The definition of a party, according to the law: "a party in Estonia is a voluntary political association of citizens with the aim of expressing the political interests of its members and associate members, and carrying out state and local authority... ."
2. Membership is open only to Estonian citizens who are at least 18 years old. However, the law lists several occupations, the representatives of which cannot belong to a party. These are:
   - judges and public prosecutors
   - police and border guard officials [guards]
   - members of the military and border guards who are in active service

   In addition to the professions mentioned above, it is not possible for the chancellor of justice and state inspector to be party members, and the president of the republic also suspends his party membership while he holds office.
3. Parties cannot have collective members.

4. Parties whose aims and actions are directed towards violent reversal of the constitutional order are forbidden.
5. The activities of a party from another country or of its structural unit are forbidden on the territory of the Estonian Republic.
6. Parties can be formed only on territorial principles.
7. A minimum of 1,000 members is necessary to register a party.
8. Organs of state or local authority cannot fund a party. At the same time, a party has the right to receive money from the state budget. Since 1997, every party represented in parliament receives money according to the magnitude of its representation. The total amount of money from the state budget that is allocated to parties is 16 million EEK (about 10 million USD).
9. A party cannot accept money from organs of state and local authority of foreign countries.
10. A party can liquidate itself or it can be closed judicially.

THE ORIGIN OF PARTIES

Relying on the classification of party origin proposed over 30 years ago by J. LaPalombara and M. Wiener,[2] we can portray the formation of Estonian parties as follows:

1. From the viewpoint of the institutional approach, as first proposed by Maurice Duverger.[3]
   a. The first possibility is that parties originate inside the governing mechanism, above all inside the parliament. None of today's parties in Estonia completely fit under this category, although the formation of Isamaaliit (Pro Patria) can largely be explained as originating within the governing structure. However, if we consider the government as an institution as well, then a good example is Koonderakond (Coalition Party), which originated in 1991 in response to the opposition of some ministers to the prime minister of the time.
   b. The second possibility proposed by Duverger, according to which the origin of a party is connected to some other nonpolitical institution outside the parliament, applies to three Estonian parties:
      - The Center Party grew out of the Popular Front, which can be classified as a political movement.
      - United People's Party took shape thanks to the Russian Democratic Movement.
      - The Families' and Pensioners' Party took its origin from the Union of Pensioners.
2. Crisis theories. According to crisis theories, the origin of parties is connected to the formation of new states or regime changes in certain countries.[4] If we base our theory on the assumption that parties strive to reestablish the sovereignty of the Estonian Republic, then we should be looking for parties that have a history that begins at the time of Soviet supremacy. Of today's parties only one—the Rural Union—was set up during Soviet supremacy. On the other hand, we can point out six parties (Center Party, Pro Patria, Reform Party, Moderates, Labor

Party, and United People's Party), a constituent part of which was set up before the independence of the Estonian Republic was regained, or that have grown out of some political organizations that existed during the Soviet times. At the same time, it is evident that at least at the moment we could consider the crisis theories applicable to the formation of all Estonian parties, since the transition period in Estonia can hardly be viewed as completed.

3. Modernization theories. As modernization stimulates the growth of level of education, urbanization, secularization, and integration, society is shaped by new circumstances that are also reflected in the origin of parties.[5] Since this theory is universal, it encompasses the formation of all Estonian parties.

To these three theoretical explanations of the origin of parties we may add that in practice the formation of many Estonian parties took place through the process of unification, splitting, and expansion. For a representation of the evolution of Estonian parties that considers this aspect of party formation, see Figure 8.1.

CLASSIFICATION OF PARTIES

Proceeding from Arend Lijphart's point of view that parties can be classified on the basis of existing dispute measurements,[6] in the case of Estonia, these dispute measurements must first be divided into two groups.

The first group consists of issues in which there is little or no antagonism between parties, such as the following:

- The religious dimension. The Christian People's Party has set itself the goal of enriching politics with Christian ethics. However, none of the other parties call themselves atheist or oppose Christian values. Although Estonian society is religiously rather diverse (of all churchgoers, approximately two-thirds are Lutheran, approximately one-fifth are Orthodox, approximately one-tenth belong to various Protestant churches, and two or three percent are Catholics), the opposition between churches is not great enough to give rise to the formation and development of different religious parties.
- Foreign policy. The most important foreign policy issue since independence has been whether or not to join the European Union, but only two parties took a stand against joining: The Christian People's Party and the Future Estonia Party. Russian parties took a cautious position but were never directly opposed.
- Support for the regime. At the moment there are no political forces in Estonia that aim at radical changes in the existing regime.
- Postmaterialistic values. Political feminism and the Green movement are represented to some extent in Estonia, but their influence in political life is very minor.
- Urban versus rural. In principle this dimension could be important in distinguishing between parties, and indeed it was so at the time of the parliamentary elections in March 1999. In recent years, however, the two rural parties have reached an agreement about the need to unite as well as to change the party

Figure 8.1 Formation of Estonian Political Parties (continued)

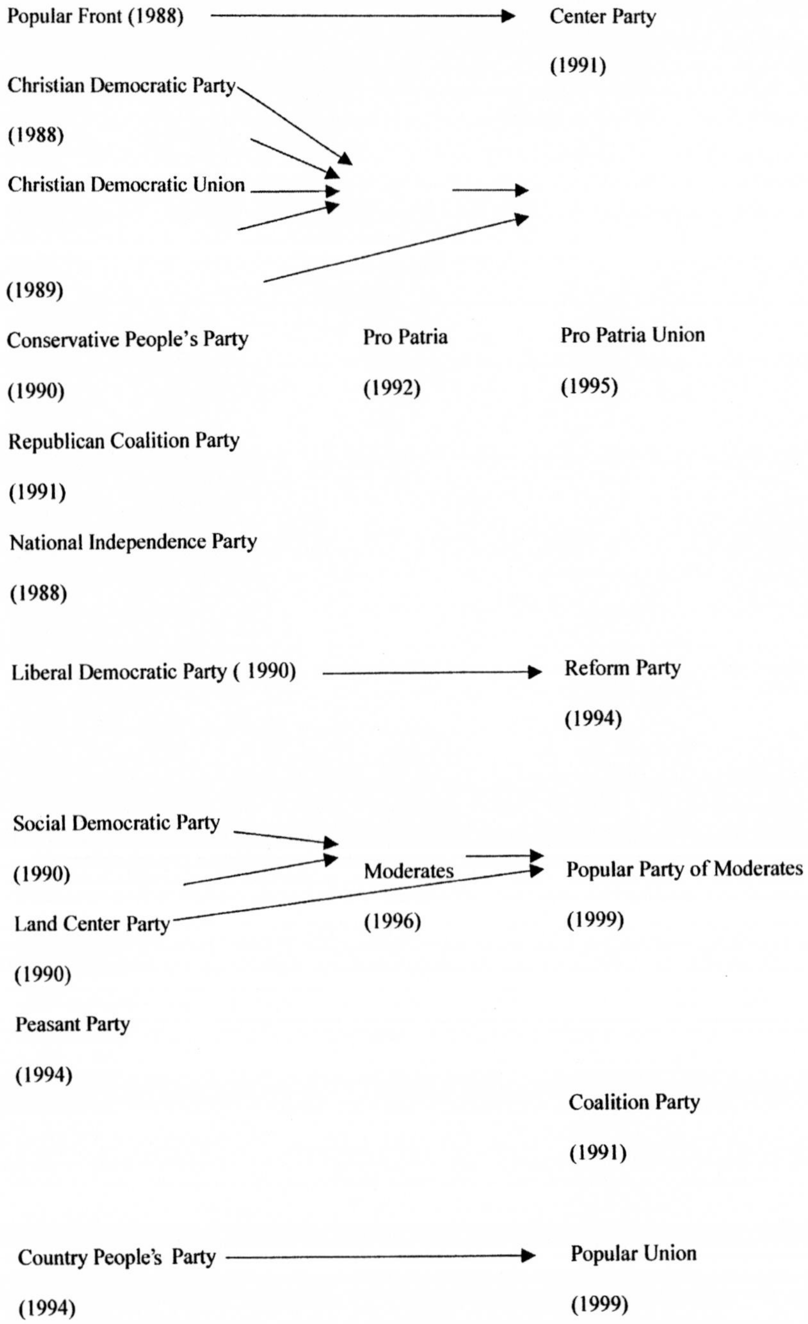

Russian Democratic Movement (1991) → United People's Party (1994)

Rural Union (1989)

Union of Pensioners' (1990) → Party of Families and Pensioners (1994)

Russian Unity Party (1994)

Communist Party of Estonia (1920) → Democratic Labor Party (1992) → Social Democratic Labor Party (1997)

Christian People Party (1998)

Blue Party (1994)

Farmers Party (1992)

Russian Party in Estonia (1994)

Center Party (1991) → Progressive Party (1996)

Pro Patria (1992) → Future Party (1993)

name to Estonian People's Union and drop its focus on protecting rural interests. With this move, the Estonian rural parties emulated Western European parties in the 1950s that changed their names to indicate that they would no longer represent the interests of a single social group.[7]

There are, however, two sets of issues on which there is serious division in Estonia:

1. The first is the socioeconomic dimension. To describe parties under this dimension it is easiest to place them on left–right scale. Estonian parties have been classified in this way by several authors.[8] Although these scholars' classifications have in common that there are more parties on the left wing, a closer look at party programs reveals that in fact most of the parties represented in the Estonian parliament can be found on the right wing, especially in the center-right sector. If we divide this scale into four parts—the leftist, center-left, center-right, and rightist parties—then the parties represented in the current parliament would divide as follows (see Figure 8.2):

- The distinction between the right and the left side is based on the attitude of parties towards a market economy. Those on the right or center-right have the program ideal of a market-economy society. The left wing consists of parties with the main goal to resist the negative influences of market economy on the Estonian society.
- The difference between the rightist and center-right parties is that the Reform Party supports the model of a liberal market economy while center-right parties advocate a social market economy.
- The United People's Party is located on the center-left, based on their own self-identification.
- Among the center-right parties, the Center Party lies on the left wing of this group, and Pro Patria on the right wing. This order is based on the tax-policy views of the parties: the Center Party strongly supports the establishment of a graduated tax, the Popular Union (former Country People's Party) and the

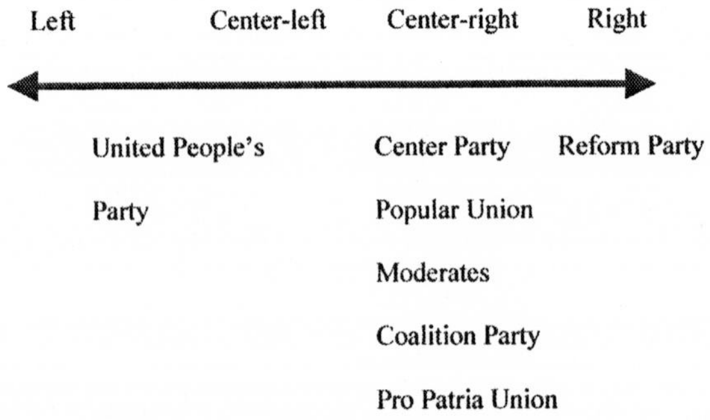

Figure 8.2 The Classification of Estonian Political Parties

Moderates have expressed this view more mildly, and the Coalition Party and Pro Patria Union are convinced supporters of proportional taxation.

This classification cannot be considered to be a fixed one in the Estonian case. Differentiation according to attitudes towards market economy seems to be characteristic only of the present time. Other criteria might change in the future as well.

Naturally, we must also consider alterations of positions in party programs. Only a few years ago, Pro Patria and the People's Party of Republicans and Conservatives, now dissolved, could have been classified as rightist parties. There have also been more parties on the center-left—the Rural Union has to a large extent given up its social democratic positions, and the Social Democratic Party has ceased to exist. It can also be claimed that many parties have, during the last four or five years, moved a bit left in their political conceptions (Center Party, Popular Union, Moderates).

2. The second parameter in which political parties take different stands is the cultural-ethnic dimension. Estonia is not a monoethnic society. It has been estimated that approximately two-thirds of Estonia's population is Estonian, and the rest is Russian. Currently there are three parties operating in Estonia (United People's Party, Russian Unity Party, and Russian Party in Estonia) that have set representing the interests of the Russian-speaking population in Estonia as one of their major goals. Bearing that in mind, we could single out the parties upholding the interests of the Russian minority in Estonia as distinct from the rest of the parties. However, such differentiation does not seem to be very fruitful.

The second option would be to place parties on a scale according to which one wing would consist of nationalist parties and the other of cosmopolitan parties. Pettai and Kreuzer[9] have used such an approach. In comparison with the previous approach, this one is more effective because is provides a possibility of comparing parties with one another.

Nevertheless, I would recommend one more approach that is based on ethnic integration. Unfortunately it involves two admissions regarding inadequate data. First, for the parliamentary elections in March 1999, although 12 parties nominated their candidates, 5 of them participated in the elections on the list of some other party and so can be taken into account only indirectly.

I have based the integration dimension on the ethnic composition of party lists. As official statistics do not list candidates by their nationality, my approach rests on names, differentiating between Estonian names on the one hand and mainly Slavic names on the other. This method cannot be considered absolute because in reality Estonians can have Russian names, and vice versa.

As to the third admission, I leave aside parties that are oriented towards the Russian-speaking population and examine only the parties that are usually considered as representing the interests of Estonians, because these parties above all should guarantee that the integration of the Slavic (Russian) minority into Estonian society be as painless as possible.

The resulting scale has at one (negative) end parties that have no candidates with Slavic names on their lists. Determining the other (positive) end of the scale is much more difficult, because it can be based on two indicators—the relative importance of the Russian-speaking population and the relative importance of the Russian-speaking citizenry. Looking at the Russian-speaking population, we could claim that parties that have approximately one-third non-Estonians on their lists have reached farther in their understanding of integration. In regard to citizenry, this indicator drops to approximately 15 percent.

Keeping in mind the number of non-Estonian candidates, we have arranged the parties in the following order:

Christian People's Party—0%	Moderates—3.0%
Farmers' Assembly—0%	Coalition Party—5.6%
Pro Patria Union—0.6%	Center Party—7.9%
Country People's Party—1.2%	Progressive Party—9.2%
Reform Party—1.5%	Blue Party—1.3%

The classification of parties on ideological grounds is somewhat easier. The distribution of parties represented in parliament refers us back to the two main ideologies with the addition of two more subsidiary ideologies.[10]

The main ideologies include, above all, liberalism, with the neoliberal direction represented by the Reform Party and social liberalism revealed best in the programs of the Coalition Party and Pro Patria Union and, to a lesser extent, in the documents of the Moderates, the Center Party, and the Popular Union.

The second most important ideology is social democracy, which can be found in the parties that appear on the list of United People's Party (UPP, Social Democratic Labor Party). Certain social democratic influences can also be traced in the positions of the Moderates, the Center Party, and the Popular Union.

In addition to the main ideologies we can also talk about nationalism, which is most characteristic of the Russian parties and also of the Pro Patria Union.

Agrarian ideology is naturally represented by the agrarian parties, Rural Union and Popular Union (formerly Country People's Party).

PARTIES IN ELECTIONS

While basically everybody could run for the first parliamentary elections in the newly independent Estonia in 1992, since 1995 the right to participate in parliamentary elections has been reserved for parties and individual candidates only. As the relative importance of the latter has proved to be practically nonexistent, in reality we can talk about party centrality.

The electoral law of Riigikogu (parliament) is rather complicated. In principle we are dealing with proportional elections, but this proportionality is restricted by a five percent threshold.

The transformation of votes received at Riigikogu elections into parliamentary seats takes place, first,

1. through a personal mandate, which is based only on the number of personally gathered votes. The candidates who exceed the quota calculated by the formula below receive a parliamentary seat:

$$Q = \frac{\text{valid votes in a district}}{\text{number of mandates in a district}}$$

Usually approximately 5,000 votes are enough to become elected. This is the only possibility for individual candidates, but so far none of them has managed to collect enough votes.

2. Second, the conversion of votes into parliamentary seats is done through district mandates. In the distribution of these seats, first, the total number of votes of a party in a district is taken into account and, second, the number of personal quotas that fit into this number is calculated. This is the way the number of seats a party gets from a given district is determined. Individually, these seats are distributed in conformity with the order of candidates formed according to the electoral results.
3. The compensation mandate is the most complicated part of the Estonian electoral mechanism. The major difference from the above-mentioned methods is that not the number of personal votes gathered by a candidate, but his/her position in a hierarchical state list that does not change during the elections is taken into account. The higher a candidate is in the party list, the bigger are his/her chances of becoming a Riigikogu member. As approximately half of the parliamentary seats were distributed like that in the 1992–1999 Riigikogu elections, it can be claimed that the wish of the electorate played only an indirect role in getting them into parliament; a large role was played by internal party politics instead.

Subsequently I will present the Riigikogu electoral results in the years 1992–1999 (see Table 8.1).

The 1992 elections were dominated by electoral coalitions. Only two parties participated under their own names and did not consider it necessary to work with other organizations—these were the National Independence Party and the Entrepreneurs Party. All other lists were in fact electoral coalitions between two or more parties or between one party and some other organizations:

Table 8.1 Elections to Riigikogu in 1992

Party	*Candidates*	*Votes*	*Votes (%)*	*Seats*
Pro Patria	101	100,828	22.00	29
Safe Home	73	63,329	13.60	17
Popular Front	103	56,124	12.25	15
Moderates	49	44,577	9.73	12
ENIP	97	40,260	8.79	10
Royalists	30	32,638	7.12	8
Estonian Citizen	26	31,553	6.89	8
Greens	14	12,009	3.71	1
Entrepreneurs	14	10,946	2.39	1
Others	121	66,983	14.60	—

Note: two parties—the Greens and Entrepreneurs Party—got their representation in Riigikogu because one candidate from each was able to gather the number of votes necessary for a personal mandate and thus be elected. In this case, it is unimportant whether a party as a whole exceeded the five percent threshold or not.
Source: Vabariigi presidendi ja Riigikogu valimised 1992, Eesti Vabariigi Valimiskomisjon, Tallinn, 1992, pp. 13839.

- Pro Patria, an electoral coalition that consisted of five parties: Christian Democratic Union, Christian Democratic Party, Conservative People's Party, Republican Party and Liberal Democratic Party.
- Safe Home, an electoral coalition consisting of two parties: Coalition Party and Rural Union.
- Popular Front, an electoral coalition that consisted of one party (Center Party) and three organizations.
- The Moderates consisted of two parties: Social Democratic Party and Land Center Party.
- The Royalists consisted of one party (Royalist Party) and one organization.
- Estonian Citizen consisted of one party (Party of Estonian Republic) and one organization.
- The Greens consisted of one party (Estonian Greens) and four organizations.

See Table 8.2 for information about the 1995 elections.

Only parties and individual candidates could take part in these elections; thus, the participation of any other organizations was forbidden, while parties were allowed to form electoral coalitions among themselves. There were three lists in which only one party participated—the Reform Party, the Center Party, and People's Party of Republicans and Conservatives. The latter used a somewhat shorter name in the elections—Right Wings. The rest were electoral coalitions of parties:

- The Coalition (Coalition Party and Country People's Union) consisted of five parties: Coalition Party, Rural Union, Country People's Party, Farmers' Assembly, and Party of Families and Pensioners.

- Pro Patria and ENIP Union consisted of two parties: Pro Patria and National Independence Party.
- Moderates consisted of Social Democratic Party and Land Center Party.
- Our Home is Estonia consisted of United People's Party and Russian Party of Estonia.

See Table 8.3 for information about the 1999 elections.

Party electoral coalitions were also prohibited during these elections. Parties were allowed to form a common list of candidates, but the list was then registered under the name of only one party. The following parties used this option:

- Coalition Party, which in addition to the main party also included members of Rural Union and Party of Families and Pensioners.
- United People's Party, which in addition to the main party also included Social Democratic Labor Party and Russian Unity Party.
- Moderates also included the Peoples' Party.

Table 8.2 Elections to Riigikogu in 1995

Party	*Candidates*	*Votes*	*Votes (%)*	*Seats*
Coalition	161	174,248	32.23	41
Reform Party	103	87,531	16.19	19
Center Party	114	76,634	14.17	16
Pro Patria and ENIP Union	109	42,493	7.85	8
Moderates	101	32,381	5.99	6
OHIE	73	31,763	5.87	6
Right-wings	101	27,053	5.00	5
Others	494	68,596	12.69	—

Source: Riigikogu valimine 5.mrts 1995, Tallinn, 1995, p.84.

Table 8.3 Elections to Riigikogu in 1999

Party	*Candidates*	*Votes*	*Votes (%)*	*Seats*
Center Party	242	113,378	23.41	28
Pro Patria Union	178	77,917	16.09	18
Reform Party	212	77,088	15.92	18
Moderates	303	73,630	15.21	17
Coalition Party	216	36,692	7.58	7
Country Peoples Party	167	35,204	7.27	7
United Peoples Party	172	29,682	6.13	6
Others	395	40,648	8.40	—

Source: Riigikogu valimine 7. mrts 1999, Vabariigi Valimiskomisjon, Tallinn, 1999, p.335.

PARTIES AND GOVERNMENTS

Due to the fragmentation of parties in the Riigikogu, it has up to now been impossible to form a single-party majority government.

Since the Estonian Republic regained its independence in August 1991, there have been eight governments. Taking into account the prime minister and parties that participated in the government, we can represent these governments as shown in Table 8.4

The absence of partners in Edgar Savisaar's and Tiit Vähi's first governments does not mean that these were single-party majority or minority governments. The last Supreme Council that acted from March 1990 to September 1992 had such a vague party composition that it is rather difficult to state which parties were active there, let alone determine which party was allied with another party. The leader party cited in the table—Popular Front—refers to the fact that the prime minister was elected into the Supreme Council with its support. Center Party means that the prime minister belonged to this party, and the same applies to Coalition Party.

The Progressive Party separated from the Center Party at the beginning of 1996 and formed its own faction in Riigikogu.

It should be reiterated that the Coalition consisted of five parties.

Starting from Mart Laar's first government, when the list was limited to six governments, most had been majority governments, although there had been minority governments as well. Mart Siimann's government was entirely a minority government. To some extent, Mart Laar's first government during its last months and Tiit Vähi's third government after the separation of the Reform Party were minority governments as well.

THE SIZE AND COMPOSITION OF PARTIES

The Party Law stipulated that parties established after Dec 1, 1994, had to have at least 1,000 members in order to be registered. The law also envisaged that all parties would have to reregister by Oct 1, 1998 and that, by that time, parties that were established before 1994 would have to have at least 1,000 members as well.

Table 8.5 presents the number of members of Estonian parties as of the autumn of 1998 and 1999.

We first notice from the table that the membership of parties had grown by approximately 40 percent in a bit more than a year. Even if we do not take the Christian People's Party, which emerged after Oct 1, 1998, into account, the increase in the membership of other parties amounts to approximately 30 percent, which should be considered a high index. Both the Riigikogu elections on March 7, 1999 and local elections on Oct 17, 1999 probably caused this increase. It can be presumed that in connection with the election campaign, parties also paid greater attention to recruiting new members.

Table 8.4 Governments of Estonian Republic, 1990–2000

Prime Minister	*Time*	*Leading party*	*Partners*
Edgar Savisaar	Mar. 1990–Feb. 1992	Popular Front, Center Party	—
Tiit Vähi I	Feb. 1992–Oct. 1992	Coalition Party	—
Mart Laar I	Oct. 1992–Nov. 1994	Pro Patria	Moderates, ENIP
Andres Tarand	Nov. 1994–Apr. 1995	Moderates	Pro Patria, ENIP, Right-wings
Tiit Vähi II	Apr. 1995–Oct. 1995	Coalition	Center Party
Tiit Vähi III	Oct. 1995–Mar. 1997	Coalition	Reform Party (until Nov. 1996), Progressive Party (from Nov. 1996)
Mart Siimann	Mar. 1997–Mar. 1999	Coalition	Progressive Party
Mart Laar II	Mar. 1999–?	Pro Patria Union	Reform Party, Moderates

Table 8.5 Membership of Parties

Party	*Autumn 1998*	*Autumn 1999*
Center Party	2,518	3,400
Moderates	1,092	3,000
Party of Families and Pensioners	2,013	2,700
Pro Patria Union	1,137	2,600
Christian Peoples Party	—	2,300
Farmers Assembly	1,114	1,500
Future Party	1,049	1,400
Coalition Party	1,244	1,400
Reform Party	1,009	1,400
United Peoples Party	1,053	1,400
Blue Party	1,145	1,300
Popular Union	1,096	1,200
Russian Unity Party	1,125	1,200
Progressive Party	1,023	1,200
Rural Union	1,042	1,100
Labour Party	1,037	1,100
Peoples Party	1,354	—
TOTAL	20,051	28,200

Note: Due to absence of data, the Russian Party of Estonia is not presented in the table.
Source:
• 1998—Signe Aaskivi, Parteiregistrid vrdluses, Snumileht, Oct 2630, 1998.
• 1999—data collected from parties, rounded to the nearest hundred.

The membership of parties as of October 1998 was analyzed[11] when all parties had to present data in order to reregister. Only three indicators can be obtained from this data—the gender structure of a party, the age structure of a party, and the residence of party members; however, we can still draw conclusions from these characteristics.

In Table 8.6 only parties that are represented in the composition of Riigikogu by members who were elected on March, 7, 1999 will be examined. The People's Party will not be examined as it united with the Moderates in the autumn of 1999.

As the table indicates, there are only three parties—Party of Families and Pensioners, United People's Party, and Russian Unity Party—where women prevail. Why this is the case with the Party of Families and Pensioners is rather easy to explain—there is quite a large number of elderly people among its members, and as population statistics show, there are almost twice as many women as men among people over 60 years of age. The deviant demographic structure is also reflected in the composition of the party.

The question as to why there are more women in parties that are oriented towards non-Estonians remains unanswered at present.

As a whole, the gender composition of parties should be viewed as an indicator of patriarchy in Estonian politics. If women wish to have more say in political decision making (and naturally they do), then above all they should start with parties.

Table 8.6 Gender Structure of Parties

Party	*Male (%)*	*Female (%)*
Center Party	52.5	47.5
Pro Patria Union	69.6	30.4
Reform Party	71.5	28.5
Moderates	58.5	41.5
Coalition Party	69.5	30.5
Party of Families and Pensioners	30.4	69.6
Rural Union	53.3	46.7
Popular Union	68.2	31.8
United Peoples Party	43.1	56.9
Social-democrat Labor Party	60.2	39.8
Russian Unity Party	41.0	59.0

Source: 1998—Signe Aaskivi, Parteiregistrid vrdluses, Snumileht, Oct 2630, 1998.

Table 8.7 Age Structure of Parties

Party	*Average age*	*Under 30 years (%)*	*30–39 years (%)*	*40–49 years (%)*	*50–59 years (%)*	*60 years and more (%)*
Center Party	48.7	16.0	13.1	19.6	23.8	27.5
Pro Patria Union	46.7	20.2	19.8	17.3	16.1	26.5
Reform Party	41.7	17.5	26.9	30.0	16.0	8.9
Moderates	47.0	12.3	16.8	25.9	25.5	19.5
Coalition Party	NA	32.4	23.0	18.2	NA	NA
Land Union	46.7	14.4	17.6	22.7	26.8	18.5
Party of Families and Pensioners	63.8	2.1	6.8	7.1	10.3	73.7
Popular Union	50.0	4.4	14.4	28.0	32.9	19.8
United People's Party	42.2	19.9	20.7	31.2	18.7	9.4
Labor Party	62.5	4.2	5.5	9.8	18.1	62.5
Russian Unity Party	37.5	29.1	27.8	26.8	12.9	3.4

Our evaluation starts with age 18 since that is the minimum age for becoming a party member.
Source: 1998–Signe Aaskivi, Parteiregistrid vrdluses, Snumileht, Oct 2630, 1998.

In Table 8.7, we focus on the future of parties and thus pay attention primarily to members under the age of 30. The low support received from this age group by two parties—the Labor Party and the Pensioners' Party—is not difficult to explain. The Labor Party grew out of the former Communist Party and, considering the Estonian political reality, it would have been surprising if young people had joined it in masses. The Pensioners' Party actually operates more as a pressure group, and it is understandable that such politics do not interest young people. Rural parties seem to be in a more complicated situation as their lack of young members can undermine their success in the future.

Table 8.8 below is based on three possible places of residence:

a. Tallinn, the capital of Estonia, where 25.5 percent of the electorate and thus also potential party members, reside.
b. Tartu, the second-largest city in Estonia (8.0 percent of the electorate)
c. All other cities and parishes—66.5 percent of the electorate

It is of course natural that the majority of the members of rural parties (Rural Union and Popular Union) come from rural areas and smaller towns. Almost all other parties can be viewed as organizations with strong capital-centrality, which essentially have been unable to spread their activities to other regions. The fact that the Moderates are not very Tallinn-centered probably derives from the circumstance that two former rural parties are strongly represented in its membership.

The under-representation of Russian parties in Tartu is most probably connected with the relatively small share of non-Estonians in the Tartu population—approximately 15 percent, whereas the share of non-Estonians in Tallinn reaches approximately 40 percent.

PARTY SUPPORTERS

The basis for determining the supporters of different parties is a questionnaire conducted by Tartu University Department of Social Sciences on the day of the Riigikogu election on March 7, 1999.[12] Approximately 1,100 people were surveyed all over Estonia. However, the results of the questionnaire should be interpreted with some caution as they included only the contingent that cast their vote on that exact day. Thus, the questionnaire could not express the opinions of the franchised citizens who did not take part in the elections or who preferred to vote at the preliminary

Table 8.8 Geographical Dispersal of Membership

Party	*Tallinn (%)*	*Tartu (%)*	*Other regions (%)*
Center Party	39.3	10.0	50.7
Pro Patria Union	38.2	16.9	44.9
Reform Party	32.4	10.9	56.7
Moderates	17.5	13.8	68.7
Coalition Party	52.5	NA	NA
Rural Union	0.9	3.0	96.1
Party of Families and Pensioners	14.2	3.3	82.5
Popular Union	5.8	4.8	89.4
United Peoples Party	60.1	2.7	37.2
Labor Party	42.0	4.8	53.2
Russian Unity Party	66.9	0.1	30.0

Source: 1998—Signe Aaskivi, Parteiregistrid vrdluses, Snumileht, Oct 2630, 1998.

elections. Taking these two aspects into account, we can claim that the questionnaire reflected the attitude towards parties of about 40 percent of the electorate.

The second aspect that should be considered in this case is that many parties took part in the elections on the list of some other party. Thus, it is not possible to determine exactly how many of those who voted for the Coalition Party would have actually preferred the Rural Union or the Party of Families and Pensioners. The same problem concerns the United People's Party—we do not know the actual preferences for the Labor Party and the Russian Unity Party represented in this list.

Next, the supporters of parties currently represented in Riigikogu are presented via five demographic indicators. Table 8.9 shows the gender representation.

The Moderates and the Popular Union strongly deviate from the average population. Support to other parties more or less reflects the gender structure of the population (approximately 45% men and 55% women).

It is striking that two parties—Pro Partia Union and Reform Party—are strongly oriented towards the younger electorate, whereas two parties count on the votes of those in the pension age (Coalition Party and Popular Union). The supporters of the United People's Party are mostly in older middle age, the Center Party is supported more by the old than the young, and only the Moderates have managed to attract all age groups equally (see Table 8.10).

Table 8.9 Gender of Supporters of Parties

Party	*Male (%)*	*Female (%)*
Center Party	41.8	58.2
Pro Patria Union	48.1	51.9
Reform Party	46.2	53.8
Moderates	30.1	69.9
Coalition Party	49.3	50.7
Popular Union	54.0	46.0
United Peoples Party	42.3	57.7

Table 8.10 Age of Supporters of Parties

Party	*18–30 years (%)*	*31–45 years (%)*	*46–60 years (%)*	*60 years and more (%)*
Center Party	15.7	17.2	34.3	32.8
Pro Patria Union	30.8	32.6	20.8	15.8
Reform Party	36.7	31.3	23.3	8.8
Moderates	22.7	25.3	25.3	26.7
Coalition Party	14.3	25.7	21.4	38.6
Popular Union	4.8	15.9	38.1	41.3
United People's Party	17.2	20.7	44.8	17.2

For comparison, we present the overall data of the whole population. As of 1999, the share of the age groups presented in the table for the whole population is as follows:

18–30 years—24.4 percent

31–45 years—27.8 percent

46–60 years—23.5 percent

60 years and older—24.3 percent

In Table 8.11, respondents were divided into four educational categories when the data were processed.

a. Persons with elementary education, which, in today's Estonia, includes those who have finished a ninth-grade primary school; however, those who graduated from the previously compulsory 6-, 7-, or 8-grade primary school were also included in this category.
b. Persons with vocational education, which includes those who have graduated from some industrial school irrespective of the duration of studies.
c. Persons with secondary education, which includes those who have graduated from a current 12-grade secondary school or former 10- or 11-grade secondary school.
d. Persons with university education, which includes those who have graduated from a university or have studied at a university for at least 3 years.

In Table 8.12, the individual monthly income of a respondent before tax deduction is taken into account. Income is given in Estonian kroons. The average monthly income at the end of 1999 was approximately 4,500 EEK. The conversion rate is: 1 USD = 16 EEK.

Respondents were divided into two groups on the basis of nationality: Estonians and non-Estonians (see Table 8.13).

At this point, we reiterate that only one party—the Social Democratic Labor Party whose membership consisted mainly of Estonians—partici-

Table 8.11 Educational Level of Supporters of Parties

Party	*Elementary (%)*	*Vocational (%)*	*Secondary (%)*	*University (%)*
Center Party	15.9	35.8	23.4	24.9
Pro Patria Union	9.0	27.1	21.7	42.1
Reform Party	7.1	26.5	22.7	43.7
Moderates	15.3	31.3	17.3	36.0
Coalition Party	21.4	37.1	18.6	22.9
Popular Union.	21.0	24.2	24.2	30.6
United People's Party	6.9	17.2	20.7	55.2

Table 8.12 Income of Supporters of Parties

Party	*Less than 1,500 EEK (%)*	*1,501–3000 EEK (%)*	*3,001–5,000 EEK (%)*	*more 5,000 EEK (%)*
Center Party	31.6	35.70	17.9	14.8
Pro Patria Union	24.6	25.1	19.9	30.3
Reform Party	22.4	17.5	20.2	39.9
Moderates	30.8	29.5	23.3	16.4
Coalition Party	33.8	32.4	14.7	19.1
Popular Union	41.0	29.5	23.0	6.6
United People's Party	14.3	35.7	25.0	25.0

Table 8.13 Nationality of Supporters of Parties

Party	*Estonians (%)*	*Non-Estonians (%)*
Center Party	92.6	7.4
Pro Patria Union	98.2	1.8
Reform Party	96.2	3.8
Moderates	98.0	2.0
Coalition Party	95.7	4.3
Popular Union	93.7	6.3
United People's Party	31.0	69.0

pated on the list of the United People's Party. The supporters of the other parties are nationally more or less homogenous, differing to a large extent from the national structure of the electorate as a whole, which is estimated as follows:

- Estonians—85 percent
- Non-Estonians—15 percent

PARTY SYSTEM

There are several criteria for describing the party system. In this survey, I confine myself to only three that seem to be most relevant regarding the present stage in the development of parties. These would be the number of parties, party organization, and the possibility of the existence of an antiparty system.

1. The number of parties

   Even when we consider only those parties that have won seats in parliament, it is clear that Estonia has consistently had a wide range of parties in the post-Soviet era. This is particularly apparent when we consider actual parties and not the coalitions in which many of them grouped themselves. Counted thus, there were 14 parties in the elections of 1992, 14 in 1995, and 12 in 1999.

Looking at the above tables concerning elections we can see that only once—in 1995—has one electoral list received more than 30 percent of the seats. Actually even this result is delusive—the contribution of the Coalition Party itself was approximately 20 percent.

The effective number of parties is also evidence of the rather high fragmentation of parties,[13] although the calculations here are based not only on the number of parties but also on the number of electoral lists:

1992—6.2
1995—4
1999—5.5

If we follow Giovanni Sartori's classification, the Estonian party system would lie somewhere between limited and extreme pluralism. There are too many parties to characterize the pluralism as limited, but on the other hand none of the characteristics of extreme pluralism are actually present in Estonia.[14] According to Alan Ware, the Estonian party system can be considered simply a multiparty system.[15]

However, in comparison with stable democracies, party fragmentation in Estonia seems to be too high. Lijphart has concluded in one study[16] that for the democracies that use the d'Hondt system, the average effective number of parties in parliament is 3.7. Thus, we have to agree with Pettai's and Kreuzer's standpoint that the Estonian party system indicates a rather low level of consolidation.[17]

2. Party organization

The following analysis is based on several criteria.

a. Dispersal of party membership over the country. Table 8.8 indicates that Estonian parties are strongly Tallinn- and Tartu-centered, while the relative importance of other regions (except for rural parties) is rather low.

b. Low number of party members. Nørgaard et al. claimed a few years ago that the party organization of the Baltic countries is weak because the party membership constitutes approximately one percent of the electorate.[18] At the end of 1999, party membership constituted approximately 3.3 percent of the electorate. Such an increase definitely shows the strengthening of party organization, but it is doubtful whether it is a sufficient indicator. For example, the same indicator in Nordic countries is as high as 15 percent of the franchised population.

c. According to Arter, a party exits its embryonic stage of development when the founders of the party leave and are replaced by a new political generation.[19] Considering this indicator, it has to be asserted that Estonian parties have not gotten very far in their development. Of the 11 parties currently represented in Riigikogu, only two (Coalition Party and Labor Party) have had a change of leadership.

d. Capability of parties at local elections. Parties on the parliamentary level are in an absolutely dominant position, but the same cannot be claimed for them at the local power level. Local governmental elections took place in Estonia in October 1999. Administratively, the Estonian Republic consists of towns and parishes, and there were 247 of them at that moment. In a society with a well-developed party organization, most of the municipal units, if not all, would be covered by parties as well. Estonia is very far from this ideal. First, only 11 parties took part in the local elections, while 7 stood aside. If we consider the parties' coverage of local areas, then the leader here was the

Center Party, which put up lists in 59 parishes and towns—still only in about one-fourth of the total. Other parties did even worse: Pro Patria Union participated in 33 locations, Moderates in 23 locations, and Reform Party and Christian People's Party in 16 towns and parishes. Other parties that came out with their own electoral lists put up candidates in fewer than 10 parishes or towns.

e. Loyalty of party members should also show the organizational strength of a party. This is reflected best by the number of renegades during parliamentary elections. On the basis of the 1995 electoral results, the organizational strength of parties could have been evaluated as rather weak by this criterion, inasmuch as 38 percent of Riigikogu members who ran for the seat again preferred to do so on the list of another party.[20] Estimating the 1999 elections in this respect, we can observe a strong shift towards stability. Ninety-five Riigikogu members ran for the seat again, and only 10 of them decided to switch parties for one reason or another; thus, the percentage of renegades dropped to 10.5.

3. When we are describing the Estonian party system, a question arises as to whether we are not dealing with an antiparty system in Estonia. According to Sartori, extreme fragmentation presupposes the existence of antiparty systems.[21] David Arter[22] claims the same about Estonia. According to him, three problems should be addressed.

Whether electors are most influenced by the programmatic stands of the party as a whole in making their decisions, or by the individual characteristics of the party's candidate. The second option suggests the existence of an antiparty system. To support his position, Arter presents the results of a public opinion survey, according to which only 31 percent of the electorate based their decisions on the programmatic stands of a party.[23] Although this survey dates back to 1992, these viewpoints have been affirmed later as well; according to a preelection survey conducted in 1998, approximately 60 percent of the respondents claimed that they proceed from the personal characteristics of a candidate in making their decision.[24] However, this finding can be contested if we proceed from questionnaires conducted on Election Day, rather than at an arbitrary time. An electoral questionnaire conducted all over Estonia on Election Day, March 7, 1999, showed that 59.6 percent of the respondents answered that the party program was a very important factor in making their decision, while the same indicator for the significance of personal characteristics of a candidate was 40.4 percent. More or less the same situation could be observed in Tartu on the day of local elections, October 17, 1999, when 63.1 percent preferred parties and 36.9 percent preferred candidates.[25] It can be concluded from these data that those who *participated in the elections* preferred party programs to personal characteristics of candidates while in *preelection* questionnaires more stress was placed on candidates.

The same distinction manifests itself less directly in the attitude towards parties. According to a survey conducted in the spring of 1998, 19.0 percent of the respondents were convinced that parties in Riigikogu acted mostly in their own interests. The survey conducted on Election Day, March 7,

1999, showed that 7.5 percent of the respondents held the view that the actions of no party corresponded to the expectations of the electorate.[26]

Low participation in the elections is the second problem raised by Arters. The participation rate in the elections held during the last 10 years has constantly dropped, as Table 8.14 illustrates.

According to Arter, we are dealing with an antiparty system if one-third of registered voters or more do not participate in elections.[27] In this respect, Estonian local elections, in which half the franchised population does not vote, are very discouraging.

The third and final problem raised by Arter is the possible existence of antiparties, that is, parties that aim at the radical restructuring of the existing political system, possibly even ready to give up party politics altogether. We do not have such parties in Estonia today, but a few examples from the recent past can be brought up. In 1992, both the Royalists and the electoral coalition Estonian Citizen received eight seats in Riigikogu. The goal of the first was (although half-jokingly) to establish a monarchist governmental system in Estonia, while the second one considered it necessary to replace the democratic Constitution of 1992 with the 1938 Constitution that had strong authoritarian elements. By now both parties have been dissolved.

In conclusion, it is clear that the party system in today's Estonia is far from fully developed. However, it is no doubt too soon to expect a stable democracy with all its characteristics to be in place The question is: what are Estonia's chances of developing a party system similar to that of the developed democratic world?

To put it simply, discourses concerning this matter in theoretical literature can be divided into two:

1. pessimistic standpoints, according to which the chances of the Baltic countries, including Estonia, developing a system where programmatic parties dominate, are rather slim[28]

Table 8.14 Participation in Elections

Year	*Elections*	*Turnout (%)*
1989	Congress of Peoples Deputies of USSR	87.0%
1990	Supreme Council of Estonia	78.3%
1991	Independence referendum	83.0%
1992	Constitutional referendum	66.8%
1992	Riigikogu	70.3%
1993	Local authorities	52.6%
1995	Riigikogu	68.9%
1996	Local authorities	52.0%
1999	Riigikogu	57.4%
1999	Local authorities	49.8%

2. cautious viewpoints, where the best is expected although the necessary conditions for this are not yet seen.[29]

What is absent are positive viewpoints. I have to admit that at the moment it is quite risky to argue that, for example, in the next 10 years, the Estonian party system will not differ much from that of Scandinavian or West-European countries. On the other hand, the rapid development of all political processes could reasonably provide a basis for such optimism. The party development in Estonia seems to have reached a stage where it can already be considered a system—it is characterized by certain stability and regulation. Estonia has come much further in its development than it was at the time of its newly gained independence, or even a few years ago. There is no point in comparing Estonia to other parts of the former Soviet Union any more. Estonia is already comparable to the rest of Eastern Europe. Keeping this in mind, there is reason to be optimistic.

CHAPTER 9

Parties and Party Politics in Latvia: Origins and Current Development

Andris Runcis

INTRODUCTION

The aim of this chapter is to understand Latvian party politics today, an aim that requires us to reconstruct the background of Latvian politics from the very beginning and to grasp the contemporary relevance of basic cleavages in society. We begin with a brief overview of party politics today, and the cleavages that are dominant, and then take a longer view, examining the development of Latvia between the World Wars and the growing impact of Soviet domination in order see the effect of this historical legacy on the nation's ability to reach the contemporary goals of independence, democratization, and change from command economy to market-oriented economy.

LATVIAN CLEAVAGES AND PARTIES TODAY: AN OVERVIEW

In their classic account, Lipset and Rokkan[1] portray parties as the principal agents of transforming societal conflicts into political divisions. They argue that political parties translate group interests into political oppositions by crystallizing and articulating conflicting interests, as well as by constructing alliances, setting up organizational networks, and devising electoral strategies, establishing a hierarchy of cleavages bases that may undergo changes from time to time.

Norgaard et al. suggest that the parties in Latvia should be placed within a two-dimensional matrix, with a radical/moderate division on the ethno-political issue and a political/economic/left/right cleavage.[2] From 1988 to 1991, the dominating cleavage was the independence issue. Later, the independence issue was very close to the ethno-political issue, which predominated when the citizenship question was discussed and which related to the inclusion/exclusion question.

Political parties have to work with the existing possibilities and resources and with the situation at hand. The creation of parties is still an ongoing process in Latvia. Some of the parties are new; some are "reborn" historical parties; some have emerged after the split of the Communist Party. Concerning parties, we can quote Joseph LaPalombara and Myron Weiner:

> The historical graveyards are cluttered with parties which dominated the political scene but which subsequently failed to adapt to new circumstances and therefore died, were absorbed by new more active movements, or withered into small marginal parties. Nonetheless the circumstances under which parties first arise in a developing political system—together with their initial tone and configuration—clearly have an important effect on the kinds of parties which subsequently emerge.[3]

In the case of Latvia, market-oriented reforms, the privatization process, and the opening of foreign trade contributed to the quick formation after independence of an entrepreneurial class within the formerly egalitarian and flattened society of Latvia. The logic of transitioning away from the post-totalitarian regime led to a powerful swing to a right-wing political orientation in Latvian society. This swing took place in the context of rapid formation and re-formation of political parties. Before the sixth session of the Latvian parliament (the Saeima), two new parties—People's Movement *For Latvia* (TKL—Siegerist Party) and Democratic Party *Master* (DPS)—had been established and gained representation. Six months before the next session several more parties emerged and two of them—People's Party (Tautas Partija—TP) and New Party (Jaunā partija—JP)—won seats in the Saeima, whereas several other parties that had won seats in the sixth session disappeared from parliament and were reduced to the status of small marginal parties. Several top-down organized parties such as *Jaunais Laiks* (New Era) and Latvia's First (ministers) party (Latvijas Pirmā partija—LPP) were established before elections to the eighth session in 2002 and gained seats. Most of the new parties are on the right; the right wing of the political spectrum is now overloaded by different Latvian parties all working in the same "dramatic narrowing of the scope of domestic political conflict."[4] During electoral campaigns these parties compete to represent the same social groups and say the same things to their electorate.[5]

However, a multiparty system as a sociopolitical phenomenon and as a constitutional institution should be differentiated. On the constitutional level several factions in the Saeima identify themselves as right-leaning, left-leaning, or center. But on the sociopolitical level, some of these parties still have a long way to go. Modeled after the Western political experience, these parties have sprung up in quite an empty space. Many of them do not reflect social, political, religious, or ideological conflicts in society. Many of these parties are weak and small, little more than "pocket" or "sofa" parties. Two-thirds of these parties, which participate in parliamentary elections, gather less than one percent of votes.

THE HISTORICAL BACKGROUND:[6] CLEAVAGES AND POLITICAL PARTIES IN THE 1920S AND 1930S

Although historically, Latvia has always been multiethnic (demographically, Latvia was the most heterogeneous state in the Baltics in the 1920s and 1930s), nonetheless between 1920 and 1940 the indigenous population was stable and formed a substantial majority. The ideological and organizational features of the inter-war political parties resulted from economic, social, and institutional circumstances. The national movement, the strong socialist movement in factories, as well as external factors after World War I, influenced the political process.

During the inter-war period, we can find several important cleavages. To begin with, the center/periphery cleavage had a tremendous importance for the political process. Conflict between centre and periphery is a fundamental part of nation building and the nation-maintenance process. Reflecting historical struggle as well as current conflicts, contemporary peripheries are most politicized when distinct identities and distinct languages are involved. At the same time, socioeconomic, urban/rural, and religious cleavages grow and further divide the nation. Several major political groups existed during the inter-war period: the socialists, the liberals, the agrarians-conservatives, and a large group of political organizations built around ethnic minorities. The multiethnic composition of Latvian society and the ethnic issue were always crucial during the inter-war period and again in the post-Soviet time. The traditional economic left/right cleavage partly overlapped with the urban/rural division. Numerous cleavages explain the ideological diversity of political parties in the political spectrum.

The first political parties emerged in Latvia in the late nineteenth and early twentieth centuries, with the dissemination of Marxist ideas in the Russian Empire, and turned into a political force by 1905. The development of political parties as real political organizations could start only when the existence of an independent state was proclaimed. These parties started to function in a political environment without a political tradition. The two largest parties at the time—the Social-Democrats and the Farmer Union—can be called social-class parties, as they represented two basic social classes—the workers and the farmers—but they could not satisfy all social strata. Freivalds[7] calculated that on the whole, three large groups of parties—Latvian citizen (23), Latvian socialist (4), and ethnic minority (17)—reflected the ideological diversity and political will of society. The main cleavage lines at that time were socioeconomic, left/right and urban/rural. The two largest parties—the Social Democrats and the Farmer Union—represented these basic lines.

Only the Social Democrats, represented by the Latvian Social Democratic Workers Party (Latvijas Sociāldemokrātiskā Strādnieku partija—LSDSP), had developed a political ideology and program. LSDSP declared itself as chieftain of the workers and landless citizens and the political representative of proletarians of all nationalities, while the bourgeoisie strata were defined as the opposition to the workers and the landless. They promoted the interests of industrial and agricultural workers employed by the wealthiest farmers. At other times, there were only two to four politically active socialist-oriented parties. LSDSP, however, was not only the biggest socialist party, but also the biggest party in Latvia. Ideological and internal problems were the main reasons this party could not overcome its social-class policy orientation.

Agrarian issues were always highly sensitive for the Latvian peasantry, because of the agrarian reform, introduced after World War I. One of the most influential parties at the time was the agrarian party—the Latvian Farmer Union (LZS). LZS dominated in the formation of the government and in Latvian political life. From 1918 to 1934, the party was represented in 15 out of 18 governments. The social basis for this party was farmers, and party leaders pointed out that land was the basis of Latvian national prosperity and that agriculture was Latvia's top priority.

Ethnic composition and issues were important as well. Non-Latvians played an important role in the Latvian state-building process. The non-Latvian citizenry was highly diverse in terms of ethnic background and religion, and social background and issues related to this diversity played an important role in the process of creating political organizations.[8] The ethnic parties' impact related not so much to the size of the different ethnic groups as to organizational strength.

The situation changed dramatically in 1940–1941, when the Soviet Union began to carry out a plan of ethnocide, or ethnic cleansing as it is called today. On one night, June 14, 1941, 15 to 16 thousand Latvians were deported to Siberia,[9] where they were meant to perish. Within two years some 34,000 Latvians had been deported,[10] and the process continued: the greatest mass deportation occurred on March 25, 1949, when approximately 119,000 people from Latvia alone, consisting mostly of successful small independent farmers and their families, were arrested and deported to Siberia.[11] After World War II, Latvia lost approximately one-third of its population for the second time in 30 years. The declining proportion of indigenous Latvians, which began in 1941, dropped from 83 percent to 52 percent in 1989.[12]

In order to fill this gap and to dilute the power and influence of the nationalistically inclined indigenous population, the Kremlin and the local government organized mass migration into the Baltic republics. Many emigrants arrived in Latvia as a result of the Soviet policies of industrialization and colonization. Because of higher living standards, industrialization, the infrastructure, and the image of Riga as a "European city" during the Soviet era, migration from the rest of the Soviet Union reached its highest levels in the 1970s and 1980s. The migration process was the key factor that changed the demographic situation in Latvia. Latvia's rapid industrialization was essentially motivated by a desire to ensure a mass migration in order to facilitate cultural assimilation and achieve political stability.[13] Ideologically, the industrial proletariat was considered superior to the peasantry and was expected to be more supportive of the Soviet regime. From a colonist imperialist point of view, industrialization offered a path for settling large numbers of Russians among the local population. Such colonization was a goal in and of itself, rather than a means of industrialization.

The Russian-dominated Latvian Communist party (LCP) carried out a social policy that was in many realms discriminatory against Latvians and the Latvian language. Issues of the use of language in the Soviet context and elsewhere are often infused with ethno-political meaning because they affect economic opportunities and group status.[14] If the regime favors one language, the native speakers of this language have a competitive edge in the economy. Moreover, as Donald Horowitz has noted, "The status of the language denotes the status of the group that speaks it."[15] By this measure, Russians have occupied a position of superior status to the Latvians, leading to considerable resentment among the latter. In the 1950s, after Stalin's death, more attention was paid to the republics' interests and demands.

Some Latvian communists sought to regulate the ongoing migration from other Soviet republics to Latvia. Others worked to foster knowledge of the Latvian language for party and government officials. These ideas were not well received in Moscow and about 2000 national communists in 1959 were purged from governing structures and lost any possibility of influencing the political processes. A Latvian historian, Ilga Apine, has summarized the negative legacy of this period: "Within a few years, there was a significant removal of cadres at all levels. Experienced and capable workers at the peak of their creative power—party and Soviet activists, scientists, journalists—were fired from active political and economic endeavors. Their intellectual potential was lost to the republic."[16] The influx of Russian speakers was reinforced by the extensive purge of Latvian national communists from the party, and, in Soviet Latvia, the Communist Party was thereafter dominated by Russians and Russian-born Latvians.[17] Attitudes towards Soviet-era immigrants had a strong influence on all political issues in Latvia, especially concerning the citizenship issue and language policy.

The non-Latvian population living in Latvia today can be divided into two groups, namely the traditional minorities and immigrant minorities. When, during the Gorbachev era, discussions of national and ethnic conflicts were no longer a taboo, Latvians strongly voiced their sense of dissatisfaction and targeted the Soviet Union's education and language policies. After regaining independence, Latvians were able to change their status from a suppressed minority to a dominant majority. Sociological survey data shows that during the last years of the perestroika period, the number of Russians in Latvia who opposed independence was almost equal to the number of Russian post-war immigrants.

During the years of Soviet power, the social structure of society was simplified, consisting of the working class, the kolkhoz peasantry, and the intelligentsia. Wessels and Klingemann[18] have described the societies of Eastern Europe as "flattened societies" as a result of the communist regime policy. The low level of socioeconomic differentiation had the consequence that the citizens' party preferences were not determined by their individual socioeconomic positions in the social structure. Such social structure survived until the beginning of the 1990s, when fast economic changes as well as social and regional changes took place. The socialist form of economics managed to satisfy the minimal economic needs of a vast majority of population groups. For a long time, the socialist system cultivated social optimism and provided a sense of stability and the satisfaction of basic needs. The subsequent variety of economic and social interests was the basis of the rise of many new parties.

THE CONSTITUTIONAL AND ELECTORAL LEGISLATION CONTEXT OF THE 1980S AND 1990S

During the Soviet era, Latvia did not have a special party law. The Soviet Constitution proposed that in the Soviet Union the main ruling force was the Communist Party of the Soviet Union. The Constitution allowed some public organizations, but citizens could be part of these organizations only with the goals of building communism.

All this changed after independence. On December 28, 1989, the Supreme Council repealed Article 6 of the Constitution of the Latvian SSR, which specified a leading role for the Communist Party. The party's official monopoly on power was gone. Now citizens could gather in parties and other public organizations, the goals and activities of which were not prohibited by the current system and Constitution. The state guaranteed free activities for parties and public organizations, and belonging to any party did not guarantee the exclusive privilege to participate in state life.

In independent Latvia, the highest-ranking law remains the Satversme (Constitution), written and adopted in 1922, and the basic elements of Latvia's election system are contained there.[19] The elections law, adopted by parliament, serves merely to provide greater specificity to these general requirements.

The most important issue here is Article 6 of the Satversme, which says, "The Saeima is elected in general, equal, direct, closed, and proportional elections." According to Dišlers, writers of the Satversme "found the principle of proportionality to be important enough to include it in the law on the Satversme"[20] and to make it one of the basic and traditional principles for elections in Latvia.

Other laws of key importance to the functioning of the electoral system include the "Law on the Saeima Elections,"[21] "On the Central Elections Commission,"[22] and "On Elections Commissions in Cities, Districts and Parishes and Commissions at Voting Precincts." Derived from the overall elections law regarding the regulation of specific areas, these laws contain very detailed rules which would not be appropriate in the general elections law.

When it comes to the participation of political parties in elections, the law "On Public Organizations and their Associations"[23] is of key importance. The elections law says that political organizations, parties, and associations can field candidates in Saeima elections, while the law "On Public Organizations and their Associations" contains a detailed definition of a political party, states the minimum number of members required to establish one, and outlines the process political parties should follow in order to register with the Ministry of Justice.

Elections on March 18, 1990, which were based on a system of plurality, led to the election of the Supreme Council of the Latvian Socialist Soviet Republic. There was no doubt that the Supreme Council was only a temporary organ of government, and its aim was to achieve full independence for Latvia and to organize free, competitive, and independent parliamentary elections. On August 21, 1991, the Supreme Council adopted a law "On the Statehood of the Republic of Latvia," declaring that the Satversme could take full effect and be established as the constitutional basis for the state. Before the Satversme could take full effect, however, a parliament had to be elected in order to set up the other governmental institutions. For various reasons, the elaboration of the necessary law and the determination of a date for the elections were delayed, and this in turn hindered the development of political parties.[24] It was not until 1993 that free parliamentary elections to the Saeima were held—the first such elections to be held freely after 50 years of Soviet rule.

The election law specified that candidate lists could be amended by voters during the voting process, that is, when one went to vote, one could amend a candidate list to include the names of candidates from other lists in the same voting district. This idea was not accepted. The new law provided for proportional representation, and it allowed voters to change the ranking of candidates within a single list by adding a + or – marking. The elections law set a four percent barrier for winning seats in the Saeima and was otherwise liberal with respect to the possibility of small or relatively informal groups being able to win seats.. It also promoted the emergence of a multiparty system. Most of the political parties that ran in the elections were established shortly after the law was passed, and most of them had very few members indeed. However, the four percent threshold (later raised to five percent) had the effect of reducing the number of parties represented in the national legislature.

NEW CLEAVAGES IN THE 1990s

Latvian society is heterogeneous not only in its sociodemographic (including ethnic) structure, but also in its political patterns and views. Several political parties that had existed before World War II renewed their activities after independence and others were formed anew. The word *party* was not particularly popular in the wake of the Communist Party era, and so the new parties did not gain much support of the population. Small groups and parties were both allowed to file candidate lists, because there would be no real difference between a small group and a political party.

In a seminal study, Lipset and Rokkan[25] used the concept of cleavage referring to a social division and analyzed the freezing of party systems. They argued "that the party system of the 1960s reflects, with few but significant exceptions, the cleavage structure of the 1920s." Cleavages affect the structure of power balance in society. Certainly this important conclusion was made about Western political party systems, but we can use this approach for the analysis of party origins and the party system in Latvia. Lipset and Rokkan pointed out that cleavages in Western societies were a result of national and industrial revolutions.

The Soviet policy of collectivization, industrialization, and migration led to the development of a "flattened" post-communist civil society.[26] This flattened civil society promoted the emergence of a large number of small political groups that tended to characterize themselves as parties.

According to Lipset and Rokkan,[27] in Western societies major waves of change—national and industrial revolutions—created social cleavages, which were reflected in the party system, which in turn structured electoral choice. One such cleavage, evolving as part of the nation-building process, was the center/periphery cleavage. Center and periphery are social and political concepts, not just geographical ones. The center contains major economic and political resources and controls the communication and decision-making process in society, whereas peripheries usually control only a few resources.[28] In the Latvian case in the early 1990s the center was the Moscow power structure, and the key issue was independence.

Smith-Sivertsen posits four basic cleavages: the independence cleavage, the ethnic inclusion/exclusion cleavage, the rural/urban cleavage, and the emerging cleavage between the disadvantaged strata versus the managing, occupational elites.[29] From our point of view, the independence and ethnic inclusion/exclusion cleavages are part of the center/periphery cleavage. The parties that emerged in the early years reflected these divisions.

POLITICAL PARTIES 1988–2000

Perestroika and the atmosphere of glasnost allowed for a limited ideological diversity and expression of social and political tensions that led to the necessity to change the usual procedure of political activities. Now it was possible not only to criticize but also to engage in the social and political activities of informal movements.

One of the first groups to take advantage of the new freedoms was the environmental protection movement, the Green Party. Its members disapproved of policies coming from the center, Moscow, which had a deleterious effect on the management of industry and natural resources and were leading to a growing recognition of the impacts of environmental pollution on public health.[30] Public concern for environmental issues was very high at the time of the struggle for independence, and toward the end of the 1980s the leading environmental movement (Vides Aizsardz bas Klubs—VAK) established the Green Party. From the second part of the 1980s, VAK played a very important role and won representation in the fifth session (the first post-independence session) of the Saeima. However, it was not successful in the next two elections, and in the eighth session it won representation only by joining a coalition headed by the Farmer Union.

In 1988, the mechanism of authoritarian power was left in the past. Instead of one authority—the Communist Party—several centers of power were formed: the Supreme Council (parliament), the government, and other parties.

The three most important parties were the Communist Party (LCP), the People's Front of Latvia (LTF), and the Latvian National Independence Movement (LNNK), which was actually a constituent part of the LTF.

The creation of the Latvian National Independence Movement (Latvijas Nacionālās Neatkarības Kustība—LNNK) in the summer of 1988 was particularly important, because this movement took the next step in the process of increasing people's political awareness and readiness to contest established authority. LNNK opposed the Soviet regime, spoke openly about the occupation of Latvia, and advocated breaking away from the Soviet Union. There were calls for the banning of the LNNK, whose "main goal was the restoration of an independent and democratic Republic of Latvia" (quoted from documents of the second congress of the LNNK in the newspaper *Jelgavas ziņotājs* on June 10, 1989). The mass media did not publish much information about the LNNK, and efforts were made to hinder its activities. In June 1989, under the influence of conservative political forces, the presidium of the Supreme Council of the Latvian SSR established a special commission to evaluate the LNNK activities. The commission's report led the presidium to conclude that the LNNK was not anti-constitutional and that it was not operating on the basis of unconstitutional methods. In short, the LNNK was legalized and the idea of Latvian independence and democracy was indirectly rehabilitated.

The People's Front of Latvia (LTF) had a more moderate program and thereby attracted broad participation—from soft-liner communists to strong nationalists. The existence of different factions within it was envisaged and even stipulated because the movement included people of quite different political views and social experience: those who had suffered from the ruling regime and those who had cooperated with it, as well as those who were in the cultural, scientific, and artistic elite of that time. They were united by the idea of national revival. On the local level, the movement was mainly run by the local intelligentsia and the most active citizens. Its major task at the beginning was to promote the development of perestroika and glasnost. Initially, LTF did not support the idea of complete sovereignty of Latvia.

LTF represented general national values rather than specific partial interests: social unity and harmony, support of the regime, and cultural-ethnic and postmaterialist values. Its members and leaders sometimes thought primarily in moral categories of the struggle of good against evil. Its internal organization was "horizontal" rather than hierarchical.

The key characteristics of LTF as a movement/party were its vague, non- or anti-ideological moralistic program and the informality of its internal structure. The LTF first emerged as the representative of civil society in a mass protest against totalitarian communist rule. Subsequently the organizational demands posed by the elections contributed to the first steps in its development as a quasi-political party. However, after the elections, when confronted with the new task of exercising power, the LTF leadership was faced with tensions among the movement's government, parliament, and grass-roots activists. The unmanageable variety of ideologies, interests, personalities, and general political objectives that they embraced lay at the root of LTF's instability.

The LTF had its own life cycle.[31] It could be said that in 1992 the cycle of life of LTF as the social movement ended. In its developing stage, from the summer of 1988 to the spring of 1989, it was characterized by cooperating relations with the supreme official political power. Official power and LTF were developing in the same direction; both supported the course of reconstruction. The second stage, from the spring of 1989 to the spring of 1990,was characterized by political conflict between official political power (LCP) and LTF. In the third stage, beginning with the elections of March 18, 1990, the LCP and LTF were no longer partners (as they had been in the elections of the USSR People's Deputies in March 26, 1989) but competitors. Participation in the first relatively free elections consolidated LTF ideologically and organizationally against the state. During this period, LTF existed de facto but de jure remained out of the system. This third stage lasted until the coup d'état of August 1991. The fourth stage was the decline of the party and the splitting away, in 1992, of several new parties formed from its ranks.

Dzintra Bungs points out that the faction of LTF and the Supreme Council could be considered an entity in itself with its own dynamics, but that the evolution and diversification of the political structures and alignments within the legislature reflected the political development in Latvia as a whole.[32]

The crisis in the Latvian Communist Party was exacerbated in 1989. In the LCP, there were two wings: conservative Stalinist, center- (Moscow) oriented communists, mostly Russians, and reform-oriented communists, mostly Latvians. In October 1989, as a result of reforms and democratization, for the first time in the history of Soviet Latvia, national-reform-oriented Latvians were nominated and accepted in the key political positions. There was a gap between the leaders of LCP (Latvians) and most of the ordinary members (Russians).

Reformists in the party found it hard to reach agreement with Stalinist communists on a program of activities that was called "On the Road Toward Latvia's Sovereignty." Both the reformists and the Stalinists made recommendations in relation to this document, but the reformists' arguments held sway over the others. In November 1989, 39 senior party officials published a document called "To the Communists of Latvia," in which they expressed their support for extensive changes in the party's structure and policies, stepping away from the constitutionally guaranteed monopoly on power. They further argued that the party must become a component in the parliamentary system. Formally, the party split on April 1990. Up to 39 percent of all LCP members in 1989 were Latvians. The political split coincided with a rift along ethnic lines, because most of the reformists were Latvian, whereas the pro-Soviet-oriented party members were mostly Russian.

The Stalinists published a different document, calling for the restoration of the party's leading role, of the party's control over the mass media, and of firm attacks against those who represented anti-socialist thinking. Both of these documents can now be seen as ones that defined the relationship between the two wings of the LKP.

In January 1991, the Latvian International Front of Workers (LIFW or Interfront) was established. The Interfront gathered together the conservative Stalinist Moscow-oriented people. Members of the Interfront were for the most part *apparatchiki* or members of the nomenclature (hard-liners), Soviet army retired officers, and family members and workers from military factories who migrated into Latvia after World War II. Interfront supported a strong centralized Soviet state with all former political structure, especially the leading role of the Communist Party, and strong control over mass media and against the autonomy of Soviet republics. Russian intelligentsia supported LTF.

In the beginning of 1990, internal conflict grew stronger and, in April 1990, LCP split into two parts: LCP (Moscow-oriented) and the Latvian Independent Communist party (LNKP). The cleavage line was based on the attitude towards Latvia's independence (center/periphery relations). LNKP later transformed itself into the Latvian Labour Democratic Party (LLDP) and then, in October 1995, into the Latvian Social Democratic party (LSDP). The Latvian Communist Party later renamed itself the Latvian Socialist party (LSP).

Numerous other parties emerged in the years following independence. A group of moderates established a center-oriented party—the Democratic Centre Party (DCP)—representing the intelligentsia and small business. In the fall of 1991, a group of more right-wing LTF radicals who had supported the reestablishment of the Republic of Latvia of November 18, 1918 organized a separate parliamentary group, Satversme, with 34 members. Most of the LNNK deputies worked with the Satversme faction. The Satversme parliamentary group, which had a special interest in agriculture and the problems of farmers, formed Agrarian factions gave rise to the Farmer's Union of Latvia (LZS). LZS made considerable progress among farmers.

Jānis Jurkāns and his supporters set up the Latvian Support Foundation. This in turn joined an alliance entitled Latvian Harmony and Economic Rebirth. This alliance emerged as one of the main forces on the left.

The election coalition Latvijas Cel̦š (LC, Latvia's Way) was founded in February 1993 by the Supreme Council factions Satversme and LTF, some former representatives of the nomenclature as well as Latvian émigré representatives from the World Free Latvian association (PBLA). As an official party, LC was established after five Saeima elections, in September 1993. LC announced itself as a liberal reform-oriented organization with a new dynamic, reform-oriented platform, and well-known leaders. Club 21 had an important role in establishing the LC. Members of Club 21 were popular public leaders and businessmen. LC's 1993 preelection program was basically concerned with economic questions, privatization, market economy, and so on.

LC was a typical cadre party with "influential persons in the first place, whose name, prestige, or connections can provide a backing for the candidate and secure him votes; experts, in the second place, who know how to handle the electors and how to organize campaign; last of all financiers, who can bring the sinews of war."[33] Important for LC was the socioeconomic ideological dimension in Latvian politics. Before the 1993 Seima elections, LC had the most developed party program, the main concern of which was economic development.

The Latvian Farmer Union (LZS) was reestablished in July 1990 as the successor of one of most influential political parties in the inter-war period. The idea to establish LZS came from the Rural Committee of Popular Front of Latvia. Later former members of LZS from the inter-war period were involved in that process. LZS was one of the first political parties in Latvia to have local branches in all of Latvia. LZS was something like a trade union of peasants.

TYPES OF ORIGIN

The new Latvian political parties can be divided into three groups according to their origins: 1) Some parties formed as a result of the split of the Communist Party (Latvia's Socialist party, Latvia's Labour democratic party, etc.). 2) Others were historical parties that existed until the coup d'état of 1934 and have now renewed their activities in Latvia (Latvian Farmer Union—LZS, Latvian Social Democratic Workers Party, Democratic Centre Party). 3) Still others were newly formed parties (Latvia's Way, Democratic Party Saimnieks (Master), People's Party, New Party, etc.).

The third kind of beginning was especially common before elections. A kind of chain reaction took place when before the elections many new parties sprang up because, as O'Donnell and Schmitter point out, "the prospect of elections brings parties to centre stage in the political drama."[34] During this "wild" stage of party formation new parties are formed without any definite social, political, or ideological basis and do not even try to shape a program. For example, two such parties even were elected to the Saeima: People's Movement For Latvia (1993) and the New Party (1995).

Maurice Duverger insists on the importance of knowing whether parties were initially created internally or externally. An internally created political party is one that emerges gradually from the activities of the legislators themselves. Duverger's theory postulates stages in party development. First, the creation of parliamentary groups takes place, then the organization of electoral committees, and finally the formation of permanent connections between these two elements.[35] Among internally created political parties are: Latvia's Way (LC), Latvian National Independence Movement (LNNK), For Fatherland and Freedom (TB), and People's Harmony Party (TSP).

Among externally created political parties are: Popular Front of Latvia (LTF), Latvian Social Democratic Party (LSDP), Latvian Unity Party (LVP), People's Movement For Latvia (Siegerist party—TKL), Democratic Party Master (DPS), Christian Democratic Party (KDS), Democratic Centre Party (DCP), Latvian Socialist Party (LSP), New Party (JP), and People's Party.

ELECTIONS

The Elections of 1993

The first free and fair elections in 60 years took place in Latvia in June 1993. They took place in the presence of Russian army troops and a population of which one-third were noncitizens. A total number of 19 parties, unions, and election coalitions competed for the 100 seats in Saeima (parliament), and turnout was high: This election cannot be looked upon as a precise indicator of the strength or weakness of one or another political party because "at a founding elections party identification is likely to be weak, surveys of public attitudes unreliable, and public opinion highly volatile."[36]

In the making of the lists of parties, special attention was paid to popular public figures. Every list had at least a few popular figures. This approach to making election lists was characteristic of most of the lists because it was expected that the voters would choose between politicians rather than between parties. The results of the survey done by the Baltic Study Centre after the elections confirmed this expectation. The answers to the question: "What and to what extent influenced your choice in the elections?" were as follows: 54 percent said that personalities strongly influenced their choice, and 27 percent said that personalities were of medium importance. The struggle was in fact between political figures. The political situation lent itself to the personification of politics. This condition is one of the main differences between the 1993 Saeima and the preceding 1990 Supreme Council elections. During the 1990 elections, the electorate had been interested only in whether Latvia would be an independent state or stay within the Soviet Union, and there were only two parties to choose from: the LTF and pro-Moscow Communists. The pro-independence-oriented LTF won the elections with a solid majority.

Another expression of the center/periphery cleavage of the time was the citizenship issue. In the 1990 elections, all permanent residents of Latvia could participate, but in 1993 only citizens could do so. Most citizens were Latvians, so the creation of Latvian parties increased the Latvian part of the electorate and changed the psychological and political climate of the elections. In the 1993 elections, one of the main issues was the attitude towards the citizenship question and the inclusion/exclusion of post-war immigrants from the political decision-making process. Latvian parties with a strong position on the citizenship issue gathered a large number of votes and were well represented in parliament. Socioeconomic issues were also important in the 1993 elections, because the deterioration of the economic situation had led to an increasing number of people living on or below the poverty line and to an increasing gap between social strata.

The Elections of 1995

A poll taken a few months before the 1995 elections revealed that only one-fourth of voters felt close to a political party. The importance of the social benefits provided by the state was emphasized now, while support for the dominance of private property in the national economy had decreased. The 1995 elections were protest elections owing to high levels of dissatisfaction with the performance of politicians and state institutions. Voters voted for new political forces. In particular, these elections were a breakthrough for the Democratic Party Master, which emphasized professionalism and support for Latvian industry. The anti- elite-oriented populist People's Movement For Latvia (Siegerist party) collected 18 seats. All together the newcomers—DPS, People's Movement For Latvia, and Latvia's Unity Party—collected more than one-third of all votes. More than 40 percent of voters made their voting decisions during the week before, or on, Election Day. Political newcomers emphasized the difference between the disadvantaged strata and the managing elite. Center/periphery and socioeconomic cleavages were easy to identify.

The People's Harmony party (TSP) emerged from the split of the union Harmony for Latvia—Revival for Economy. This party, which supported the interests of Russian speakers and a more liberal citizenship law, gained six seats. The Latvian Socialist Party, also a party of the Russian-speaking population, was ideologically a left-wing party; it won five seats. The Latvian parties—LNNK, For Fatherland and Freedom, Latvian Farmer Union, and Christian Democratic Union—emphasized the national issue. They were less successful in the elections than before. The success of the Latvian Unity party, People's Movement For Latvia, and the Latvian Farmer Union showed the importance of the urban/rural cleavage.

The Elections of 1998

The 1998 elections were dominated by amendments to the Citizenship law. But election results show that the socioeconomic issue was important too. The non-Latvian voters were more influenced and consolidated by the preelection campaign than the Latvian voters. Half of them voted for the People's Harmony Party proposal. From 1995 to 1997, the Latvian economy experienced a banking crisis. (Another economic hardship in Latvia's dealings with Russia emerged in the spring of 1998. However, at the time of the elections the voters had not felt its consequences yet.)

Shortly before the 1998 elections, two new parties were established: the People's Party (TP), led by former prime minister Andris Škele and New Party (JP), led by a well known businessman, Ainars Šlesers. These political newcomers were quite successful. TP collected the majority of votes and received 24 seats out of 100. JP was less successful and received 8 seats. Election results show that voters were more stable in their political preferences and not as emotional as in 1995. Their electoral choice was more rational, and people voted for better-known politicians. For example, the leader of the People's Party, Andris Škele, had already been the prime minister several times; the leaders of the Social Democratic Party were well-known politicians too. Center- right-wing parties—the People's Party, Latvia's Way, and For Fatherland and Freedom/LNNK (TB/LNNK) advocated for market-oriented economic policy and reforms, as well as less state influence in economics. TB/LNNK merged from two parties, For Fatherland and Freedom and the Latvian National Independence Movement, parties that had similar programs and competed for the same voters. But public opinion polls showed that at least half of the voters thought that the state sector in the economy should be larger. Supporters of all parties—Latvians and non-Latvians—expressed the attitude that the state must take care of welfare and social security, making it clear that the supporters of right-wing parties were quite far from traditional rightist values.

The time of the voting decision was important as well: around 40 percent of voters made their decisions a long time in advance or at least one month before the election day. This time there were fewer floating voters than in 1995. The voters of the Party Fatherland and Freedom/LNNK were more stable and predictable: 57 percent of them made their decision long before and 17 percent one month before the election day; in the case of the People's Party, 46 percent of decisions were made more than one month before and 28 percent one month before the elections; 43 percent of voters for the Social Democrats made their decisions more than a month before, and 21 percent one month before the elections; for LC, the figures were 40 and 22 percent; for the People's Harmony Party, 37 and 24 percent. LC and TB/LNNK voters were more retrospective and more satisfied with the ruling parties' performance. The who voted for political newcomers, the Social Democrats and the New Party, were more future oriented.

Attitudes towards the ethnic issue stabilized voting priorities—70 percent of the People's Harmony Party and 55 percent of the TB/LNNK supporters made the same choice in 1998 as they had in 1995. Nevertheless, a large group—31 percent—could still be characterized as floating voters.

Election results indicated that Latvian voters were easy to manipulate because of a lack of political experience and knowledge about democratic politics. Candidates with solid financial capital and popularity found it relatively easy to enter party politics. Election results showed that the center/periphery cleavage (or the inclusion/exclusion line as an expression of it) was still very important.

The Elections of 2002

During the next national elections we can observe a similar pattern of party development. Several right-wing parties—New Era (Jaunais Laiks, JL), Latvia's First (Ministers) Party (Latvijas Pirmā partija, LPP), and the election coalition Greens and Farmers (Zaļo un Zemnieku savienība, ZZS)—were created and subsequently received representation in parliament. The leader of the Jaunais Laiks was Einars Repše, the "godfather" of Latvia's currency, and the chairman of the Central Bank of Latvia from 1991 to November 2001. He was one of the founders of the Latvian National Independence Movement and a member of the Supreme Council in 1990–1991. Shortly after the announcement of the party's emergence, he was the leader in public opinion polls. Thus, the socioeconomic and elite/mass cleavages had become more important because the questions of independence and ethnic inclusion/exclusion were basically solved. Politicians' personalities remained important for voters.

SOCIAL DEMOCRACY IN LATVIA

Social democracy was a very interesting phenomenon in Latvia and deserves a section of its own. The idea of social democracy was popular at the end of the 1980s, but from 1990 this idea was strongly attacked by right-wing parties. The main argument was that Social Democrats were successors of the Communist Party. Latvia appeared to have the necessary social basis for social democracy. Given that there were many poor people in need of help, social democratic and socialist parties defended the interests of the poor and insisted on a strong role of the state in dealing with socioeconomic problems. Many people in Latvia felt the same way, and their reasoning went beyond the subjects of work, food, and housing. Still, Social Democrats never managed to gain control of the government. An event of significant political importance was the congress that was held by the Latvian Social Democratic Workers Party (LSDSP) in December 1989.

The party considered itself to be the successor of the LSDSP, which had been formed in 1904 and was the largest party in Latvia during the inter-war period; hence, the December 1989 event was billed as the twentieth party congress. After World War II, the party had continued its operations in emigration. The honorary chairman of the party was Bruno Kalniņš, who was a well-known party activist before World War II, but the persons who reinstated the organization did not have close links to the LSDSP of the inter-war period. The ideas of the Social Democrats were popular in society, but during the first few years of its existence, the party's leadership was weak. The leaders did not have a sufficiently precise and clear idea of the place and role of social democracy in society. One of the founders of the party, Valdis Šteins, was a national radical not interested in the idea of social democracy. He had a strong anticommunist position. A more moderate group of party members quit the party because of the idea of banning former members of the Communist Party of the Soviet Union from joining the LSDSP.[37] As a result of this lack of clear direction, the party split up, then reunited, and did not win great electoral success.

Around this time, the LCP broke up, too. The Latvian Independent Communist Party (LNKP) emerged first, followed by the Latvian Democratic Labour Party (LDDP). Both tried to occupy the political niche that had been taken by the LSDSP before. None, however, found sufficient support among the public, and even though numerically they were among the largest parties in Latvia, they did not have much influence at all.

In the elections in 1993, Social Democrats did not win any seats at all—the LSDSP won a measly 0.6 percent of the vote, while the LDDP got 0.9 percent. The main reason was that many citizens automatically associated the word *socialism* with the previous regime and sought to avoid anything that had to do with the old system. The parties lacked highly regarded and striking political personalities and suffered from the split that had taken place. Several candidate lists sought the same electorate. There was also a fundamental difference in the way in which parties perceived the legal succession of the Republic of Latvia. The LDDP spoke of the second republic and the creation of a new country, while the LSDSP stood in support of the idea that contemporary Latvia was a direct successor to the republic that existed between the two world wars. These factors all served to ensure that the parties did not win sufficient support among the public.

In 1995, the Social Democrats began to talk about a merger, understanding the fact that two social democratic parties in Latvia could not hope for much of a future. The parties also began to cooperate with labor unions, as they were a chief source of support for social democratic parties elsewhere in Europe. The changes came too late, however, and the Social Democrats did not win any seats in the 1995 election. A joint candidate list took 4.67 percent of the vote (parties require 5 percent of the national vote to win any seats in the Saeima). People who voted for the party were in many instances poor people, as well as those who had been defrauded by the numerous financial pyramid schemes that existed in Latvia at that time. In fact, financial fraud was so pervasive that there was a candidate list that was called "Justice—the Party to Defend Defrauded People."

During his term in office (1995–1998) Jānis Ādamsons, elected from the LC list, left that party to join the Social Democrats. This allowed the LSDSP to gain a foothold in the Saeima, even though it had not won sufficient support in the election.

The Latvian Social Democratic Union (Latvijas Sociāldemokrātu apvienība, LSDA), set up by the Latvian Social Democratic Workers Party (LSDSP) and the Latvian Social Democratic Party (LSDP), emerged shortly before the election of 1998 and became one of the most important social democratic political forces in Latvia. Over time, the two component parties drew closer together, and, in 1998 they filed a joint candidate list and a joint program of operations. At that time, the two parties were expected to merge into one. However, any process of merger and dissolution is a complex one. There was a lack of agreement on the legal succession of the Republic of Latvia—the LSDSP saw the country as a direct successor to the pre-war state, while the LSDP, and particularly its leader Juris Bojārs, stood for the establishment of a new state without legal links to the First Republic. A second and major difference related to the attitude of the two parties with respect to former members of the Communist Party. Third, there were differences of opinion in regard to the party's organizational structure and traditions. The LSDSP sought to implement a democratic style of administration. The party had no distinct leader, and its leadership rotated. Theoretically, at least, any party member had a chance to rise up to the top of the structure.

Despite all this, the consolidation process proceeded, and the two parties produced nearly identical party programs. The merger of the two parties took place in 1999 on the basis of these programs, and the LSDA rapidly become a serious political force. They won seats in the 1999 election, despite the fact that they had no positive political image and that they had run a fairly dull campaign. Much of the electorate in Latvia was not particularly firm in terms of its views and many people voted for any party that had not been in power before. The time when people were scared of the word *socialism* was gone, even though some other parties sought to represent social democracy as a great evil. The prime minister at the time, Andris Škele, went so far as to call on people not to vote for the Social Democrats, who supposedly had been kissing Soviet tanks in June 1940. Issues of the day included pensions, the privatization of monopoly companies, as well as other aspects of egalitarianism. The leaders of the party made peace with one another to a certain extent in advance of the election.

Also on the ballot in 1999 was the Labour Party, which filed a joint candidate list with two other small parties but did not win any seats in parliament (it later won representation in the Rīga City Council).

Why were the Social Democrats successful in 1999? We should look at the social structure of the society and at the cleavage lines. One of the main cleavage lines was the disadvantaged strata versus the managing, occupational elites.[38] The voter base of the Social Democrats has been fairly indistinct. It is hard to determine any particular groups in society that automatically support the Social Democrats, because people seek to identify themselves with a certain social group without any truly objective justification for doing so. There are, however, certain trends in this situation:

- Most of the people who vote for the Social Democrats are older people, pensioners, as well as people who are of preretirement age. Most of these people are poor, and they are not competitive in a market economy. This makes them uncertain about their future. The Social Democrats promised social guarantees and aid for the poorer strata in society, and this won them support.
- Some of the supporters of the Social Democrats are people who can be associated with the sentiment of equality, who are disappointed in liberal reforms and who see them as inhuman. These voters are also noncompetitive in the market economy and they also see the Social Democrats as a force that will protect and support them. Sociological surveys after the election showed that many voters thought that the party would defend their interests by regulating economic issues and reducing the level of social differentiation.[39]

The Social Democrats were not a part of the governing coalition following the election, but they did collaborate with the government on the basis of a special agreement between the prime minister, Vilis Krištopans, and the LSDA faction. The agreement concerning collaboration was aimed at reaching the goals that were set out in the Cabinet of Ministers' declaration of operations. There were 19 strategic missions and principles on the list, including the introduction of an antipoverty program and a national program on employment, increases in the budget financing education and science, a raising of the minimal wage, the elaboration of a system to protect the legal rights of people who rent or own flats, as well as other social democratic priorities. The document also stated that the LSDA faction would take responsibility for the field of agriculture, and LSDA member Pēteris Salkazanovs served as the Minister of Agriculture in the Krištopans government. The LSDA promised to support the governing coalition and its draft legislation. It would refuse to support opposition amendments to the national budget, to tax laws or to any other laws that relate to the budget without the agreement of the Coalition Council. The Social Democrats would also refrain from proposing or supporting any vote of no-confidence in the Cabinet of Ministers or any individual minister without the agreement of the prime minister (the agreement was published in *Brīvība,* March 1999).

In short, the Social Democrats in the new parliament engaged in limited work in the government, although one of their members served as deputy of the chairman. Social Democrats chaired several parliamentary commissions and the party had the right to nominate candidates for positions in various government institutions, company councils, and so on.

Shortly before the 2002 elections, the LSDA split into two parts—LSDSP and the Social Democratic Union (SDS). Why? In the four parliamentary elections since 1993, experts have always said that winners and losers could be attributed to the image of candidates and parties, because durable voter loyalty had not yet been achieved for many parties. This is partly a question of time, but there is also the matter of a certain lack of political skills. The only party in Latvia about which one could say that it had achieved the loyalty of a certain segment of the electorate was the left-wing For Human Rights in a United Latvia (PCTVL). PCTVL merged from three parties—the Latvian Socialist Party, the movement Equal Rights (Līdztiesība), and the People's Harmony Party (Tautas Saskaņas partija, TSP). The achievements of other parties have had everything to do with hot-button issues such as citizenship and the state language, which were issues that benefited the right-wing For the Fatherland and Freedom/LNNK party, a party which also focused on the need to fight against corruption and bring greater order to the government (issues that were addressed by several other parties as well). The party system was still new, and voter loyalties were not fixed. Both the achievements of the Social Democrats in the 1999 elections and in the subsequent Rīga City

Council election, as well as their unexpected loss of all parliamentary representation in the elections of 2002, were all very normal phenomena in Latvian politics.

However, it is also true that the Social Democrats have not yet been able to come up with a clear program or with a skilful and far-sighted leadership. Unemployment, inequality, and the absence of true social security are real problems in Latvia, and they should theoretically create a good foundation for social democratic thinking. The Social Democrats could have used these issues to find new voters and supporters. Instead, the leadership of the Social Democrats spent the period before the 2002 election on a foolhardy project of writing a new constitution for Latvia, a topic of little interest to the voters. There were problems with the party's leadership style, and there were internal conflicts; when these led to a split just prior to the elections, the poor results of the party were not surprising.

Does social democracy have a future in Latvia? If the Social Democrats find a way to move beyond mere criticizing of the current situation, and if they formulate a clear explanation of why these problems still exist and how they can be solved with a new program or a fresh approach toward socioeconomic issues, then they would find their niche in Latvian politics. The LSDSP needs more modern approaches and leaders.

CONCLUSION

Although the traditional categorization of political parties does not adequately portray the political spectrum in Latvia, some things are clear. First, parties of the moderate right have been the most consistently successful. Second, political parties and party politics form around two basic cleavages: center/periphery or independence/ethnic and socioeconomic. The ideological difference among them is minor. The urban/rural and religious cleavages are not so important.

Further political development, in terms of mastering the art of cooperation and compromise, as well as the continuing formation of coalitions that will eventually lead to the development of larger political parties, is still needed in order to develop a stable democracy. Creating a stable democracy will take some time because it requires successful economic reforms and the formation of a cohesive body of citizens. A large portion of the Latvian population still consists of noncitizens. The ability of representatives of major oppositional parties to cooperate with the government on certain issues in 1993–2003 is a good sign of progress. Political stability can be expected to increase, as more of the population is included in the political decision-making process, and thereby become more familiar with the ways of democracy and develop greater tolerance for one another's views.

But despite these advances, serious problems remain. One is the continuing importance of the role of personalities in politics. Some parties are organized from the top down and serve simply as campaign organizations to promote particular candidates' reelection. Voters still trust in personalities. The presence of a large Russian-speaking population keeps nationalist issues alive, although in the 2002 elections, the national conservative party TB/LNNK gathered fewer votes than before and was represented by only seven seats in the parliament.

The defense of Latvian nationalism and the belief in radical market reforms are majority positions, whereas the forces of economic moderation and the interests of Russian speakers are small and scattered. The most important parties are close together in ideological terms, that is, in terms of national identity as well as in terms of economic policies, whereas the minority parties tend to be single-issue parties with high-profile policies relating to a single cleavage. Personal clashes between the leaders of central parties and economic groups of interests are the main reasons for government changes.

To sum up, Latvian party politics are still characterized by instability, fragmentation, high electoral volatility, and protest voting. Latvia is on the way to becoming a stable democracy, but it still has a long way to go.

CHAPTER 10

Lithuania's Political Parties and Party System, 1990–2001

Algis Krupavičius

Political parties play an exclusive role as the intermediate structures between citizens and governmental institutions in the internal political environment of all contemporary democracies. Rapid development of political parties and stability of the party system in new democracies of Eastern Europe are necessary for the consolidation of democracy.

Lithuania represents an example of negotiated transition. From the path-dependency perspective—an approach that connects the "*ancient regime*" and the most viable strategic choices within a new political order—the multiparty system in Lithuania would be expected to be comprised mostly of clientelist and programmatic parties as the country exited from national accommodative communism.[1] The idea of a negotiated transition presupposes that the reformist part of the old elite is willing to, and does, take an important role in the democratization, especially in helping to delegitimize the old regime and to facilitate the accommodation of different political forces. However, in Lithuania, the anticommunist opposition remained a major source for new parties.

More than a decade after the restoration of Lithuania's independence in 1990, Lithuanian party politics is often described as a political pendulum in constant fluctuation between left and right. However, Lithuania can hardly be classified as an example of two-partyism; it is rather as a case of moderate pluralism with three to five parties as the leading political actors. After the 2000 Seimas elections, among core players of the country's party system were the Lithuanian Social Democratic Party, New Union (Social Liberals), Homeland Union (Lithuanian Conservatives), Christian Democratic Party, and Liberal Union.

There is an obvious need to explore the wider political context and the positions of the existing parties in Lithuania's party system. Among the main issues to be traced here are the historical origins of the political parties, the rebirth of multiparty competition, and the structure of the party system.

THE HISTORICAL ORIGINS OF LITHUANIA'S PARTIES AND THE REVIVAL OF A COMPETITIVE PARTY SYSTEM

Lithuania, as a second attempt at democracy, has a history of competitive party politics, and this historical experience mattered when it came to establishing a post-transitional party system. The significance of its historical parties in the current political situation can be illustrated by several important facts. The most influential historical parties, the Lithuanian Christian Democrats and the Social Democrats, have been constantly represented in parliament since 1990. After the local elections in 1995 and 1997, the Christian Democrats entered into the ruling coalition with the Lithuanian Conservatives in many municipalities. From the end of 1996 almost until the end of 2000, the Christian Democrats have been partners of the governing right-wing coalition on a national level. The Lithuanian Social Democratic Party was obviously the strongest historical party on the left side of the political spectrum since 1990, having as many as 9 MPs even in the constituent parliament in 1990–1992. Since mid-2001, after merging with the Lithuanian Democratic Labor Party (LDLP) in February 2001, the Lithuanian Social Democratic Party (LSDP) was part of the ruling center-left coalition together with New Union (Social Liberals).

During the national elections of 1992 and 1996, the historical parties received 22.8 percent and 26.7 percent of the total votes and occupied 23 and 35 seats in Lithuania's Seimas respectively. In the 2000 parliamentary elections, the share of historical parties was difficult to calculate since the LSDP was out of the game because of its coalition with the Labor Democratic Party. The so-called historical parties have found enough followers to stay active on the Lithuanian political stage, despite the fact that the political weight and representation of historical parties decreased in the 2000 Seimas elections. Still, previous political trends demand a short examination of the historical heritage of the pre-war party system in Lithuania. See Table 10.1.

Much like many other countries in Western Europe, Lithuania's early party system was shaped by national and socioeconomic conditions, similar to those described in the concept of social cleavages developed by Rokkan and Lipset in the late 1960s.[2] Where Lithuania differed from most Western European countries was the timing of its national and industrial revolutions. As a consequence, the structure of Lithuania's multiparty system was mainly affected by three sets of cleavages: church versus the state,

Table 10.1 Political Weight of Historical Parties, 1992–1996

	Parliamentary elections 1992			*Parliamentary elections 1996*			*Parliamentary elections 2000*		
	No. of MP's	*Share of seats (%)*	*% of votes*	*No. of MP's*	*Share of seats (%)*	*% of votes*	*No. of MP's*	*Share of seats (%)*[1]	*% of votes*
LChDP	10	7.1	12.2	16	11.6	9.9	2	1.4	3.1
LSDP[3]	7	5.0	5.8	12	8.7	6.6	—	—	—
Other historical parties	6	4.2	4.8[2]	7	5.1	10.2	5	3.5	10.3
Total	23	16.3	22.8	35	25.4	26.7	7	4.9	13.4

[1]Calculated from 137 MP's who were elected to the Seimas in October and November 1996.
[2]Excluding the votes for the National Progress Movement, which started to search for historical roots only in 1993 as a source of legitimacy; the votes for Nationalists Union and the Democratic Party are not calculated because they participated in the elections in coalition with nonhistorical parties.
[3]In the 2000 Seimas elections LSDP took part as a member of the Social Democratic Coalition together with the Lithuanian Labor Democratic Party and had the support of 31.1 percent of voters.

land interests versus the state, and workers versus the owners. At the end of the nineteenth and the beginning of the twentieth century, the traditional political parties of the left–right ideological continuum emerged. Among these early parties were the Social Democratic Party (founded in 1896), the Democratic Party (founded in 1902), the Christian Democrats (1904), the Nationalists Union (1916, but known as the National Progress Party until 1924), and the Peasants Party (1922).

A fully functioning multiparty system was introduced after Lithuania gained independence in 1918. Between 1919 and 1926, the strongest political force was the Lithuanian Christian Democratic Party (LChDP) together with its satellite organizations, such as the Labor Federation and the Farmers Union. The LChDP and its allies had the majority of seats in most parliaments, except during the third Seimas that was elected in 1926. A major competitor of the LChDP was the so-called People's Coalition, which initially included the Lithuanian Socialist People's Party and the Lithuanian Peasants' Party. The Lithuanian Social Democratic Party, a party that had overcome the "disease of communism" in 1918 and 1919, represented the third major political group. Later, the LSDP joined the left-wing coalition led by the social-liberal Peasants People's Party.

The steady expansion of parties in the multiparty system was reversed dramatically after the coup d'état led by the Nationalists Union in December 1926. Just after the coup d'état of 1926, only the Communist Party of Lithuania was banned, and all other parties survived until November 1935, when open political activity from all other parties, except the LNU, was prohibited. Increasingly, the international instability around Lithuania in 1938 and 1939 forced the Nationalist government to go back to its pre-1936 policy of so-called soft suppression of political opponents. For example, throughout the Nationalists' rule, an opposition press was allowed. Some newspapers were linked to opposition political parties, such as the *Mintis* [Mind], *Rytas* [Morning], *Lietuva* [Lithuania], *Lietuvos žinios* [News of Lithuania].

After the Soviet occupation of Lithuania and the introduction of the Communist Party dictatorship in 1940, the possibility of existence of any independent party was totally destroyed. However, although the Communist Party dominated Lithuania's internal political stage for almost 50 years, former political loyalties and preferences were still alive in the people's cultural and social consciousness. A clear indication of this was the reestablishment of most of the major historical parties after 1988.

Historical party traditions had a significant influence on the revival of competitive party politics in Lithuania, but a more immediate effect was the reconstruction of the multiparty system in itself.

Alfred E. Senn described a power pyramid in the former Soviet system, which was characterized in terms of the interactions between the power of the party and constitutional authority. A striking feature of the Soviet one-party system was that it institutionalized the authority of the party above the constitutional order.[3] Gorbachev's policy of perestroika changed the relationship between the party's authority and the constitutional order, slightly increasing the importance of the latter but still preserving the basic pattern (see Figure 10.1). Since the middle of 1988—the establishment of Sąjūdis—the first noncommunist political movement organized in the form of a wide popular front—contradictions between the influence of the Communist Party and constitutional institutions were made quite explicit, as was reflected in numerous discussions on the new constitution. The Supreme Soviet of Lithuania was used as a battleground for some of the conflicts between the Lithuanian Communist Party and Sąjūdis. At the end of 1989, after the Lithuanian Communist Party broke away from the control of the Kremlin, its authority was based primarily on the Soviet pattern of power distribution, but the growth of the independence movement in 1989 and 1990 led to an exchange of Communist Party authority for the authority of the nation (see Figure 10.2).

Despite this, political parties started to reemerge on Lithuania's political stage in 1988 and 1989, even though they lacked a certain degree of constitutional legitimacy. After the constituent elections of 1990, followed by major economic, political and social reforms, many political parties acquired their much-needed legitimacy. Between 1990 and 1992, the Supreme Council was only one of the institutions that could legalize parties, but it became the cradle of party politics. Two aspects of this process are extremely important. On the one hand, the Supreme Council was a place for the institutionalization of party organizations. As early as March 1990, the informal Sąjūdis faction established in the constituent parliament what might be described as a protoparliamentary faction of Sąjūdis. But due to its internal ideological differences (within Sąjūdis), this pro-

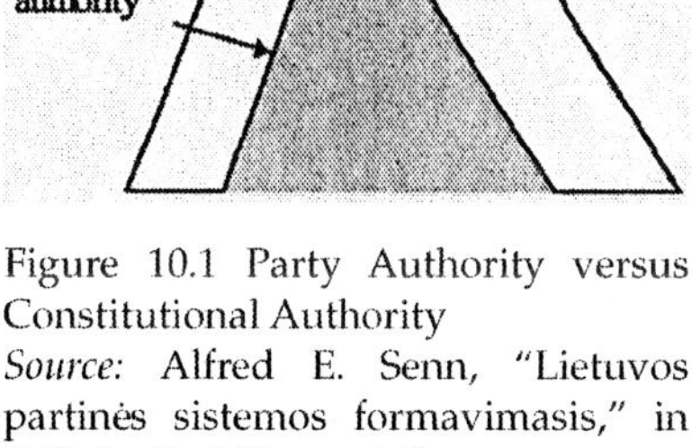

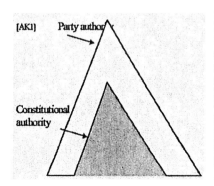

Figure 10.1 Party Authority versus Constitutional Authority
Source: Alfred E. Senn, "Lietuvos partinės sistemos formavimasis," in *Politologija*, 2(8), pp. 4, 7.

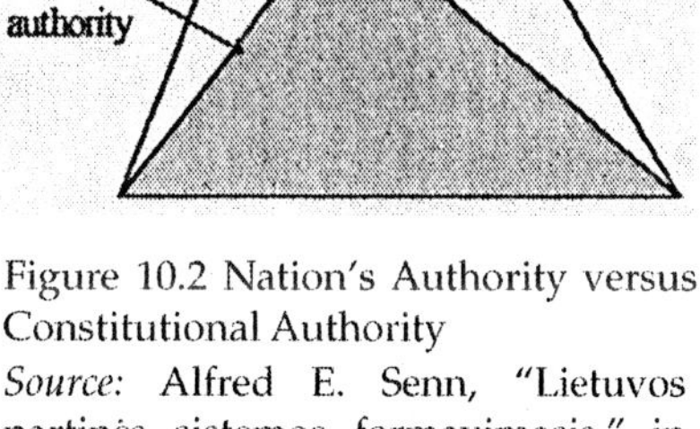

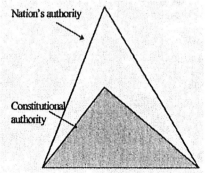

Figure 10.2 Nation's Authority versus Constitutional Authority
Source: Alfred E. Senn, "Lietuvos partinės sistemos formavimasis," in *Politologija*, 2(8), pp. 4, 7.

cess continued until the first multiparty elections in 1992. Finally, seven factions, most of which were loosely connected with extra-parliamentary political organizations, were founded on the basis of their elected representatives in parliament. They entered the Supreme Council on Sąjūdis' list in 1990 with the two remaining factions representing the Labor Democratic Party and the Lithuanian Polish Union.

The constituent parliament played an exceptional role in the ideological consolidation of these would-be political parties. The process was primarily based on ideological differentiation within the Sąjūdis parliamentary group. The outcome of this process was that parliamentary factions in the Supreme Council have represented all major traditional ideological trends since early 1992 (see Table 10.2).

Looking at the different methods of party development, we can distinguish four separate modes. Moreover, party developments were closely related to their historical roots. All of the historical parties were reconstituted outside of parliament initially, and only after the multiparty elections of 1992 did they form independent parliamentary factions. The so-called post-mass opposition parties (in the case of Lithuania, post-Sąjūdis parties) came about after the very gradual disintegration of the umbrella movement in the constituent parliament. The mainstream of Sąjūdis was reorganized into the Homeland Union (Lithuanian Conservatives) in May 1993. However, on the eve of the general elections of 1992, Sąjūdis still confronted the *ancient regime* and was not prepared for a new era of party politics.[4] In the same way, the various centrist political groups could be regarded as successors to the moderate wing of Sąjūdis, which was unable to develop into representative parties and remained as amorphous political movements prior to the elections of 1992. All in all, the fragmentation of Sąjūdis was an extremely positive process for the institutionalization of a multiparty system, and at the end of the system's reform and introduction of basic democratic institutions, as well as adoption of a new constitution (in the last months of 1992), representative parties and

Table 10.2 Factionalism and Ideology in the Supreme Council, 1992

Parliamentary faction	*Ideological orientation*
United Faction of Sąjūdis	conservative
Concord Faction (Sąjūdis)	moderate conservative
Nationalist Faction	nationalist
Moderate Faction	moderate liberal
Center Faction	social democratic and moderate liberal
Liberal Faction	liberal
National Progress Faction	moderate nationalist
Democratic Labor Party's Faction	social democratic
Faction of Polish Union	nationalist

other would-be parties became the principal players that shaped electoral choice in Lithuania.

Quite a different story is the case of the ex-communist Democratic Labor Party. From a Baltic perspective, the Lithuanian Communist Party was substantially different from its counterparts in Estonia and Latvia. As a consequence of its differences, the role and evolution of the Lithuanian Communist Party during the transitional period is only marginally comparable to the fate of the Communist Party in the neighboring countries.

A crucial factor in the exceptional role of the Lithuanian Communist Party was its ethnic composition. The Lithuanian Communist Party (LCP) was a "Lithuanized" party vis-à-vis the "Russified" Communist parties in Estonia and Latvia (see Table 10.3). The native population not only dominated the LCP, but also the proportion of former members of the Soviet Communist Party among the adult population was lower than in Estonia and Latvia respectively Thus it was possible for the Lithuanian Communist Party to achieve a relatively high level of legitimacy on the domestic political stage, compared to what transpired in the other Baltic countries, where the Communist Party was perceived, for the most part, as an external and alien institution. Lithuanian reform communists were supported by the opposition forces from the very beginning and came to the top of the Lithuanian Communist Party quite easily in 1988. Furthermore, between 1989 and 1990, the Lithuanian Communist Party was able to transform itself into a representative parliamentary party, whereas attempts to reform the former Communist Party in Estonia and Latvia failed.

However, the differences in the ethnic composition and level of legitimacy of the former communist parties in the Baltics was not the only reason why the Lithuanian CP survived the democratization and its counterparts in Estonia and Latvia did not. In the latter states, citizenship laws, which excluded from electoral processes a significant number of the reform communists from ethnic minorities; the strength of alternative parliaments elected by legal citizens, which confronted the founding parliaments in 1990–1991; the absence of charismatic or, at least, very attractive leadership; and the greater strength numerically of hard-line communist opposition all worked to foster political mobilization of voters by the new or revived noncommunist parties, formed within or in close relation to

Table 10.3 The Ethnic Composition of the Baltic Communist Parties in 1989

	Estonia	*Latvia*	*Lithuania*
Members of the CP in 1.000 of adult population	98	92	78
Representatives of titular nations in the CP (%)	50	40	71
Russians (%)	39	43	17
Others (%)	11	17	12

the mass opposition movements and not by the soft-liners in the former Communist Party. On the internal political stage, the changes within the Lithuanian Communist Party could be described as a gradual transformation, or even as an evolution. The final phase of this transformation was reached at the end of 1990, when the Independent Lithuanian Communist Party adopted a moderate social democratic program and was renamed the Lithuanian Democratic Labor Party.

Along with the parties that developed from larger political entities, such as Sąjūdis and the Lithuanian Communist Party, and through the revival of historical political organizations, there were several other groups of parties that should be mentioned. These are the new parties that entered the political arena without any roots in Lithuania's history, or an established connection with either Sąjūdis or the Lithuanian Communist Party. Among these parties are the Liberal Union and the Green and Women's Parties (see Table 10.4).

It is clear from the timetable of party developments (see Table 10.5) that among the Lithuanian political parties, both the post-Sąjūdis and former Communist organizations were transformed successfully into representative parties. However, this transformation occurred much later than in the case of the historical parties. While five out of seven historical parties were reestablished in 1988 and 1990, the major post-Sąjūdis parties emerged between 1992 and 1993. The so-called new parties emerged in two phases. The Green Party was founded in 1989 along with a few other political groups, which later disappeared from the political arena. The second wave of new parties started in late 1992 and is not over yet. On the eve of each of the last two parliamentary elections in 1992 and 1996, between three and five new political organizations were registered with the Ministry of Justice, but the majority of them completely disappeared after the elections.

Table 10.4 Types and Ways of Party Development in Lithuania

Type of party	*Way of development*	*Example*
Historical parties	Revival	LSDP, LChDP, LDP
Post-Sąjūdis parties	Disintegration	HU(LC), LCU
Ex-communist parties	Transformation	LDLP
New parties	Establishment	LLU, Green Party, LWP

Table 10.5 Dynamics of Development of Lithuanias Parties, 1988–1999

	1989	*1990*	*1991*	*1992*	*1993*	*1994*	*1995*	*1996*	*1997*	*1998*	*1999*
Historical	5	1	1	2	0	0	0	0	0	0	0
Ex-communist	0	1	0	0	0	0	0	0	0	0	0
Post-Sąjūdis	0	2	1	1	1	0	0	0	0	0	0
New	3	0	0	1	1	3	4	4	0	1	3
Total	8	4	2	4	2	3	4	5	0	1	3

Only a few of them proved their ability to survive in competition with the historical, post-Sąjūdis and ex-Communist Party. Among them are the Liberals, Polish Electoral Action, and the Women's Party, which have been represented in Lithuania's Seimas and in local government.

The first and major crisis of the post-transitional party system occurred in the 2000 Seimas elections when the relatively old and established mostly right-wing parties such as the HU/LC, LChDP, and Lithuanian Center Union (LCU) lost their positions to a newcomer, New Union/Social Liberals, as well as to Liberal Union, which struggled to become a parliamentary party in 1992 and 1996. These changes are well reflected by a comparison of the percentages of votes for new parties in two subsequent parliamentary elections, 1996 and 2000. In 1996 new parties that had never before taken part in the Seimas elections were able to gain only about 14 percent of total votes, which resulted in very few MP seats, since under the proportional representation (PR) system most of these votes were distributed among small parties unable to garner sufficient votes to win access to parliament. But in 2000 the share of votes for new parties reached slightly more than 24 percent of total votes and new parties secured more than one-fifth of seats in the 2000–2004 Seimas. An even more profound decrease in incumbency rates of individual MPs reflected a shift in favor of new parties and a crisis of the established center-right parties. By 1996 reelection rates had begun to stabilize around 50 percent, but this trend was reversed in the 2000 Seimas elections, when the incumbency rate decreased to less than 30 percent. The reasons for the success of the new parties are numerous and complex, with the two most significant being the poor performance of the ruling parties and the lack of coalescent behavior among ideologically similar parties on the center-right flank of the political spectrum.

Despite the fact that the total number of political parties is relatively high (for instance, during the Seimas elections of 1996 the number of parties competing for parliamentary seats increased from 24 to 28 compared to previous general elections, but again declined to 15 party lists in 2000), the number of major parliamentary parties has been relatively stable since 1992. All in all, no more than five parties were able to enter Lithuania's Seimas and form single-party factions in accordance with the proportional formula of the parliamentary elections.

While the number of political parties on Lithuania's political stage is still quite impressive (in 2001 it was equal to 40, including some unregistered political groups), the period between the two parliamentary elections of 1992 and 1996 could be called the initial phase of party system consolidation. This trend is obvious, despite the fact that before every parliamentary election since 1990 at least a few newly established parties attempted to enter the national political stage. Most of these attempts failed. One of the most successful was the case of New Union/Social Liberals established by A. Paulauskas at the time of the 1997 presidential elections. Although Paulauskas lost the election to V. Adamkus he did so by a margin of less of one percent of total votes and the New Union/Social Liberals (NU/SL) was among the winning parties during the 2000 local and parliamentary elections.

Indeed, from the perspective of the key evaluation criteria traditionally used in analyses of political parties, such as the level of membership, ideological identity, legal and organizational institutionalization, connections with social and interests groups, political efficiency, and relations with international party organizations, Lithuanian parties adapted quite rapidly to Western European standards of political behavior and ideological traditions.

The best way to consider the maturation of Lithuania's political parties is to look at their ideological distribution along the left-right continuum—along the variables presented by Lane and Ersson: that is, name, program, appeal, and international relations.[5] Lithuanian political parties can be classified into nine ideological groups:

1. parties of ethnic minorities, such as Polish Electoral Action and the Russian Union of Lithuania (which were created to represent the interests of the ethnic minorities)
2. nationalist parties, such as the Nationalists Union, National Progress Party, and some others, or those seeking to represent the interests of specific nationalist groups
3. conservative parties, which include the Homeland Union (Lithuanian conservatives), the Union of ex-Political Prisoners and Deportees, and the Union of Moderate Conservatives
4. the Christian Democratic political space, represented by the Christian Democratic Party, the Union of Christian Democrats, and the Union of Moderate Christian Democrats
5. liberal parties represented by the Liberal Union and Center Union (political organizations clearly oriented around liberal and social-liberal ideas)
6. the LSDP and the Democratic Labor Party, which belong to the camp of social democratic parties
7. the Peasants Party, the only agrarian party
8. parties such as the Greens and the Women's Party, which can be called protest parties because they emerged as a reaction to particular problems (the Green Party lobbied for environmental protection, the Women's Party was founded in reaction to the under-representation of women in Lithuania's politics)
9. the group of populist parties, including organizations such as the Freedom Union and the Republican Party

Ideology has a certain impact on timing and ways, or when and how political parties appear on the political stage. After the first multiparty elections in 1992,[6] new protest, populist, and single-issue parties tended to enter the political scene very regularly on the eve of every new election and sometimes to disappear almost the next day after the election. Mainstream liberal, social democratic, Christian democratic, and conservative parties were established in the late 1980s and early 1990s. Newcomers within these party families, if they appeared at all, in most cases resulted from internal disagreements and splits within respective mother-parties. There are a few exceptions from this rule, most evidently the New Union/ Social Liberals. However, from the ideological point of view, the NU/SL was based on an ideological mix of liberalism and social democracy.

A traditional ideology is a strong preventive force against the multiplication of political competition within a single ideological sector after the first signs of party system consolidation appear. As long as a certain party occupies the traditional ideological niche, all new challengers from outside in the same ideological sector experience a double pressure, that is, from the senior party of same family (an intra-ideological competition), as well as from the rest of the political parties (an inter-ideological competition). This explains why new parties within traditional ideological niches emerged exclusively on the basis of splits within the inner circle and in most cases because of personal rather than ideological disagreements in the leadership of existing parties. Traditional ideologies not only played a constraining role against new parties but also turned into a force of unification among similar ideological parties. The process of uniting ideologically similar parties was started by the unification of the LDLP and LSDP in January 2001. The same pattern was followed by the merger of the Lithuanian Christian Democratic Party and the Lithuanian Christian Democratic Union during the spring of 2001, and the establishment of Lithuanian Right-wing Union by four "dwarf" right-wing parties in October 2001. In most cases new challengers to the existing parties have had a limited number of options from the ideological perspective. On the one hand, they could establish themselves by mixing several traditional ideological approaches or accepting extreme ideological positions; on the other hand, they could base themselves on structural cleavages and/or on nonideological grounds.

There are other ways to measure the relative consolidation of the parties, one of which is the level of individual party membership. If a medium-sized party organization in Estonia and Latvia has below 1,000 members, its equivalent in Lithuania has more than 4,000 individual members. In 1995, the Estonian Center Party numbered 1,407 members, the National Independence Party 1,200, and the Coalition Party only 452; despite this, all of these parties were strongly represented in parliament. The largest Latvian party, the Farmers' Union, was able to mobilize only 4,225 members, but the other parties were far behind the LFU.[7] Moreover, while in 1993 only 1.3 percent of all eligible voters were members of political parties, at the end of 1996 the overall individual party membership increased to 2.8 percent (twice the original number).[8] At the beginning of 2001 the two largest Lithuanian parties, that is, the LSDP and Homeland Union/ Lithuanian Conservatives (HU/LC), had more than 15,000 individual members each. At the same time the LChDP declared a membership of 10,500, and LCU and NU/SL numbered 3,500 citizens.

A clear indication of a certain degree of organizational stabilization of parliamentary parties is the substantially decreased rates of interfaction mobility in the Seimas since 1992 (see Table 10.6). However, two notes are appropriate here. Surprisingly, the intergroup mobility was higher in the period of 1996–2000 than in the period of 1992–1996. The general assumption that the time factor almost automatically might help to decrease interfaction mobility in new democracies is not valid enough.

A sounder explanation here might be based on the ideological leanings of parties that tend to fragment most frequently (see Table 10.7). Lithu-

Table 10.6 Inter-group Mobility in Lithuanian Parliamentary Parties, 1992–1996 (Number of Dissent MP's)

	1992	*1993*	*1994*	*1995*	*1996*	*Change*
Faction of Lithuanian Democratic Labor Party	73	73	70	70	60	−13
Sąjūdis Faction*	14	14	—	—	—	0
Faction of Homeland Union (Lithuanian Conservatives)	—	—	24	24	24	0
Faction of Lithuanian Christian Democratic Party	10	10	12	12	12	+2
Faction of Lithuanian Democratic Party	4	4	3	3	3	−1
Faction of Lithuanian Social Democratic Party	7	7	7	7		7

Notes: *In 1994, the Faction of Homeland Union (Lithuanian Conservatives) was established on the basis of the Sąjūdis Faction.
Source: Alvidas Lukošaitis, Lietuvos Respublikos politinės partijos, Vilnius: LR Seimo kanceliarija, 1993, 1994, 1995, 1996; Darius Žėruolis, "Lithuania," in *The Handbook of Political Change in Eastern Europe*, ed. Berglund Sten, Hellen Thomas, and Aarebrot Frank H., London: Edward Elgar, 1998, p. 145.

Table 10.7 Inter-group Mobility in Lithuanian Parliamentary Parties, 1996–2000

Year	*HU(LC)*	*LDLP*	*LChDP*	*LCU*	*LSDP*	*LLU*
1996	70	12	16	14	12	3
1997	70	12	16	15	12	3
1998	67	13	16	16	11	—
1999	65	13	16	18	11	—
2000	49	13	12	17	7	—
Change	−29	+1	−4	+3	−5	0

Source: Alvidas Lukošaitis, Lietuvos Respublikos politinės partijos, Vilnius: LR Seimo kanceliarija, 1996, 1997, 1998, 1999, 2000.

ania's experience allows us to hypothesize that the right-wing parties were more fragile than the left-wing parties and that the level of dissent within them more often led eventually to a splitting up of the party. The right-wing parties appear to be more subject to internal dissent—and to more serious dissent—than the left-wing parties. This was very true for Sąjūdis in 1990–1992, and for the HU/LC and LChDP in 1996–2000. Disagreements on the leadership level are common to all types of political parties, but parties that have charismatic leaders and are able to achieve success on the national level work to sustain unity, as was in case with the LDLP under A. Brazauskas's leadership in 1990–1996.[9] On the other hand, high personalization of party politics seems to be counterproductive for party unity and produces high dissent rates within the party. The HU/LC was an excellent example of personalized leadership in 1993–2000, and this party was still unable to escape splits in 1999–2000. As a matter of fact, the Homeland People's Party and Union of Moderate Conservatives were established as a consequence of the personal disagreements within the HU/LC. In the decade from 1990 to 2000, only Social Democracy 2000 was established as a direct consequence of a split (in this case, within the LSDP).

In the right-wing parties, on the other hand, in the period 1996–2000 both the Homeland People's Party and Union of Moderate Conservatives split away from the HU/LC between 1996 and 2000, and the Union of Moderate Christian Democrats emerged as a result of the breakup of the Lithuanian Christian Democratic Party, not to mention that since 1992 the LChDP was competing with the Lithuanian Christian Democratic Union, which emerged on the Lithuanian political scene by soliciting some of the LChDP members. Overall, the behavior of the left-wing parties was much more pro-unity and coalition-oriented. As early as 1992 the LDLP managed to form a preelection coalition with a number of small leftist organizations, despite the fact that the LSDP—the main competitor on the left wing—stayed outside of it. Before the 2000 Seimas elections the LSDP and LDLP managed to form the first preelection coalition based on an equal partnership between coalition parties, which finally led to the unification of these two parties and the establishment of the united Lithuanian Social Democratic Party at the beginning of 2001.

THE LEGAL CONTEXT OF LITHUANIAN PARTIES: THE CONSTITUTION AND ELECTORAL LAW

In new democracies, the process of party institutionalization might be described on the basis of at least two parameters:

- formal or legal and institutional regulations of party development, including the legal basis of party formation
- the electoral system as it conditions parties' electoral performance

The legal regulation of party activities is an essential point in the analysis of party structure and performance. Moreover, these laws are initiated and formulated by political groups and organizations, which means that all the laws necessarily reflect the interests of certain groups.

Political parties are mentioned only twice in the 1992 Lithuanian Constitution. Article 35 states that "citizens have a right freely to unite themselves into communities, political parties, and associations, if their goals do not contradict the Constitution and [Lithuania's] laws."[10] The same article remarks that other laws regulate the formation and activities of political parties. Article 83 of the Constitution refers to political parties rather negatively: "the person who is elected President of the Republic must terminate his activities in political parties and political organizations until the following electoral campaign for President of the Republic."[11]

Despite the brevity of these direct references to political parties, the Constitution establishes very definite guarantees for collective and individual political self-expression in Lithuania. It includes the freedom of thought, the right to privacy, the principle of equal treatment before the law, the right to vote, and the right to representation, as well as the right to criticize the government and governmental officials, and so on, in other words the guarantees that constitute the basis of group and individual autonomy *from* and influence *on* political institutions.

The Constitution is the only general legal document that allows and regulates party activities. But nonetheless the road traveled to attain this document was long and rough. Sąjūdis, founded in June 1988 as the first mass opposition movement, was an illegal organization according to the Soviet legal code. Furthermore, the only way to legalize Sąjūdis was for it to be registered as a social movement. Articles 6 and 7 of the Constitution of Soviet Lithuania stated that the LCP was "an integral part" of the Communist Party of the Soviet Union (CPSU) and that the latter was the only legal political party, playing "the leading and directing role" in society. These articles of the Constitution were removed entirely in December 1989.

However, the de facto reconstruction of multipartyism was started only by and through Sąjūdis. In late 1988 and early 1989, such historical organizations as the Democratic, the Christian Democratic, and the Social Democratic parties, as well as the Nationalists Union and Young Lithuania formed their initial groups and announced that they were the continuation of their inter-war predecessors. At the same time, a few new parties, such as the Humanists and the Greens, were established. In April 1989, Sąjūdis passed a motion that the LCP must be transformed into an autonomous political party, and that all other parties should be legalized and receive equal treatment under the law.[12]

The actual rebirth and formation of political parties was speedier than were the changes in legal regulations. The 1989 legal changes served to codify changes that had already taken place and practices that had become more or less customary.

Major efforts to introduce formal legal regulations governing political parties were made by the Constituent parliament in September 1990 through the adoption of the Law on Political Parties and Political Organizations. The law described the rules and procedures of party formation and activity. The so-called Parties' Law granted the right to all citizens of Lithuania to form and participate in the activities of political parties. The law suspended the right of party membership only for military and police servicemen, staff of national security agencies, and judicial officials during the period of their service or employment. Requirements and procedures of party formation and registration included five basic elements:

- at least 400 founding members
- a party statute and basic program
- elected leadership
- party institutions formed at a conference or congress of the founding members or their delegates
- the registration of the political party with the Ministry of Justice

Lithuania's rules of party registration can be characterized as strict because each new party was required to present a list of founders with names and signatures, as well as information about their citizenship, addresses, personal codes, and professions, plus confirmation that they were not members of another party, a protocol of the founding conference, party statute, and even designs of party symbols.

Electoral rules in the narrow sense have a two-fold effect on political parties, that is, on the stability of party government and the structure of the party system. The first postcommunist election law was passed by the Constituent parliament in July 1992. The 1990 founding election in Lithuania was based on the inherited Soviet majority system of representation. The debate over a new profile of an electoral system was extremely heated and controversial in 1992. The right wing of Sąjūdis argued for a two-round system, while the moderates of Sąjūdis and the left-wing parties expected to get dividends from a proportional list system. Both opposing groups believed that the different electoral systems promoted by them would at least allow them to secure their parliamentary seats and would restrict political fragmentation in the parliament through cutting off the entry of small extra-parliamentary parties into the Seimas.

After a prolonged political crisis from April to July of 1992, a mixed-member proportional electoral system was introduced in Lithuania. This decision was an outcome of political compromise. Nevertheless, the mixed-representation system was one of the best options available to provide a balance between representation and fragmentation in the parliament after the first multiparty elections of 1992.

The law on the Seimas elections fixed that 71 members would be elected in single-mandate constituencies, and 70 seats of the parliament would be filled on a proportional party list basis. All parties needed at least four percent of total votes to enter the Seimas, except the political organizations representing ethnic minorities. After the amendments to the law in June of 1996, the threshold for a single party was increased to five percent and for an inter-party coalition to seven percent. The special threshold of two percent for minority ethnic parties was abolished. These changes were made by the efforts of the strongest parties—the LDLP, HU(LC), LChDP—and reflected their desire to tighten the circle of electoral competition around a small set of competitors. Moreover, the higher threshold for party coalitions compared to single parties could be cited as violating a principle of equal opportunity in representative democracy. By increasing the price of preelection inter-party coalitions, the law has almost eliminated the opportunities of smaller parties to compete against their larger competitors.

The outcomes of the 1992 and 1996 parliamentary elections regarding the effects of the mixed system disappointed the major competing groups. The expectations of the right-wing Sąjūdis failed because the two-round representation yielded seats in the Seimas for 13 parties in 1992 and 14 in 1996—hardly the expected reduction of small parties' influence. With the exception of the LSDP, the moderates failed to enter into the parliament in 1992 under the proportional representation part of the system. And in both elections only five political organizations were able to enter the Seimas through the proportional formula. This means, contrary to the well-known theoretical assumptions, that the two-round system produced party fragmentation and proportional representation decreased it in Lithuania's parliament.

Before the 2000 Seimas elections under the initiative of the HU/LC, but with the silent support of the LDLP, the two-round formula in the single-mandate districts was changed to the simplest form of plurality—the majority electoral system (First Past the Post). However, this change had no major effect on party seats distribution on Election Day.

The law on local elections, passed by the Seimas in 1994, established proportional representation, with parties the only entities able to nominate candidates. A four-percent threshold was set for entry into local self-government bodies.

The differing electoral systems on the national and local level allowed for the majority of parties to be represented on one or another level of government as well as to reach a modus vivendi between multiple parties and to secure the representation of various political identities of voters. On the other hand, the large number of competing parties in the elections indicated that all of them played consequential roles for interest articulation, and even major parties were still in trouble with respect to their capacity to aggregate interests. For instance, two winning parties in the national election of 1996—the HU/LC and LChDP—received only 15.76 and 5.24 percent[13] support from the eligible electorate.

If the mixed-member proportional electoral system is to be maintained in the future, one can try to predict that, with the ongoing stabilization of the party system, voters' behavior may change considerably. We may expect the electoral learning process to yield such change. The proportional formula, with the five-percent threshold presumably favoring major party lists, ignored the desires of almost 36 percent of voters in 1996, and 23.4 percent of voters in 2000 (the percentages of votes going to parties failing to pass the threshold). The present electoral rules will eventually lead a significant portion of voters to change their behavior and turn to split-ticket voting, that is, to vote for different parties along the proportional and plurality formulas.

The picture of parties' legal bases would be incomplete without mentioning their status and influence in the Seimas, especially since all new parliaments carry a double burden of responsibility, acting as agents of political socialization for the parliamentary elite while simultaneously performing standard legislative functions.[14] Nevertheless, the essential structures of parties' representation in the parliament are parliamentary factions.

The first parliamentary factions were established in the Supreme Council in the early 1990s. On the eve of the 1992 elections, there were nine parliamentary factions. Among them, seven were founded on the basis of Sąjūdis, and the other two represented the Polish Union and the LDLP. The majority of these factions could hardly be characterized as parliamentary parties because of their lack of connections to the extra-parliamentary organizations, low internal discipline, and ideological differences among members of same faction.

The standing orders of the Supreme Council took little notice of the parliamentary factions in the legislative process. Despite the fact that during the founding elections some candidates mentioned their party affiliation on the Sąjūdis list, the Sąjūdis label overshadowed it.

The position of parliamentary factions has changed fundamentally after the first multiparty elections in 1992. From that moment on, the Seimas was organized along party lines. The most obvious indicator of the increasing strength of parliamentary parties was a sudden decrease in the number of nonaffiliated MPs from 22.1 percent in 1990 to 4.9 in 1992, and to nil in 1996. Even independent MPs joined parliamentary factions in 1996 because they, along with the Seimas committees, turned into the most influential centers in the legislative process. A relatively low requirement for parliamentary faction membership—only three members of Seimas are required to register a faction—facilitated the unification of all MPs into factions in 1996.

According to the Statute of Lithuania's Seimas, parliamentary factions perform the following formal functions:

- prepare the agenda for the Seimas plenary sittings and Seimas sessions
- propose candidates for membership on parliamentary committees, commissions, and the Board of Seimas
- submit drafts of decisions

- may declare themselves the parliamentary opposition and announce an alternative to the government's program[15]

From this brief overview of the reemergence of political parties in Lithuania since 1988, it is obvious that a competitive party system has become a political reality. But is it possible to say the same about the stability of Lithuania's party system?

PROFILE OF THE PARTY SYSTEM FROM 1992 ONWARD: STRUCTURAL AND VOTER DIMENSIONS

Most scholars agree that a major function of a political party in a representative democracy is to define and present electoral alternatives. However, the actual political weight of the parties in the competition for votes, and in shaping the electoral choice, is unequal. The political weight of each party constantly changes. Russell J. Dalton pointed out that "party systems are in a state of flux, and it is difficult to determine how fundamental and long lasting these changes will be,"[16] even in advanced liberal democracies.

Another difficulty when discussing party systems lies in the area of academic conventions. From the viewpoint of system analysis, it is quite obvious that a system is a set of certain objects, including attributes and interactions between these objects. In the case of party system analysis, it "consists of a set of political parties operating within a nation in an organized pattern, described by a number of party system properties."[17] This is the only point on which scholars agree, because different researchers identify different sets of party system properties. M. Duverger, in his classic study on political parties, classified party systems on the basis of the electoral strength of parties. Since Duverger's study in 1954, this variable has been popular among scholars. Circumstances changed slightly after G. Sartori, in the mid-1970s, proposed the concept of a relevant party as an important element of party system research.[18] In 1994, J.E. Lane and S. Ersson presented a new detailed summary of the variables needed in analyzing party systems. They developed a detailed list of criteria to describe party systems on the basis of two dimensions: that is, electoral participation and ideological distance.[19]

Ideological differences appeared on Lithuania's political stage as early as 1988, and proto-parties started to emerge at the same time, but political discourse was dominated by macro- and medium-level political choices such as the struggle for independence, the introduction of democratic institutions, and the rule of law. The reconstruction of economic bases and the reintroduction of private ownership were underway. During the earliest phases of transition, political parties were unable to implement their traditional functions such as interest aggregation or elite recruitment. They lacked the ideological identity, experience, organizational skills, and infrastructure to mobilize voters.

A departure point for analysis of Lithuania's party system is 1992. In 1992 a new constitution was adopted, which meant that the transformation of political institutions was coming to an end; parliamentary elections were called, with clearly expressed competition between political parties, internal ideological and organizational consolidation, and speedy development of political discourse on micro-level political issues, such as inflation versus unemployment, the social protection of minority and disadvantaged groups, and so on.

The most important characteristic of a newly developing party system is not its composition based on the number and/or profile of relevant political actors but rather its general stability. Voter turnout is a key variable for assessing party system stability. Looking at electoral participation in Lithuania between the two consecutive parliamentary elections in 1992 and 1996, we can see that up to 23 percent of eligible voters became politically inactive. Moreover, during the third set of multiparty elections the failure of major parties to mobilize voters increased again. This cannot be explained as the effect of certain institutional factors such as electoral competitiveness and proportionality, unicameralism versus bicameralism, multipartyism, or the electoral laws.[20] A frequent change in voter turnout suggests that Lithuania's party system has experienced a high degree of instability (see Table 10.8).

Another indicator, the index of the efficient number of parties, measured by the Laakso-Taagepera formula,[21] was equal to 3.3 points (in 1996) compared to 4.15 in the Czech Republic, 4.13 in Estonia, and 3.89 in Poland (in 1996);[22] even compared with the average for Western Europe, which was equal to 4.3 (between 1985–1989), the number of effective parties in Lithuania was relatively low, which means that the party system was dominated by relatively few political actors (see Table 10.9).[23]

Table 10.8 Voter Turnout in the Parliamentary Elections, 1990–2000 (%): The Baltics Perspective

	The founding elections	*First multiparty elections*	*Second multiparty elections*	*Third multiparty elections*	*Average*
Estonia	78	67	70	57	68
Latvia	80	89	72	72	78
Lithuania	72	75	52	57	64
Total	76.6	77.0	64.6	62.0	

Table 10.9 The Efficient Number of Parties in Lithuania, 1990–2000

	1990	*1992*	*1996*	*2000*
The effective number of parties	1.9	2.98	3.32	4.20

As a consequence of this situation, the largest party was able to secure an absolute majority of seats in the parliament. The 1996 and 2000 elections scenario was very different, and the share of votes received by the largest party decreased to around 30 percent. In 1996 the HU/LC was able to win the Seimas election only because of two circumstances: voter turnout decreased by more than 20 percent, and the share of votes for parties that did not meet the threshold required for parliamentary seats increased more than twice, to over 30 percent[24] in comparison to the 1992 elections. This trend of intensifying party competition since the 1996 elections had a twofold effect on party system stability. On the one hand, it was a sign of democratic developments within the party system, where new political actors could expect to receive quite extensive electoral support and enter into the still open political stage. On the other hand, all this signified that the major parties lacked credibility and confidence among the voters. Moreover, voters consistently evaluated the performance of ruling parties in power as unsatisfactory and poor.

The contradictory character of Lithuania's party system is stressed by the index of fractionalization. This index simply counts all the parties represented in the parliament. In Lithuania's case, this index reached 13 and 14 parties in 1992–1996 and 1996–1997 respectively. After the 2000 parliamentary elections, the number of parliamentary parties increased to 16. At the same time, such a high number of parliamentary parties has existed only in a few Western democracies, such as 15 in Switzerland, 14 in Italy, and 13 in Spain (1985–1989).[25] But the situation in some other post-communist countries was quite similar to that of Lithuania: in Estonia's parliament 10 parties were represented, 12 in Romania, and 13 in Slovakia (in 1996).[26]

The share of votes and the Seimas seats received by the largest parliamentary party might also reflect the degree of party competition within the party system. Here the same trend of fragmentation and consequently of higher competition was observed since 1990 (see Table 10.10).

The above-mentioned trends were well reflected in electoral volatility scores (see Table 10.11). Again this was the most obvious sign of the unfinished institutionalization of Lithuania's party system. Total volatility is a measure of the electoral instability of the party system, and most new democracies have high scores here. The following calculations

Table 10.10 Share of Votes and Seats of the Largest Parliamentary Party (%), 1990–2000

	1990		*1992*		*1996*		*2000*	
	Votes	*Seats*	*Votes*	*Seats*	*Votes*	*Seats*	*Votes*	*Seats*
Share of votes and seats of the largest party	N/A	68.5	42.5	51.77	29.7	51.1	31.1	36.17

Table 10.11 Electoral Volatility in Lithuania, 1992–2000

	% of votes in elections 1992	*% of votes in elections 1996*	*% of votes in elections 2000*	*Score of volatility, 1996*	*Score of volatility, 2000*
LDLP*	42.5	9.5	31.1	16.5	7.5
HU(LC)	20.5	29.7	8.6	4.6	10.5
LChDP	12.2	9.9	3.1	1.15	3.4
LSDP	5.8	6.6	0	0.4	-
LLU	1.5	1.9	17.3	0.2	7.7
NU (SL)	0	0	19.6	0	9.8
LCU	2.4	8.1	2.9	2.8	2.6
Total	83.4	63.8	82.5	25.6	41.5

*The volatility scores of the LSDP and the LDLP coalition in the 2000 elections were calculated by summing up the shares of the two parties in the 1996 parliamentary elections.

according to a formula initially developed by A. Przeworski[27] show that the score of electoral volatility—25.6 points for the leading Lithuanian parties in 1996—was slightly higher than in Poland and Slovakia (22.78 in 1991–1993, and 24.68 in 1992–1994, respectively), but lower than in Hungary (28.02 in 1990–1994).[28] In the 2000 parliamentary elections, and after the first post-transitional turnover of the Lithuanian party system, the volatility score almost doubled: it was 41.5 points for the mainstream parties. Moreover, in the 2000 Seimas elections total volatility was equal to 46.2 points,[29] if calculated for all Lithuanian parties that took part in the elections deciding the distribution of seats proportionately. These scores are far behind Western European countries' volatility scores.[30] Despite the fact that the methodology for the evaluation of volatility is not a perfect one,[31] it is obvious that efficient political mobilization of voters must become a major issue for Lithuania's leading parties in the forthcoming years.

Bloc volatility indicates the electoral strength of party blocs and has implications for the office- and policy-related maneuvering capabilities of political parties.[32] Bloc volatility of the left-wing parties in Lithuania was very low. A real challenge for the left-wing parties were the electoral losses in favor of other party blocs. In 1996, LDLP and LSDP (the largest leftist parties) lost votes to the center-right and right-wing parties. However, in 1996, volatility scores did not reflect real voting behavior. Most potential left-wing voters simply did not take part in the elections, and voter turnout decreased by more than 20 percent compared to the 1992 Seimas elections. During the 2000 parliamentary elections, the social-democratic coalition suffered from a voting swing in favor of center-based parties. Even among those who in 1996 voted for the LDLP or LSDP, in 2000 as much as 24.9 percent chose the NU/SL and 19.1 percent the Liberal Union.[33] The right-wing parties were in a more complicated situation. Bloc volatility of the main right-wing parties was equal to 30.27 points in the 2000 Seimas elections.

Nevertheless, new trends toward the stabilization of party loyalties since 1997, compared to the period of multiparty system institutionalization in 1992–1996 (see Table 10.12), might signal a certain stability within the party system. On the other hand, this is only partly true because increasing party loyalties might be shared by a number of various parties, and possibly not by those who for some period of time have dominated the political stage.

On average, party attachments in the period 1992–1996 seem to be relatively well reflected by absolute figures quite comparable to the data from the era of partisan dealignment in the 1980s and 1990s in the advanced Western democracies. According to R. Dalton's estimates, by 1994 nonpartisans "accounted for more than 30 percent among Westerners."[34] Meanwhile, one serious difference needs to be mentioned in contrast to Western Europe, that is, a substantial instability of attachments towards individual parties. Of course, instability of party attachments strongly affects voting choices, but it does not mean that partisanship and vote are always bound together. On the contrary, "partisanship generally is a political orientation that continues over time, even in face of vote defections."[35]

In case of Lithuania, in the period 1992–1996, the share of voters who were able to define their party preferences was on average equal to 52.3 percent (excluding the data from post-election surveys, because, following elections, the numbers of voters having party preferences tend to increase substantially above the average). But measuring the stability of party attachments on the basis of standard deviation allows us to conclude that a fluctuation in the range of approximately 10 percent is high even in absolute terms. The change of voter preferences for major parties was equal to 10.2 percent, exceeding the average level of deviation. Nevertheless, the share of voter preferences for the largest parties—93.4 percent—was very impressive.

After the 1996 Seimas elections, some qualitative changes towards greater stability of party attachments seem to have taken place. First of all, there was an increase in the share of voters who were able to define their party preference, from 52.3 (1992–1996) to 66.7 (1997–2001) percent on average (see Table 10.13). But more importantly, the stability of party preferences was higher as well. However, a certain stability of party preferences was achieved not only through increasing voter identification with the major parties but also through growing attachment to minor parties, because the total share of loyalty to major parties in fact slightly decreased from 48.9 to 46.7 percent on average.

It is not clear what electoral outcomes (the impact on voting choices in particular) this new situation might have in relation to the increased party identification. However, change is an implicit feature of democracy, and stability is always a relative phenomenon. Traditional parliamentary par-

Table 10.12 Party Preferences in 1992–1996 (%)

	Jan. 1992	*Mar. 1992*	*June 1992*	*June 1993*	*Dec. 1993*	*May 1994*	*Dec. 1994*	*Feb. 1995*	*June 1995*	*Sept. 1996*	*Average*
Percentage of respondents with definite party preferences	52.4	64.0	60.2	71.5	54.1	43.1	49.2	52.0	70.5	51.9	52.3
Respondents preferring the largest parties*	38.7	49.4	45.3	67.8	51.0	38.7	41.7	38.4	48.1	30.3	48.9
No party preference/do not vote	47.6	36.0	39.8	28.5	45.9	56.9	50.8	48.0	29.5	48.1	47.7

*Until 1993, considered as the largest parties were LDLP, Sajūdis, LSDP, and LChDP; since 1992 LCU has been recognized as a major party; from May 1993 to May 1994 preferences for both Sajādis and HU (LC) were included.
Source: Vilmorus data, 1992–1996.

Table 10.13 Party Preferences in 1997–2001 (%)

	Feb. 1997	*June 1997*	*May 1998*	*Sept. 1998*	*Nov. 1998*	*Dec. 1998*	*June 1999*	*Jan. 2000*	*Sept. 2001*	*Average*
Share of respondents with definite party preferences	65	64.6	68.5	64.5	61.8	65.4	63.9	77.6	69.3	66.73
No party preference/do not vote	35	35.4	31.5	35.5	38.2	34.6	36.1	22.4	30.7	33.27

Source: Vilmorus data, 1997–2001.

Table 10.14 Number of Party Votes, 1992–2000

	Year of the election and number of votes					
Party	*1992*	*1995*	*1996*	*1997*	*2000 (local)*	*2000 (parliamentary)*
HU/LC (in 1992 Sąjūdis)	393,500	315,000	409,585	331,000	159,163	126,850
LDLP	817,331	214,000	130,837	122,000	120,622	457,294*
LChDP	234,368	185,000	136,259	102,000	68,996	45,227
LCU (LCM)	46,908	59,000	113,333	92,000	130,729	42,030
LSDP	112,410	52,000	90,756	85,000	98,550	—
LLU	28,091	26,000	25,279	43,000	176,615	253,823
LPP	28,091	53,000	22,826	42,000	127,815	60,040
NU/SL	—	—	—	—	224,925	288,895

Source: Table compiled by Alvidas Lukošaitis, except the 2000 elections.
*Votes for the LDLP and LSDP coalition.

ties—HU(LC), LChDP, LDLP, LSDP, and LCU—tend to lose, or, at best, have "frozen" electorate, as the 2000 local and parliamentary elections indicated (see Table 10.14).

Among the main challengers to the mainstream parties were the New Union/Social Liberals, the Lithuanian Peasants' Party, and the Liberal Union. These three political organizations were able to win as many as 529,000, or 37.5 percent, of the total votes in the 2000 municipal elections. During the 2000 Seimas elections, the total share of these parties increased to 602,000, or almost 41 percent of valid votes.

The central point to be made regarding these changes relates to the behavior of the individual voter. Classical views of individual political participation suggest to us at least four complex variables that directly affect individual involvement in politics, the formation of party identities and loyalties, and stable voting behavior: Individual political participation is (a) a function of external stimuli, that is, group identity, alienation, cynicism, trust or distrust towards political leaders and authorities; (b) a function of personal factors, including attitudes and beliefs, individual psychology, and the degree of socialization and extraversion; (c) a function of social position, that is, being in the center or periphery of society and class, living place, organizational network, communal identity, age, gender, and race; and (d) a function of larger societal variables, that is, the level of modernization, political violence, rules of social and political interactions, and the party system.[36] A detailed investigation of all of these factors is beyond the scope of this study. However, it is important to note that whereas the party system is an independent variable in the context of individual behavior, it turns into a dependent variable in the context of mass political behavior.

Mass political behavior in general and voter party linkage in particular strongly depend on the quality and means of mass communication. In order to stabilize their connection with the electorate, political parties in new democracies need to rely more and more on new means of electronic mass media. From a rational choice perspective, electronic media are pushing down procurement costs of political information and thus create a rationale for political actors to invest in the area of political communication. Because of trends towards the individualization of politics when, in the words of R.J. Dalton, an eclectic and egocentric pattern of citizen action is developing, a change that signifies a shift away from electoral decision making based on social group and/or party cues toward a more individualized and inwardly oriented style of political choice,[37] new media might have an unexpectedly high influence on individual political choices in the medium and long run. Certainly, the scale of current party investments to reach individual voters by means of computer communications basically depends on the general level of computerization of a particular society, and studying the presence of parties on the Internet is the simplest, though incomplete, way to examine party strategies for using new electronic media in their attempts to mobilize party electorates.

Political information was among the most attractive and readable material on the Internet in Lithuania, as is confirmed by the fact that Lithuanian Seimas was the second-most-visited Web site after the site of the daily *Lietuvos Rytas.* Moreover, an elections Web site established by the Central Electoral Commission in 1996 almost instantly became an extremely popular site, despite the fact that the degree of computerization at that time in Lithuania was very low and users of the Internet usually browsed the Web from the computers installed in their workplaces.

The HU/LC was the first Lithuanian party about which some information appeared on the Internet as early as 1996. However, before the forthcoming parliamentary elections, the HU/LC Web page was designed by a Norwegian follower of this party, without the knowledge or consent of party leadership.

Soon after the 1996 Seimas elections, the Lithuanian Liberal Union created a party Web page. This effort was a conscious act of the party. Early exposure of the liberals to the Internet seems to stem from the fact that this party enjoyed considerable support from the youngest cohort (18–29 years old) of the electorate and that the most of the party leaders were in their mid-30s. The next step was the development of a Web page by the Lithuanian Movement of Young Centrists, an associate of the Center Union. Lithuanian Social Democratic Party, Lithuanian Center Union, and Homeland Union/Lithuanian Conservatives followed these early examples only in 1997–1998. Many more party Web pages appeared in connection with the 2000 local and parliamentary elections. In total, 18 political parties managed to create and maintain their own sites on the Internet in 2000.

Lithuanian political parties might draw several conclusions looking at the emerging use of new electronic media. Liberal and center parties were most exposed to the use of the Internet because of the convergence of two circumstances: first, a substantial part of their followers were very young and highly exposed to the Internet, and second, most of the leaders of these parties were young and well-educated and did not underestimate the importance of communication with potential voters via the Web as early as 1997–1998. During the second phase, or in 1999 and 2000, all major parties from traditional ideological camps started to deliver their messages to the electorate through the Internet.

However, the structural contents of party messages, the popularity of certain Web sites, as well as the pattern of party actions through the Internet varied widely. Among the parties that had established discussion forums and other interactive features, only a few were updating information on a regular basis, for example the Social Democratic Party and Liberal and Center Union. The Internet was already a part of the communication strategy for these parties. HU/LC, NU/SL, and the Union of Moderate Conservatives made up the second group of parties, for whom the Internet was a place to provide fairly complex information on the organization and to receive feedback from Web users, mostly during the election periods. The third group included such parties as LChDP and Party of New Democracy, which managed to create and update Web pages only with basic information. Finally, the fourth group consisted of the parties that managed to present themselves before the 2000 Seimas elections but did not use the Internet as a link to voters. The statistics on the popularity of party Web sites partially reflected the division of parties into three groups based on the party–Internet relationship (see Table 10.15).

Unfortunately, even some well-maintained party Web sites gave no statistics regarding number of visitors to the site, and the presented calculations are very incomplete. Still, we can suggest that several factors

Table 10.15 Popularity of Party Web sites as of October 31, 2001*

	Number of visitors
New Union/Social Liberals	65,915
Lithuanian Liberal Union	40,870
Lithuanian Social Democratic Party	25,595
Lithuanian Nationalists Union	2,907
Union of Moderate Conservatives	2,853
Party of New Democracy (former Women's Party)	1,943
Lithuanian National Democratic Party	1,281
Union of Political Prisoners and Deportees	694

*Only the Web sites that have statistics of visitors are included.

Table 10.16 Patterns of Internet Use by Lithuanian Political Parties

Contents of Internet information	*Intensity of internet use*	
	Fragmental	*Permanent*
Basic	Only once (Nationalists Union)	Regular update (LChDP)
Complex	Election upheaval (HU/LC, NU/SL)	Internet as an integral part of communication strategy (LLU, LSDP, LCU)

matter for a party's access to the means of electronic communication: general strength and resources of the political party (more established parties tend to use the Internet more intensively), the structure of the party electorate (a younger and better-educated electorate is more exposed to the Internet),[38] and conscious strategies of the party elite. General patterns of the use of the Internet by Lithuanian parties might be summarized in two parameters: intensity (sporadic vs. permanent) and contents (basic vs. complex) (see Table 10.16).

In summing up the role of new electronic media in establishing party–voter linkage, we need to stress that it played a marginal role in voter mobilization in recent years. Because of the ability of new information technologies to bring political issues and party agenda closer to individual voters, political parties have started to invest their efforts in this area, expecting profits only in the future.

Last but not least, we ought to look at Lithuania's party system through a typology of the party system developed by G. Sartori.[39] Lithuania had developed a competitive party system; however, after the parliamentary elections of 1992 and 1996 two parties[40] succeeded in achieving single-party majorities in different Seimas. Nonetheless, it would be difficult to define Lithuania's party system as a two-party system. After the Seimas elections of 1996, the Lithuanian Conservatives were invited to join the Christian Democratic Party in the parliamentary majority. The LChDP accepted this invitation and concluded a formal agreement on the governing coalition. Since 1992 the Lithuanian parliament has been dominated by five political parties: the HU/LC, LDLP, LChDP, LCU, and LSDP. From this point of view, Lithuania's party system can be described as a three- to five-party system, according to Sartori's classification. Moreover, it can also be characterized as a moderate multiparty system from an ideological angle, because antisystemic parties were represented in the parliament only by a few MPs. Lithuania's party system stability was seriously challenged in both local and parliamentary elections in 2000 by the entry onto the political stage of the Liberal Union and NU/SL; however, neither of these newcomers can be considered an antisystemic party. Nonetheless, the general stability of Lithuania's party system has been disturbed by recent electoral volatility, as well as by decreasing voter turnout.

CONCLUSION

The competitive party system is a political reality in Lithuania as well as a significant factor in the success of ongoing democratic consolidation. Some aspects of party performance, such as the problems of voter volatility and political mobilization, some ambivalence in the relationships between parties and interest groups, and emphasis on the vertical versus horizontal relationships inside parties were clear obstacles to further institutionalization and stabilization of the party system. However, the overall conclusion is that Lithuania's parties are well on their way towards institutionalization and towards a successful performance of the functions of the intermediate structures in the context of Lithuania's consolidating democracy.

CHAPTER 11

Conclusion: Party Building in Post-Soviet Space: Between Imitation and Simulation

Susanna Pshizova

At the end of the 1980s and the beginning of the 1990s, during the stormy period of democratization in Eastern Europe, a French political scientist wrote: "In the times we live in, any questioning of democratic legitimacy is tactless."[1] However, it became clear very soon that there was some room for doubt—if not of the legitimacy of democracy, then of its triumphant procession throughout the world. These doubts intensified as political systems in postcommunist countries became institutionalized.[2] The concept of democracy gradually lost its clarity and needed more and more specification. The old discussion about the nature of democracy flamed up with new force.[3] Western theorists began to insist on the distinction between liberal democracy and electoral democracy[4] and to describe new regimes as illiberal democracies,[5] pseudodemocracies, or competitive authoritarianism.[6] Political scientists in some post-Soviet countries prefer to speak about guided democracy, implying the capability of authorities to manipulate democratic procedures to provide for their own interests. The heart of the problem is to differentiate political regimes in which official democratic procedures (foremost electoral) are fulfilled but fundamental rights of persons and groups are not guaranteed, and there is no real representation of interests, from regimes where all these things work more or less well.

Actually, the present process of global democratization has made urgent the fundamental question of the correlation of political form to its content. Certainly, the shifting of political institutions and power relations patterns takes place in almost any historical period. The question is: what exactly is pulled out of context and transferred to a new ground? The distance between the perception of the pattern by the subjects of the transportation and the pattern's real embodiment could well be great. In defiance of the subjective reformers' will, the ground (social and cultural context) could turn down institutions seen as unfit. Something is rejected deliberately, or otherwise changed during reception. How well does the result of political transplantation meet our expectations? The chapters of this book partially answer this question for seven post-Soviet nations.

The collected materials concern the rise of political parties and party systems in a large region, occupying a noticeable part of the "third wave of democratization." A little more than 10 years ago these societies were parts of a common political system but diversified in their socioeconomic characteristics. They started to build their independent political systems simultaneously but undertook very different ways of reform. Comparing the processes of post-Soviet transformation in parts of the former single country, one can see some factors determining the formation of democratic institutions in the modern world. Analyses of party systems are particularly important since the character of political parties is the key point that determines a regime's type today, and "few would deny that full appreciation of the operation of modern liberal democracy requires an understanding of the political challenges facing political parties and how successfully they deal with them."[7]

These factors are both general and specific. The most general is the idea of the indispensability of party building itself, based on the experience of Western democracies. The ambition to duplicate an attractive Western pattern was the main stimulus of the process of reforms not only in post-Soviet territory; it was common for all postcommunist countries. During the recent wave of democratization, the introduction of Western patterns of political institutions (elections, parliaments, constitutions, political parties, etc.) took place everywhere in political practice as well as in the analytic kit of newly established national schools of political science. This idea of imitation totally dominated post-Soviet territory. Yet as politicians worked on the carcasses of the Soviet political system, their perception of their own benefit and expediency and their apprehension of how it should be, based on the practice of Western democracies, obviously clashed. Researchers, in their turn, applied Western models to the realities of new democracies in order to determine how ripe and close they were to the exemplar. Discrepancies were (and often are) interpreted as transitional provisional costs, resulting from the incompleteness of the process. The nations covered in this book are not exceptions.

The destruction of the single Soviet political system was carried out in the name of a single ideal. But it was not an ideal expressed only in principles. It was an ideal with concrete political forms and traits.[8] Among the obligatory attributes of this ideal were (and continue to be) political parties. Democracy was (and is) thought of as requiring a multiparty system.

Political parties are associated with fundamental functions that determine the existence of liberal democracies themselves: structuring the popular vote, integration and mobilization of the mass of the citizenry, aggregation of diverse interests, recruitment of leaders for public office, and formulation of public policy.[9]

As a matter of fact, modern democratic rule is party rule, and only in this form is it recognized as legitimate. That is to say that parties are the crucial agencies of the institutional legitimization of democracy. However, "the leaders whom parties recruit, the policies which they formulate, and the governments that they seek to control can be legitimized only to the extent that the parties themselves are legitimized: hence the relevance of the mass party."[10] It was the popular base of parties that was to ensure their legitimacy: "Parties reflected the public will and provided the crucial linkage between the citizenry and the state. They did so as mass organizations, for it was as mass organizations that they belonged to the society from which they emanated. In effect, and above all else, the twentieth century has been the century of the mass party."[11] The main indices of the mass character (hence the legitimacy) of parties were their numerical strength and (or) stable adherence to substantial segments of the electorate (grassroots), the influence of party members and large interest groups on the formation of party politics, as well as independence from a state based on the voluntary support of the citizenry and financed by fees and institutional donations. Such was the model for imitation.

Chapters of this book reflect, first, the efforts made in practice to transplant this model onto post-Soviet ground, and second, the research done to trace progress along the path to this aim—as well as the real outcomes of both of these efforts.

What is most striking is that parties in new democracies do not much look like the ideal seen in transitional projects. They are not mass organizations. They do not have numerous members, despite the requirement of a certain minimal strength as a condition for party registration in most countries. More precisely, their numerical strength is often in direct proportion to what the law demands, and there are few if any signs of growth over time. These organizations look like tadpoles; their bodies are almost entirely situated in capitals. Instead of the enthusiasm of crowds of members and activists, they use the services of paid, hired personnel and consulting firms.

From the point of view of ideology, the situation is no less problematic. Party leaders label themselves in accordance with a foreign ideological spectrum, while researchers try to place their parties on the right–left scale following the Western pattern, albeit without great success. The lack of correspondence between the two systems is often quite evident. As a rule certain ideologies are written on party banners but not determined by real social cleavages and not confirmed by real policy.

The surface multiplicity of political parties in these nations is striking, and nowadays they continue to appear (and, naturally, disappear). Largely this is also connected with the idea of imitation. The desire to reproduce Western patterns has led to the formation of many political organizations before the initiation of or even without any preconditions for their activity. For example, since there are powerful social-democratic parties in respectable elder democracies, this kind of party model is very popular among theoreticians and post-Soviet politicians. As a result, we see many social-democratic (or, with the same result, say, conservative) parties fabricated by small groups of party builders. Since these parties do not have any real basis for their activity, they soon disappear or drag out a miserable existence, collecting one to two percent of votes, or even less.

In fact, it appears that modern conditions do not stimulate the rise of firm ideological divisions in society that are then reflected in party systems. One may hardly ascertain linkages between social cleavages and party systems in new democracies. The only newly formed parties that look more or less like traditional ones and are based on social cleavages are ethnic parties. Incidentally, in the West this kind of party also changed little during the last decades.

Politicians in post-Soviet countries, as well as the contributors to our book, often refer to the pre-Soviet democratic experience. But those cleavages and parties did not recur in post-Soviet times. The same situation is visible in Eastern and Central Europe.[12] Those kinds of cleavages lost their importance in the West as well, though tradition and historical memory continue to work. Everybody knows who those old political actors on the political scene are: who are on the left and who are on the right. It may well be that they are not really so left and so right, and the difference between them is not so apparent today. But a tradition tells voters in the West who is who. As a result, a considerable number of voters are still led by ideological party labels. The charm of political leaders is not so crucial, and political advertisement is not so effective.

There is no such historical memory in the new democracies. All players on the political scene are new, and they do not have a durable reputation. The only exceptions are splinters and successors of the Communist Party of the Soviet Union. These are the parties that most resemble the Western pattern as organizations, and they have a large number of ideologically motivated followers as well, loyal to them from preindependence days. The remaining voters are guided by the images of leaders presented to them by the mass media.

Generally speaking, there are many more political leaders who want to head political parties than there are ideologies. To serve these ambitions, parties continue to come into being and pretend to ideological peculiarity. However, this is always only self-labeling, sometimes self-suggestion, and more often mere electioneering tactics. The ease that characterizes the transfer of activists from one party to another and the formation of the most inconceivable alliances show that all this is not more than simulation.

These factors determine the instability of party systems in the countries under examination. New parties arise before nearly every election. The fragmentation of party systems is high even in the Baltic States. Not long ago the political forces in those states were divided in accordance with their attitude towards the former Moscow metropolis. However, recent elections in Lithuania, Latvia, and Estonia brought success to new actors and changed the party disposition on the scene. Unexpectedly for many experts, the consolidation of party systems did not occur. One can say that continuing discussions about the consolidation of new democracies have been belied by the ongoing destabilization of the party systems. In other cases the consolidation of regimes after the first years of radical party pluralism have meant a greater (in Belarus) or lesser (in Russia) decline of democracy.

Simultaneously, widespread hopes that the establishment of parliamentary systems (versus the "perils of presidentialism") would promote democratic development were not realized.[13] After communists came to power in Moldova (one of the few parliamentary systems in the former Soviet Union), political competition has been reduced. Institutional design has facilitated party strength in the Baltic States as well as in Moldova but has not been favorable for party building in Ukraine, Russia, and Belarus. Institutional conditions should not be overestimated; they are not decisive. The problem is not how to make the government responsible to the parties in parliament, but rather to make them both—parties and government—responsible to the citizens.[14]

Meanwhile the linkages between parties and citizens are very weak in all post-Soviet countries. The firm view that political parties serve their own interests instead of the interests of their voters is so widespread that it seems to be true. Disappointment with the ineffectiveness of democratic institutions, including political parties, has helped to strengthen the successors of the Communist Party in many post-Soviet countries. Even the success of Lukashenko's attack on democracy in Belarus can be explained to a considerable extent by the citizens' attitude to newly formed democratic parties. After coming to power, post-Soviet parties have mainly worked as individual or group lobbyists upholding particular private interests in legislative or executive bodies. It is hardly worth explaining that the little public trust in political parties is only "a reaction against the earlier enforced communist 'partyism.'"[15]

This is quite natural, taking into account the fact that political parties in new democracies do not depend on society in large part. In the best case they financially depend on the state, in the rest of the cases on private business, and frequently on both, but with dominance of the second. With sponsors' help and through mass media, parties manipulate mass consciousness during elections and receive legitimization through democratic procedures. However, in the final analysis they are instruments in the struggle between different parts of the elite, and above all of the economic elite. The reason lies in the inseparability of power and property in post-Soviet territory.

The monopoly on state property was practically ubiquitous in the Soviet Union. The process of privatization that followed was and still is going on under the rules assigned by state bureaucrats. Therefore business is highly connected with and depends on the state, giving rise to corruption and widespread lobbying activity. In addition, this lobbying activity, by force of historical circumstance, is poorly regulated. Quite naturally, part of the Soviet bureaucracy (nomenclature), which had controlled state property, kept for itself a great deal of authority and converted it into private property. Hence powerful parties of power have risen above ideological distinctions. This continuity of elites determined the continuity of very important social structures. The members of the elite brought with them not only former connections, but also habits, traditions, and business ethics in general. The more radical change of the elite during revolutions, determined by national history and by the view of communist rule as foreign supremacy, limited the influence of these factors in the Baltic countries and led to a more successful establishment of liberal regimes.

Nevertheless, most parties are still created by different parts of the economic elite. Impulses from other strata are practically nonexistent. Their interests are deeply secondary. No wonder electoral participation is not high, public trust in political parties is very low, and vote volatility is permanent almost everywhere in the post-Soviet states. The lack of strong intermediate structures as well as of any forms of citizens' political activity and public control over parties beyond elections make the gap between the rulers and the ruled particularly tangible. The desire to make up for these shortcomings by the intensive use of market-campaign technologies produces a more radical version of the electoral professional party model known in the West.[16]

Meanwhile, the traits of political parties so much desired by post-Soviet reformers refer in the best case to the past of Western democracies and often represent a theoretical norm that had never existed in practice even in the West. It is no mere chance that recent research in transitology bears a strong resemblance to the resourcefulness of Soviet social science, which tried to explain the delayed advent of communism by making necessary ever new stages on the road to it: first "building of the bases" of socialism, then "construction of socialism completely and definitively," then "developed socialism." If the Soviet system had not been dismantled, apparently some more stages on the path to the great aim would have been substantiated theoretically. In transitologists' theory, *communism* is replaced by *liberal democracy*, but the logic is roughly the same: the achievement (sometime or other) of a normative pattern is not called into question. True, in this case the pattern is not so utopian and even has actual historical realization. However, torn out of the contemporary context (which also means the process of global interactions and transformations), it assumes the character of a myth. This myth-making process is seen in all the nations discussed in this book.

The new organizations do not look like parties of mass integration at all. Newly formed parties in new democracies bear much more resemblance to the new tendencies in party development in the West than to the above-mentioned authoritative pattern. They can be called label parties because they serve simply as trademarks for electoral promotion.

The role of leaders is crucial everywhere. As a rule new parties are organized around leaders and represent a kind of personal clientele. Squabbles between leaders or unsuccessful changes in a leader's career may provoke a party split or the disappearance of an organization. More often parties are much more interested in having famous politicians as party members than these politicians are in being associated with any party. This is often true even for communist parties, which may be quite useful for campaigning but undesirable later on. When promoted, a leader aims to get rid of his party label. As a matter of fact, prominent politicians do not need parties. On the contrary: parties need them. Parties compete with each other to invite well-known leaders to become their "face."

It is not mere chance that presidents in some post-Soviet states are not affiliated with a party. Their campaigns are waged beyond any party structures with the help of hired professionals. Even if they rest upon some party or parties during elections, they prefer to remain outside any organization. Regional leaders in Russia, for example, do not like to be connected in public opinion with any definite party. If elected by party lists, after winning they seek, under this or that pretence, to avoid party control, to the point of leaving an organization.

So-called new political technologies (political marketing) and the services of political consulting firms are used very actively. These firms, hidden behind parties and politicians, organize the whole electoral process: they collect signatures if necessary, do preliminary research on the political market, and determine strategy and tactics, as well as manage the campaign, produce advertisements, and so on. The only thing left for citizens to do is to vote. And what is more, in contrast to traditional parties' modus operandi, instead of seeking to persuade voters about their political projects, new parties work out their electoral proposals (visual images) in accordance with the results of marketing research, which reflect the transient demands of the market. Thus, the relations between parties and citizens have changed directions. Electoral tactics absolutely dominate over programs, making possible the rise of the rule of representations instead of representative rule.[17] The ways of financing are also similar to the recent trends in old democracies, with all the consequences mentioned above.[18]

These tendencies worry political scientists and politicians in the West. The 1990s will be remembered not only as years during which new democracies emerged, but also as "the years during which serious questions were raised about the future of the main instruments of liberal democracy, the political parties, in many, if not in all Western European countries."[19] Researchers write about the general decline of party membership.[20] In spite of the declared aspiration to reinforce ordinary members' and non-party voters' influence on the elaboration of party decisions and candidate selection, actually quite the reverse is happening. Yet the leaders' roles increase. More and more frequently they appeal over party members' heads directly to the voters, who in their turn are not able to control the activity of professional politicians effectively. At the same time citizens' political allegiances have become much more volatile; stable identifications with parties are noticeably declining.[21] New conceptual models are proposed, such as the electoral-professional party, cartel party, or party–business firm.[22] They are based on changes in party organization, in the system of ties between state and society, in ways of finance and ways of campaigning, and so on.

Newly formed parties in post-Soviet countries are not moving towards a similarity with old powerful Western organizations, and less so with their previous historical models. If one looks at them closely, they are much more similar to newly formed parties in the West, the parties that have arisen recently or are arising before our eyes. The process of this kind of party formation seems to have a global character.

It is clear that the contemporary world where the democratization of post-Soviet countries is going on is not quite the same as the world in which Western democracies arose. The common feature of this group of countries is that all of them are carrying out radical reforms in a postindustrial globalizing world, where factors like new ways of communications work everywhere, cross frontiers, and deeply influence processes inside a country irrespective of historical traditions and the level of economic development.

Among the factors that have determined the process of the "third wave of democratization," S. Huntington has noted the "demonstration effects," or, in other words, the contagious, diffusive, and emulous character of the process—the snowball phenomenon. In his opinion, the reason behind the formerly unprecedented importance of demonstration effects during the third wave is "the tremendous expansion in global communications and transportation that occurred in the decades after World War II and particularly the blanketing of the world by television and communications satellites in the 1970s."[23] As a result, it became "increasingly difficult for authoritarian governments to keep from their elites and even their publics information on the struggles against and overthrow of authoritarian regimes in other countries. Thanks in large part to the impact of global communications, by the mid-1980s the image of a 'worldwide democratic revolution' undoubtedly had become a reality in the minds of political and intellectual leaders in most countries of the world. Because people believed it to be real, it was real in its consequences."[24] How the demonstration effects worked in the Soviet Union, as well as inside post-Soviet territory, is apparent in the chapters of this book.

However, it is also evident that side by side with the process of globalization, which is so much written about, the very real revolution in the means of political communication should be taken into account in analyzing political processes in new democracies. This revolution not only gives rise to demonstration effects in Huntington's sense, which means following Western patterns, but also forms an environment if not identical, then in some sense reflective of factors transforming political institutions in old democracies now.

New ways of communication have had a great impact on political parties in the West, largely giving rise to the process of power virtualization, the growing priority of leadership, electoral-professional changes in organization, and the dominance of marketing forms of campaigning. All post-Soviet countries had started the party-building process in a globalizing world and in a modern communicative situation. Therefore, quite unexpectedly for our Western colleagues, some phenomena not only similar to the most contemporary tendencies but also radical could arise here. These radical forms do not mean the best for the functioning of democracy as a political regime. Simply put, the restrictions (structures, traditions, and relations) inherited by Western countries from the past that are able to neutralize to some extent the undemocratic effects of certain modern factors are absent or extremely weak in the new democracies. While institutions that have a long history and that sprang up in different conditions are slowly transformed and adapt to new circumstances, their newly formed copies can be more susceptible to new trends, including primarily the negative ones.

According to Huntington, "the impact of the demonstration effects did not depend significantly on the existence of economic and social conditions favorable to democracy in the recipient country." Due to the demonstration effects the speed of democratization accelerated like a snowball: "In Poland, as the phrase went, democratization took ten years, in Hungary ten months, in East Germany ten weeks, in Czechoslovakia ten days, and in Romania ten hours."[25] However, new political forms and technologies did not plunge into the same social and cultural environment everywhere. The results of these transplantations may greatly differ from each other.

It is evident today that the overthrow of communist governments by no means led to the establishment of liberal regimes everywhere. Many characteristics of the new governments were determined by contexts and by "the existence of economic and social conditions favorable to democracy."[26] In some post-Soviet countries early democracies degenerated into autocracies of different kinds, where democratic institutions kept their form but lost content. In these cases political parties became mere facades.

However, there are some common trends inherent in the contemporary development of democracy. Summing up the research of political parties in Eastern and Central Europe, Kay Lawson writes: "The forces at work—the impact of the global economy, the ever more open pursuit of political power as an instrument for controlling the distribution of a nation's wealth, and the developments in modern communication—are forces that are presently changing the nature of cleavages, party politics, and voter responses across the globe."[27]

It has turned out that "the third wave of democratization" is something much more complicated than simple quantitative and territorial expansion of democracy. However "scholars are only now groping their way towards taking stock of the ambiguous implications of globalization for democratization."[28] We see how the military-political, financial, and criminal sides of globalization outstrip its institutional, legal, and democratic aspects. The formation of global society is not a mechanical expansion of Western influence. We are dealing with the process of *global change,* which possesses unity and universality. Not only yesterday's dictatorships but also yesterday's democracies are in transit now. The results of these transformations are still hard to describe exactly, although they are obviously not identical with the old system of mass representative democracy.

It almost seems as if in the very course of the presumed wave of democratization the representative democratic paradigm is losing out. This paradox shows itself specifically in the ineffective attempts made by postcommunist countries to reproduce the classic patterns of political institutionalization in Western liberal democracies. The political regimes that have arisen from these efforts differ greatly from each other. They could, and even should, be ranged in accordance with the level of liberty. That is what Freedom House does successfully.[29] However, even the most liberal among them could hardly be considered fully democratic, if by this we mean the pattern they tried to imitate when beginning their reforms. That pattern was based on the traditional view of democracy as the rule of the majority of the population acting through institutions of representation. The fruits of the process of imitation differ from this ideal. Parties and elections have been put through the most difficult trials. These institutions, which had played a key role in the formation of mass representative democracies in the West, are now seriously transformed. The failure of the attempts by new democracies to make their own versions following antiquated twentieth-century European models is already quite evident. Even the most liberal (according to Freedom House classification) postcommunist countries have not succeeded in reproducing them, unlike the dictatorships that were democratized after the Second World War or the countries in Southern Europe that started the so-called third wave. Instead, it is being discovered that the desired pattern has been left irrevocably in the past. Although the Western democracies may bear the stamp of the past, new trends in their development require new efforts at comprehension and new theoretical approaches as well.

However, not only politicians but also political scientists still declare that in the future voters will become more active and more civic, that parties will be more rooted in society, that they will receive ideological peculiarity and a stable organizational structure and will represent the interests of wide social strata. In practice, all participants in the recent wave of democratization have moved from more or less diligent *imitation* of traditional democratic patterns to its intentional or unintentional *simulation*.

Not long ago Phillipe Schmitter wrote about "a near-total absence of experimentation with new institutions in these neodemocracies," and about their tendency to imitate what is usually considered the democratic norm, but what actually is to a large extent the "absolutely routine practices of Western democracies" already in discredit and decline. To his mind, such creative sterility and emphasis on the imitation of Western patterns could bring at best the emergence of "a rather pale reflection" of Western institutions.[30] However, the emphasis on imitation may in fact mean the mere simulation (deliberate or not) of the Western pattern, masking the rise of absolutely new practices.

At one time, rulers of medieval Europe aspired to reproduce the experience of the ancient Roman state, which struck them as very successful. They tried to transfer to their native ground the admired patterns by imitating Roman political symbols and ceremonies, by the diligent adoption of Roman power institutions and relations. It is well known today how much the fruit of these efforts differed from the "normative model." Nevertheless, it is doubtful that today anybody would venture to call it a "pale reflection" of the pattern.

Notes

CHAPTER 1

1. We are using the definition of *politics* from Kay Lawson, *The Human Polity*, (Boston, New York: Houghton Mifflin Company, 1999), p. G–9.

2. *Nations in Transit 2003: Democratization in East Central Europe and Eurasia*, Rowman & Littlefield Publishers, copublished with: Freedom House, 2003. http://www.freedomhouse.org/research/nattransit.htm.

Freedom House publishes annual assessments of the state of democratization by assigning each of 27 countries of Central and Eastern Europe and the former Soviet Union the status of "Consolidated democracies," "Democracies (some consolidation)," "Transitional governments or hybrid regimes," "Autocracies," or "Consolidated autocracies" by averaging of ratings for Electoral Process, Civil Society, Governance, and Independent Media ratings. Those whose ratings average up to two are generally considered "Consolidated democracies," two to four are "Democracies," four to five are "Transitional governments or hybrid regimes," five to six "Autocracies," and six to seven "Consolidated autocracies."

3. *Nations in Transit 2003*, p. 498.

4. Jacques Rupnik, "The Postcommunist Divide," *Journal of Democracy* 10 (1) January 1999: 57–62.

5. Thomas Carothers, "The End of the Transition Paradigm," *Journal of Democracy* 13 (1), January 2002: 5–21.

6. Kenneth Janda, *Political Parties: A Cross-National Survey* (New York, London: The Free Press, 1980), p. xiii.

7. Seymour Lipset and Stein Rokkan, "Cleavage Structure, Party System and Voter Alignments: An Introduction," in *Party Systems and Voter Alignments: Cross-National Perspectives*, ed. Seymour Lipset and Stein Rokkan (New York, London: The Free Press, 1967).

8. Rupnik, "The Postcommunist Divide," p. 57.

9. Amanda Schnetzer, "Nations in Transit 2003: Milestones," in *Nations in Transit 2003*, p. 9.

10. *Nations in Transit 2003*, p. 127.

11. Ibid., p. 435.

12. Ibid., p. 607.

CHAPTER 2

1. Viktor Sogrin, *Politicheskaya istoriya sovremennoi Rossii. 1985–2001: ot Gorbacheva do Putina.* (Moscow: Izdatel'stvo "Ves' Mir", 2001) (Political History of Contemporary Russia), p. 41.

2. Michael McFaul, Nikolai Petrov, and Andrei Ryabov (eds.), *Russia in the Course of 1999–2000 Election Cycle* (Moscow: Carnegie Center; Moscow: Gendalf, 2000), http://pubs.carnegie.ru/english/, p. 611.

3. *Nations in Transit 2003: Democratization in East Central Europe and Eurasia* (Rowman & Littlefield Publishers, copublished with Freedom House, 2003), http://www.freedomhouse.org/research/nattransit.htm, p. 5.

4. The notion "authoritarian-bureaucratic regime" has been introduced by Lilia Shevtsova in "Between Stabilization and a Breakthrough: Interim Results of Vladimir Putin's Presidency," *Briefing Paper* 1, January, 2002 (Moscow: The Carnegie Moscow Center): http://pubs.carnegie.ru/english/.

5. The chapter develops ideas presented in Anatoly Kulik and Susanna Pshizova, "Political Parties in the Post-Soviet Space: A Unique Response to the Context or a Future of the Western Model?" prepared for the XVIII World Congress of the International Political Science Association, 1–5 August 2000, Quebec, and in Anatoly Kulik, "To Prosper in Russia: Parties Deep in the Shadow of the President," in *When Parties Prosper*, ed. Kay Lawson and Peter Merkl (in progress).

6. Viktor Sogrin, 2001.

7. Spravochnik (Izdatel'stvo RAU Press, 1991), 43, 74.

8. Rossiya Segodnya, Politicheskii portret, 1985–1990 gg./Otv. red. B.I. Koval (Moscow: Mezhdunarodnye otnosheniya, 1991), 29.

9. The Public Opinion Foundation, a nonprofit organization for conducting public opinion surveys in Russia in the fields: Politics, The State, Society, Persons and some others,http://english.fom.ru/.

10. In 2003, 48 percent of Russians judged the events of August 1991 as merely one episode in the wrestling for power among the top leadership of the country, 33 percent as having tragic consequences for people and the country, and 9 percent as the victory of democracy (WCIOM Press-release #23, August 18, 2003. http://www.wciom.com).

11. Facing this broad rejection of ongoing transformation, Yeltsin was compelled to distance himself from his own former declarations: "What I want to say to those who proclaim as though Russia is going to capitalism, is that we do not lead Russia to any capitalism. Russia is simply unable to be capitalist. It will not be either in socialism, or in capitalism." See *Argumenty i facty*, 1992, 45.

12. Later the leading role in leftist opposition went over to CPRF, the CPSU successor, reestablished in February 1993. The main issues of its agenda were the reconstitution of state-socialism and the revitalization of Russia as a great world power.

13. *Izvestiya*, June 13, 1992.

14. So, Democratic Party of Russia decreased from about 50,000 members in early 1992 to less then 15,000 by the end of the same year. See Vladimir Gel'man, Grigorii Golosov, and Elena Meleshkina (eds), *Pervyi elektoral'nyi cikl v Rossii (1993–1996)*, (Moscow: Iz-vo "Ves' mir," 2000), p. 92 (The first electoral cycle in Russia, 1993–1996).

15. Viktor Sheinis, "Rossiiskii parlament: desyat' let trudnogo puti," [Russian Parliament: Ten Years of the Hard Way], in *Parlamentarizm i mnogopartiinost' v sovremennoi Rossii*, ed. Vladimir Lysenko (Moscow: ISP, 2000), p. 75.

16. Chapter 1. Article 13. The Constitution of the Russian Federation. http://www.democracy.ru/english/library/laws/constitution_eng/.

17. Vladimir Lysenko, "Desyat' let sovremennogo rossiiskogo parlamentarizma: nekotorye itogi i perspektivy," in *Parlamentarizm i mnogopartiinost' v sovremennoi Rossii*, ed. Vladimir Lysenko (Moscow: ISP, 2000), p. 219 (Ten Years of Contemporary Russian Parliamentarianism: Some Results and Prospects).

18. As Gorbachev mentioned, "A politician may today be in the list of one [electoral] bloc, tomorrow—of another, and the day after tomorrow—on the third list. Utter, cynical pragmatism. Only to get pork, nothing more. So, people get engaged in corruption. ..." *See* Mikhail Gorbachev, "Mnogopartiinost': istoriya i sud'ba," in *Parlamentarizm i mnogopartiinost' v sovremennoi Rossii*, ed. Vladimir Lysenko (Moscow: ISP, 2000), p. 140 (Multiparty System: A History and a Fate, in Parliamentarianism and Multiparty System in Contemporary Russia).

19. The motto "Great Power, Empire, Viva Russia" found support of 65 percent of a national sample with 17 percent against (Monitoring VSIOM #1(21) 1996: 18).

20. Monitoring VSIOM, Monitoring obschestvennogo mneniya: economicheskiye i sozialnye peremeny [Monitoring of the Public Opinion: Economic and Social Changes], no. 2(22) (Moscow: VSIOM, 1996): 5.

21. Lysenko, p. 217.

22. The success of LDPR in the 1993 elections contributed to its growth and made it very attractive for many dubious businessmen with criminal ties as well. See Yurii Korgunyuk, *Sovremennaya rossiiskaya mnogopartiinost'* (Moscow: INDEM, 1999) (Current Russian Multiparty System), p. 287.

23. Russia Votes 2003/2004: A Joint Project of Centre for the Study of Public Policy, U. Strathclyde (Director: Professor Richard Rose) and VCIOM Analytic Agency (Director: Yuri A. Levada), http://www.russiavotes.org/.

24. Monitoring VCIOM #2(22) 1996: 15.

25. "Vlast' i narod. Chto pokazal vserossiiskii opros," *Rossiiskaia Federatsia*, No18/94, 9–11.

26. Monitoring VCIOM #2(22) 1996: 5.

27. A. Dmitriev, "Korrupciya i vlast' v sovremennoi Rossii'," in *Tehnologiii vlasti i upravleniya v sovremennom goudarstve*, (Moscow: MGU, 1999), p. 22.

28. One of the main campaign managers of OVR, Sergey Yastrzhembskii (later Putin's aide on Chechenya) accused the Kremlin of offering $700,000 to one of the principal nominees for leaving the OVR list two weeks before the ballot. *See* http://www.polit.ru/documents/149401.html.

29. Sogrin, p. 231.

30. *Nezavisimaya gazeta*,12 July 2000 (http://ng.ru/politics/2000-07-12/3_show.html).

31. Justifying this action the CPRF leader declared in a TV interview that "democracy is the power of the majority."

32. McFaul et al., p. 380.

33. *Argumenty i Fakty* (21), 2000.

34. Sogrin, p.239.

35. Shevtsova.

36. McFaul et al., p. 611.

37. Vladimir Putin, Speech to Campaign Supporters, February 12, 2004 (In English): (http://putin2004.ru/english/authorized/402D773F).

38. See the official Web site of the Party United Russia: http://www.edinros.ru.

39. From official Internet site of the State Duma: http://www.duma.ru/deputats/fraction.htm.

40. *Izvestiya*, 2 December 2004.

41. Lysenko, p. 221.

42. "Rossiiane o vyborakh v Gosdumu" (Russians on the elections to the State Duma), VCIOM-A Press release #27, 21 November, 2003, www.vciom-a.ru.

43. Thomas Carothers defines this kind of politics as Dominant-Power Politics in "The End of the Transition Paradigm," *Journal of Democracy* 13 (1): 5–21.

44. Central Electoral Commission http://www.izbirkom.ru/izbirkom_protokols/sx/page/protokolin.

45. Obshestvennoe mnenie—2002. Moscow: VCIOM, 2002 (Public opinion—2002) http://www.wciom.ru/vciom/info/cnew/opinion2002.htm.

46. Public Opinion Foundation poll from 4 November 2000, http://www.fom.ru/reports/frames/d002932.html.

47. The Labor Codex of Russian Federations, adopted in December 2001, bestows privileges to Federation of Independent Trade Unions, the descendant of decorative Soviet trade unions that inherited their dependence on government.

48. Vladimir Rimskii, "Nuzhny li Rossii politicheskie partii?," in *Parlamentarizm i mnogopartiinost' v sovremennoi Rossii*, ed. V. Lysenko (Moscow: ISP, 2000), pp. 151–52 (Whether Political Parties Are Needed in Russia).

49. Vladimir Rimskii, "Parlamentarizm v poskommunisticheskoi Rossii: nadezhdy i razocharovaniya," in *Parlamentarizm i mnogopartiinost' v sovremennoi Rossii*, ed. V. Lysenko (Moscow: ISP. 2000), p. 39 (Parliamentarianism in Post-Communist Russia: Expectations and Disillusion).

50. Michael McFaul and Audry Ryabov, eds., *Russian Society: The Establishment of Democratic Values?*, September 1999, p. 206 (http://pubs.carnegie.ru/english/).

51. E.I. Bashkirova, "Transformaciya cennostei rossiiskogo obshestva," *Polis*, 2000, (6), http://www.politstudies.ru/fulltext/2000/6/5.htm.

52. *Izvestia*, 5 March 2004.

53. VCIOM 2002: 53.

54. R. Inglehart, "How Solid is Mass Support for Democracy—And How We Can Measure It?" *Political Science and Politics* 36 (1), 2003, p. 53.

55. *Rossi'skoe obshestvo nakanune prezidentskih vyborov* (Moscow: VCIOM, 2004), http://www.wciom.ru/files/040212.doc, p. 31.

56. Putin.

CHAPTER 3

1. S. Huntington, *The Third Wave: Democratization in the Late Twentieth Century* (Norman: University of Oklahoma Press, 1991).

2. In accordance with the data of research carried on in the Republic of Belarus by the Russian Sociological service database of the "Fond obsrestvennoie mnenige" [Public Opinion Fund] in April 1994, http://www.fom.ru.

3. The left wing, by the results of the parliamentary elections, looked quite strong. Five parliamentary factions were formed in the Supreme Soviet of the 13th call: communists (45 people), agrarians (49 people), liberal Grazhdanskoe deistvie (Civic action) (18 people), propresident faction Soglasie (Agreement) (61 people), social-democratic faction Sojuz truda (Union of Labor) (15 people).

4. At the elections to local councils in April 1999 there was already a tendency of sudden switches in party preferences of the electorate. Trust in the representatives of political parties reduced visibly, as did the activity of the parties. Parties made up only 4.8 percent of the candidacies and won only 3 percent of the vote. In 2000, 97 people's deputies were elected to the Chamber of Representatives of the National Council of the Republic of Belarus. The representatives of eight political parties and public unions received deputy mandates. In the parliament six people represent the propresident Communist Party of Belarus, five the Agrarian Party, two the Republic Party of Labour and Justice, one the Social-Democratic Party of People's Agreement, one the Social-Sportive Party, one the Liberal-Democratic Party, one the United Civic Party, and one the Belarusian Public Union (Apple). It is necessary to note that a part of the opposition parties boycotted elections in 1999 and 2000.

5. If in April 1996 the opposition managed to bring to the streets more than 100 thousand people, at the present time a 10-thousand-people demonstration in Minsk (with the population of two million) is a great success. Ratings of all the political parties without exception are very low, and the opposition parties did not manage to persuade the European politicians of the necessity to continue a politics of isolation in respect to Belarus—the Belarusian parliament is accepted to the Parliamentary Assembly of Europe. Local councils elections (March 2003) took place practically on a non-alternative basis—a significant number of the deputies is made up of the employees at local administrations and nonparty (teachers, doctors) deputies; the representatives of political parties and democratic movements received only about one percent of mandates.

6. The essence of the constitutional reform happened to be perverted. A change to the parliamentary republic was necessary for Voronin to become president, after which he gained control over all the institutions of power. As a result the constitutional principle of power division is observed only nominally.

7. In accordance with the data of the poll "Public opinion barometer," carried out by the Institute of Public Policy in December 2001. (Moldavian Vedomosti 70 [413], 5 Dec. 2001).

8. In Tiraspol 27 Feb. 2003 there took place for the second time in 2003 a round of negotiations in a five-side format (Russia, Moldavia, Pridnjestrovie, Ukraine, and OSCE) about regulation of the Pridnjestrovie conflict. Participants of the meeting worked on the project of the future status of Pridnjestrovie on the basis of the project of agreement about federalization of Moldova, suggested by the mediators in conflict regulation in July of the previous year in Kiev. The project of agreement provides for the creation of the federation of subjects in Moldova. In accordance with the documents, preservation of single currency, army, security bodies, or customs with differentiation of powers between the center and subjects of federation are envisaged. (27 Feb. 2003 INTERFAX).

9. It should be noted that the first parliaments in Ukraine, Moldova, and Belarus were elected in the Soviet period, and representation of the Soviet party-economic nomenclature was extremely strong, and that the first parliamentary elections in the independent states took place in Moldova and Ukraine in 1994 and in Belarus in 1995. Nevertheless, the influence of the representatives of people's fronts in the parliaments of all three states before the first national democratic elections was extremely strong. During the first years of independence their programs were realized almost completely and the movements of national revival exhausted their potential. Unpopular economic reforms were strongly connected with these parties in mass consciousness, which led to a rapid loss of their authority in the political process.

10. In 1995 in Belarus the communists and the agrarians formed the largest factions in the Supreme Soviet of the XIII call. In Ukraine the communists and socialists had strong positions in the parliament in 1994, and they got even stronger in 1998; their strong representation is preserved in the Supreme Rada after the elections of 2002. In Moldova the communists participated successfully in the elections of 1998, in 2000 they won parliament, secured their candidate in the office of president, and formed the government. In 2005 they won 46.1 percent of the votes. In Belarus, Moldova, and Ukraine the communist parties are the only political organizations with a developed, strictly structured network of primary party structures, inherited from the Soviet times, which provides them with constant and reliable contact with the population.

11. In parallel with the administration's efforts to strengthen executive power, taking place on the pretext of "strengthening of the president's vertical [axis]," the Supreme Soviet of the XIII call also made attempts—unsuccessfully—to transform the legislation in a cardinal way: to change to a parliamentary republic, including completely annulling the post of the president and changing the electoral system to a proportional one, and also reducing the voters' attendance barrier to the electoral districts. As a result, in November 1996 two projects of constitutional changes were proposed for the referendum—one packet was developed by the parliament, the other by the administration of the president. However, the parliament was in informational isolation at that time and did not have the administrative resources for controlling the organization of the voting procedure and the calculation of votes, which was why the victory of the president's project of changes in the constitution was predictable.

12. In accordance with the new election code, passed before the last parliamentary elections (2000), persons who committed administrative offenses could not register as candidates, which automatically excluded the majority of opposition leaders (who were repeatedly subjected to political arrests) from participation in the election process. Just before the elections of 2003 to the local councils (during the period of the candidates' nomination) the central electoral committee "interpreted the spirit of the law," explaining that there must exist officially registered primary organizations in the administrative units where party candidates will be nominated, though the legislation did not require them to register.

13. The conflict between the branches of power in Belarus led to the most tragic consequences for the political parties. The representation of the party deputies in the parliament was reduced from 52 percent in 1995 to 18.5 percent in 2000 owing substantively to manipulation of the majority system by the executive power at the parliamentary elections.

14. Moldova is a sphere of strategic interests of Ukraine, a partner in numerous bilateral and multilateral projects. A range of agreements about cooperation was signed between the countries (about non-visa trips of citizens, about mutual acceptance and equivalence of documents, about academic and scientific degrees, about economic and scientific-technical cooperation in the sphere of agriculture, about cooperation between the Ministries of Justice, etc.).

15. The Central European initiative is a forum for provision of cooperation in the region and one of the elements of stability and cooperation in Europe; it does not substitute for any other mechanisms of cooperation and does not influence the international obligations of the member states. The activity of CEI develops in the following directions: as transport, environmental protection, science and technology, struggle against organized crime and international terrorism, problems of national minorities, migration, youth exchanges, and inter-border cooperation.

16. There is a lot of evidence that the opinion of the electorate is hardly interesting for any political leaders during the period between elections: legitimate parliament was dismissed in Belarus and mass actions are put down severely; in Moldova, achievement of tactical interests of the most influential political groups was accompanied by losing the possibility for the population to elect the president directly; in Ukraine, because of the threat to the clan interests, the parliament dismissed the government of V. Jushcenko, which achieved significant success in the sphere of economic reforms, in spite of the fact that the activity of the government was positively assessed by more than half of the population, and the level of trust for the Superior Rada was extremely low.

CHAPTER 4

1. Official results of the presidential election in Belarus, September 9, 2001: Alexander Lukashenko: 75.6 percent, Uladzimir Gancharik: 15.4 percent, Siargei Gaidukevich: 2.5 percent, Turnout: 83.9 percent (Radio Free Europe/Radio Liberty Newsline, Vol.5, No.171, Part II, 10 September 2001).

2. Best examples are the infamous "alternative" presidential election in 1999, organized by the opposition to overthrow the illegitimate president, scandalous parliamentary elections in 2000 with opposition parties boycotting the regime, and in culmination, the persuasive victory of President Alexander Lukashenko, in the rigged election of 2001.

3. See summer issues of Radio Free Europe/Radio Liberty, 2001 for allegations made against OSCE Ambassador Georg Wieck, and the U.S. Ambassador Michael Kozak (http://www.rferl.org/newsline). Lukashenko's preelection popularity score remained reasonably high and stable (42–45 percent), despite alleged accusations of abducting and assassinating his political opponents. See E. Korosteleva et.al. (eds.), *Contemporary Belarus: Between Democracy and Dictatorship* (London: Curzon Press, 2002).

4. Within the structure-oriented framework the following directions can be identified: (a) the neoinstitutionalist approach views political instability as a dysfunction of the institutional environment that fails to provide complex realization of political participation and to meet rising public expectations of the modern world; (b) the structural approach sees parties signifying important political cleavages, which should channel mass protest with leadership representation; and (c) cultural analysis that regards political systems as expressing the ethos of a given

social milieu, and consequently dependent on the cultural mode and long-lasting traditions and legacies of society in the process of consolidation. An alternative theoretical perspective that views the mode of transitions and the outcomes of the regime change as path-dependent is the process-oriented approach. Within this framework the most notable structured analytical attempt belongs to rational choice theory, which sees political actors as responding rationally to the opportunities provided by formal institutional settings within a given social environment.

5. See S. Huntington, *The Third Wave: Democratization in the Late Twentieth Century* (Norman: University of Oklahoma Press, 1991); G. O'Donnell, "Delegative Democracy," *Journal of Democracy* 5 (1), 1994: 55–69; J.J. Linz and A. Stepan, *Problems of Democratic Transition and Consolidation: Southern Europe, South America and Post-Communist Europe* (Baltimore, MD: Johns Hopkins University Press, 1996).

6. D. Furman et al., *Belorussiya i Rossiya: Obschestva i Gosudarstva* (Belarus and Russia: Societies and States) (Moscow: Prava Cheloveka, 1998); D. Marples, *Belarus: The Denationalized Nation: Post-Communist States and Nations* (Amsterdam: Harwood Academic Publications, 1999); V. Silitski, "Explaining Post-Communist Authoritarianism in Belarus," in Korosteleva, *Contemporary Belarus,* ch.3, etc.

7. Independent nationalist movements in Belarus started formally in 1902 with the emergence of the Belarusian Revolutionary Hramada, which was subsequently renamed the Belarusian Socialist Hramada in 1903. Apparently, the idea of nationhood had become dominant long before the beginning of the century with the emergence of mass nationalist movements such as Land and Freedom and Talk. The Belarusian Socialist Hramada, though, was the first exclusively Belorusian party, with a definite program and a clear nationalist stance. In temporal alliance with the communists (to secure national statehood) it mobilized most of the population of Belarus, of which 74.6 percent considered themselves Belarusians. See S.L. Guthier, "The Belorussians: National Identification and Assimilation, 1897–1970," *Soviet Studies,* 29(1,2), 1977. During the Revolution period other nationalist political parties and organizations emerged such as the Belarusian People's Hramada, the Belarusian Autonomous Union, and the Christian Democratic Union.

8. H. Kitschelt, "The Formation of Party Systems in East Central Europe," *Politics and Society* 20 (1), 1992: 7–50; H. Kitschelt, "Formation of Party Cleavages in Post-communist Democracies: Theoretical Propositions," *Party Politics* 1 (4), 1995: 447–73.

9. J. Zaprudnik, *The Historical Dictionary of Belarus* (Lahman, MD, London: The Scarecrow Press, 1998); D. Marples, *Belarus*; Silitski, "Explaining Post-communist Authoritarianism in Belarus," ch.3, etc.

10. A full description of events can be found in E. Korosteleva, *Explaining Party System Development in Post-Communist Belarus,* Ph.D. thesis, University of Bath, 2001; Korosteleva, *Contemporary Belarus.*

11. The president's measures against trade unions included alterations in the procedure of paying membership fees, taking away unions' traditional privileges on distributing discount holidays and service for members, expropriating unions' buildings, through-the-roof taxation, and so on.

12. Lukashenko's pledges to defend his loyal deputies were fully fulfilled at the parliamentary elections of 2000. The first runoff was passed by the majority of nonpartisan candidates, two members of the Communist Party of Belarus, three from the Agrarian Party, one from Party of People's Accord (PNS) and one from Social-Sport Party—all progovernmental organizations. For details, see http://

www.rec.gov.by, retrieved in November 2000 (subject to administered access by Belarus' authorities); or http://www.agora.it/elections/election/belarus.htm, retrieved June 2001; or the British Helsinki Committee Report on 2000 elections at http://www.bhhrg.org/belarus/belarus%202000/startpage.htm, retrieved in June 2001.

13. Michael Chigir was a former Prime Minister, who was dismissed by Lukashenko for his liberal views.

14. Silitski, p. 27. See also: Zenon Pozniak, "Praekt yhir," *Naviny* 12, March 1999: 2.

15. D. Rotman, A. Danilov, "President and Opposition: Specific Features of the Belarusian Scene," in Korosteleva, *Contemporary Belarus.*

16. G. Sartori, *Party and Party Systems: A Framework for Analysis,* vol.1 (Cambridge: Cambridge University Press, 1976), p. 72.

17. M. Duverger, *Political Parties* (London: Methuen, 1954).

18. In 1999 the BNF literally withdrew its candidate and refused to participate in the election race because it found that OGP was dishonestly trying to promote its own candidate on others' behalf. In 2001 the fragmented opposition finally agreed to support Vladimir Gancharik, a relatively conservative trade union leader who is not affiliated with any political party; this belated consensus was reportedly only achieved under considerable pressure from the U.S. government. Overall, the United States provided aid of about $50 million to various opposition organizations. See I. Traynor, "Belarusian Foils Dictator-Buster ... for Now," *Guardian,* 14 September 2001, on the alleged activities of the US ambassador to Belarus, Michael Kozak.

19. Huntington, 174, 190.

20. The 2001 presidential election proved its working. What the opposition nevertheless missed is a unity, not the last-moment push into a fickle and temporary alliance of antiestablishment forces.

21. K. Lawson and P.H. Merkl (eds.), *When Parties Fail: Emerging Alternative Organizations* (Princeton, NJ: Princeton University Press, 1988).

22. O. Manaev, "Belorusskii Electorat: Za i Protiv Presidenta" (Belarusian Electorate: For and against the President), *NISAPI News* 1: 22.

23. D.G. Rotman, E.A. Korosteleva, et al., *Kakoy Mi Vidim Nashu Belarus? Dannye operativno-socioloogicheskisch oprosov 1994–1995* [What Kind of Belarus Do We See? The Results of Sociological Observations 1994–1995] (Minsk: Belarusian State University, 1996), Part 3; D. Rotman, "Kakoi mi vidim Belarus?"[What Belarus Can We See?], *Narodnaya Gazeta* [People's Paper], 21 October, 1997: 1, 3; D. Rotman, *Sociological Report 1998-99* (Minsk: Belarusian State University, 1999).

24. Rotman, "President and Opposition."

25. According to other surveys, the number of undecided votes is 47.9 percent (Manaev, 1998) or 54 percent (Belapan, http://www.belapan.com,November 1999), which suggests that about 50 percent of the population on average do not have a clear political stance and may well form a pool of supporters for one of the camps: governmental or oppositional.

CHAPTER 5

1. J. LaPalombara and M. Weiner, *Political Parties and Political Development* (Princeton, NJ: Princeton University Press, 1966), p. 30.

2. On the history of Moldova see Helen Fedor, ed., *A Country Study: Moldova,* The Library of Congress, http://lcweb2.loc.gov/frd/cs/mdtoc.html.

3. Among the illegal political organizations were: Marksmen of Great Stefan (Soroca, 1945–1947), Sword of Justice (Balti, 1947–1948), Party of Freedom (Lapusna, 1949), and Black Army (Ungheni, 1949).

4. Political parties of the Republic of Moldova by Association for Participatory Democracy (Political Parties, Legislation, Elections, Electoral Blocs), http://www.parties.e-democracy.md/en/legislation/politicalparties/i/.

5. The parameter of splits and mergers testifies, according to Lane and Ersson, to the institutionalization of political parties. J.-E. Lane and S.O. Ersson, *Politics and Society in Western Europe,* 2nd ed. (London: Sage Publications, 1999), p. 113.

6. R. Rose and T.M. Mackie, "Do Parties Persist or Fail? The Big Trade-Off Facing Organizations," in *When Parties Fail: Emerging Alternative Organizations,* ed. K. Lawson and P.H. Merkl (Princeton, NJ: Princeton University Press, 1988), p. 536.

7. M. Duverger, *Political Parties: Their Organization and Activity in the Modern State* (London: Methuen, 1964).

8. S. Lipset and S. Rokkan, "Cleavage Structures, Party Systems and Voter Alignments," in *Party Systems and Voter Aligments,* ed. S. Lipset and S. Rokkan (New York: Free Press, 1967), pp.1–84.

9. A. Lijphart, *Democracies: Pattern of Majoritarian and Consensus Government in Twenty-One Countries* (New Haven, CT: Yale University Press, 1984).

10. R. Dahrendorf, "Reflectii asupra Revolutii in Europa," *Editura Humanitas.* (Bucuresti, 1993), pp. 63–64.

11. Political Parties of the Republic of Moldova by Association for Participatory Democracy (Political Parties, Legislation, Elections, Electoral Blocs), http://parties.e-democracy.md/en/legislation/politicalparties.

12. *Political Transformation and the Electoral Process in Post-Communist Europe.* Web site of the Project Based in the Department of Government at the University of Essex, UK. Moldova—Legislation, Election Results, Constituency Data, Candidate Data, http://www2.essex.ac.uk/elect/database/legislationAll.asp?country=moldova&legislation=md94const.

13. La Palombara and Weiner, *Political Parties and Political Development,* p. 23.

14. J. Sartori, *Parties and Party Systems,* vol. 1: *A Framework for Analysis* (Cambridge: Cambridge University Press, 1976).

15. M. Laakso and R. Taagepera, "Effective Number of Parties: A Measure with Application to West Europe," *Comparative Political Studies* 12 (3), 1979.

16. One of the criteria of entry into this group of countries is the stability of the party system. The stability of the party system depends, in J. Blondel's opinion, on the ideological configuration of the party system, represented by the way parties are situated on the left–right political plane (see J. Blondel, "Party Systems and Pattern of Government in Western Democracies," *Revue canadienne de science politique* 1 (2), June 1968: 183–90). In the construction of this table, we use the classification, ideological continuum, and quantitative distinction of the relative importance of political parties that J. Blondel gives in this work. Accordingly, the political party that collected more than 40 percent of votes is a *strong* party (S); that which collected more than 20 percent is an *average* party (a); that which collected approximately 15 percent is an *intermediate* (between average and small) party (i);

that which collected less than 10 percent is a *small* party (s); and that which collected less than 10 percent is an *other* small party (o).

17. Lijphart, *Democracies.* This parameter is obtained as follows: a complex "of cultural-ethnic measurements" ("center-periphery" cleavage)—1; a complex "religious measurement" ("state-church" cleavage)—1; a complex "measurement on the character of settling" ("city-village" cleavage)—0.5; a complex of "social-economic measurement" ("owners-workers" cleavage)—1; a complex "support of the regime"—1; a complex "external measurement"—1; a complex "post material measurement"—0.

CHAPTER 6

1. A. Renney, *Governing of Men* (Manchester: Manchester University Press, 1989) p. 312.

2. S.M. Lipset and S. Rokkan, *Party Systems and Voter Alignments: Cross-National Perspectives* (New York: Free Press, 1967).

3. *Verkhovna Rada of Ukraine: Paradigms and Paradox,* Issue 1 (Kiev: Ukrainian Perspective, 1995) [In Ukrainian], pp. 7, 10.

4. *The Law of Ukraine "About Election of the People's Deputies of Ukraine"* (1997), September 24, [1]541/97-VR. Art. 1, 42 [In Ukrainian].

5. *Verkhovna Rada,* p. 6.

6. A. Tsibenko, *Political Party in Parliament of Ukraine: The Principals of Organization and Functioning* (Kiev: KIS, 1997), p. 26 [In Ukrainian]; *Verkhovna Rada of Ukraine: Informational Reference* (Kiev: NISD, 1998 [In Ukrainian], pp.23–24.

7. *Verkhovna Rada of Ukraine: Paradigms and Paradox,* Issue 4, 1996 (Kiev: Ukrainian Perspective, 1996) [In Ukrainian], pp. 31–32.

8. Calculated from the data provided in the collection: *Vybory '98: Yak Ukraïna Rolosuvala* [Election '98. As Ukraine voted] (Kiev: KIS, 1998) [In Ukrainian].

9. M. Tomenko, "Results of Parliamentary Elections in Ukraine: Political Orientations and Preferences of the Population, *Polis* (3), 1998: 75 [In Russian].

10. It is necessary to note that after the change of Verkhovna Rada's leadership at the beginning of 2000, political parties have maintained their influence in the legislature: the speaker, his first deputy, and the majority of the heads of parliamentary committees represented political parties.

11. Constitution of Ukraine: adopted by the Verkhovna Rada of Ukraine, June 28, 1996 [In Ukrainian], Art. 78, 113, 114, 115, 118.

12. *Newsletter of the 4th Session of the Verkhovna Rada of Ukraine of 12th Convocation* (1991) Sitting Dec. 5. Kiev [In Ukrainian], p. 7.

13. Calculated from the official data of ballot results of the first round of presidential elections 31 Oct. 1999, displayed on the Central Electoral Committee official Web site [www.cvk.ukrpack.ua].

14. *The Government Courier* June 24, 1997 [In Ukrainian].

15. M. Duverger, *Political Parties: Their Organization and Activity in the Modern State* (London: Methuen, 1954; New York: Wiley, 1963).

16. M. Laakso and R. Taagepera, "Effective Number of Parties: A Measure with Application to West Europe, *Comparative Political Studies* 12 (3), 1979.

17. M. Eagles and L. Johnston, *Politics: An Introduction to Modern Democratic Government* (Peterborough, Ontario: Broadview Press, 1999), p. 330; R Taagapera

and M. Shugart, *Seats and Votes: The Effects and Determinants of Electoral Systems* (New Haven, CT: Yale University Press, 1989).

18. A. Lijphart, *Democracies: Patterns of Majoritarian and Consensus Government in Twenty-One Countries* (New Haven, CT: Yale University Press, 1984).

19. S.P. Huntington, "Political Development and Political Decay," *World Politics* 17: p. 394.

20. K. Janda, *Political Parties: A Cross-National Survey* (New York: Free Press, 1980).

21. J.E. Lane and E. Ersson, *Politics and Society in Western Europe.* 2nd ed. (London: Sage Publications, 1999), p. 113; R.H. Dix, "Democratization and the Institutionalization of Latin American Political Parties," *Comparative Political Studies* 24, 488–511; Janda, pp. 143–44, 155.

22. R. Rose and T.M. Mackie, "Do Parties Persist or Fail? The Big Trade-Off Facing Organizations," in *When Parties Fail: Emerging Alternative Organizations*, ed. K. Lawson and P.H. Merkl (Princeton, NJ: Princeton University Press, 1988), p. 536.

23. Tomenko, p. 79.

24. A. Lijphart, "Constitutional Alternatives for New Democracies," *Polis* (2), 1995 [In Russian]: 140; M. Wallerstain,"Electoral Systems, Parties and Political Stability, *Polis* (5–6), 1992 [In Russian]: 162; J.J. Linz, "The Perils of Presidentialism," *Journal of Democracy,* 1, 1990: 51–69; S. Mainwaring, "Presidentialism in Latin America," *Latin American Research Review,* 25(1), 1990: pp. 157–79.

CHAPTER 7

1. Michael McFaul, *The Fourth Wave: Democracy and Dictatorship in the Post-Communist World,* paper prepared for delivery at the Annual APSA meeting, San Francisco, August 30–September 2, p. 2.

2. Claus Offe, "Capitalism by Democratic Design? Democratic Theory Facing the Triple Transition in East-Central Europe," in *Economic Institutions, Actors and Attitudes: East Central Europe in Transition,* ed. Gyorgy Lengyl, Claus Offe, and Jochen Tholen (Budapest: University of Economic Sciences, 1992), p. 14.

3. Frank Aarebrot and Terje Knutsen Terje, "Introduction," in *Politics and Citizenship on the Eastern Baltic Seaboard: The Structuring of Democratic Politics from North-West Russia to Poland,* ed. Frank Aarebrot and Terje Knutsen (Kristiansand: Nordic Academic Press, 2000), p. 21.

4. For instance, see: Frank Aarebrot and Terje Knutsen, "Comparative Perspectives," in Aarebrot and Knutsen, *Politics and Citizenship on the Eastern Baltic Seaboard*, p. 307.

5. Sten Berglund, Tomas Hellen, and Frank Aarebrot, "Foundations of Change," in *The Handbook of Political Change in Eastern Europe,* ed. Sten Berglund, Tomas Hellen, and Frank Aarebrot (London: Edward Elgar, 1998), p.10.

6. Ibid., p. 9.

7. Ibid., p. 10.

8. Ibid., p. 11.

9. Tomas Hellen, Sten Berglund, and Frank Aarebrot, "The Challenge of History in Eastern Europe," in Berglund et al., *The Handbook of Political Change in Eastern Europe,* pp. 21–22.

10. Darius Žėruolis, "Lithuania," in Berglund et al., *The Handbook of Political Change in Eastern Europe*, pp. 126–27.

11. Ibid., p. 139.

12. Hans Petter Svege and Christer D. Daatland, "Estonia," in Aaarebrot and Knutsen, *Politics and Citizenship on the Eastern Baltic Seaboard*, p. 66.

13. Heidi Bottolfs, "Latvia," in Aaarebrot and Knutsen, *Politics and Citizenship on the Eastern Baltic Seaboard*, p. 90.

14. Herman Smith-Sivertsen, "Towards Parties of Elites—or Popularism?" in *Revue Baltique* (8): 27.

15. Mikko Lagerspetz and Henri Vogt, "Estonia," in Berglund et al., *The Handbook of Political Change in Eastern Europe*, p. 76.

16. Leonardo Morlino, "Political Parties and Democratic Consolidation in Southern Europe," in *The Politics of Democratic Consolidation: Southern Europe in Comparative Perspective*, ed. Richard Gunther, Nikiforos P. Diamandorous, and Hans-Jurgen Puhle (Baltimore, MD: The John Hopkins University Press, 1995), p. 315.

17. Yonhyonk Choe, *Institutional Trust in East and Central Europe: A Macro Perspective*, paper prepared for the ECPR General Conference, 6–8 September, 2001, Canterbury, UK, p. 12.

CHAPTER 8

1. For an English translation of the Estonian constitution see the Web site of the consulting company, Vnesh Expert Service: http://www.vescc.com/constitution/estonia-constitution-eng.html

2. Joseph LaPalombara and Myron Wiener, "The Origin and Development of Political Parties," in *Political Parties and Political Development*, ed. Joseph LaPalombara and Myron Wiener (Princeton, NJ: Princeton University Press 1966), pp. 7–21.

3. Maurice Duverger, *Political Parties: Their Organization and Activity in the Modern State* (London: Methuen, 1954, 1969), pp. xxivxxx.

4. Klaus Von Beyme, *Political Parties in Western Democracies* (Aldershot: Gower 1985), pp. 18–22.

5. Seymour Lipset and Stein Rokkan, "Cleavage Structure, Party System and Voter Alignments: An Introduction," in *Party Systems and Voter Alignments: Cross-National Perspectives*, ed. Seymour Lipset and Stein Rokkan (New York: Free Press, 1967), p. 47.

6. See Arend Lijphart, *Democracies: Patterns of Majoritarian and Consensus Government in Twenty-One Countries* (New Haven, CT: Yale University Press, 1984), pp. 127–41.

7. Von Beyme, p. 114.

8. David Arter, *Parties and Democracy in the Post-Soviet Republics: The Case of Estonia* (Aldershot: Dartmouth, 1996, p. 233; Ole Nørgaard, Dan Hindsgaul, Lars Johansen, and Helle Willumsen, *The Baltic States after Independence* (Cheltenham and Brookfield: Edward Elgar, 1996), p. 100; Vello Pettai and Marcus Kreuzer, "Party Politics in the Baltic States: Social Bases and Institutional Context," *East European Politics and Societies* 13 (1), Winter 1999, p.170.

9. Pettai and Kreuzer, "Party Politics in the Baltic States," p.170.

10. Rein Toomla, *Eesti erakonnad, Eesti Entsüklopeediakirjastus,* (Tallinn: Eesti Entsükeopeediakirjastus, 1999), p.272.

11. Signe Aaskivi, "Parteiregistrid võrdluses," *Sõnumileht,* October 26–30, 1998.

12. Marti Taru and Rein Toomla, *Ülevaade valijaskonna eelistustest Tartu linnas,* October 1999, unpublished paper; Marti Taru, "Valimispäeva küsitluse tulemusi," in Rein Toomla et al. (eds.), *Riigikogu valimised 1999* (Tartu: Tartu Ülikooli kirjastus, 1999).

13. Rein Taagepera and Matthew Soberg Shugart, *Seats and Votes: The Effects and Determinants of Electoral Systems* (New Haven, CT: Yale University Press, 1989).

14. Giovanni Sartori, *Parties and Party Systems: A Framework for Analyses,* Vol. I (Cambridge: Cambridge University Press, 1976), pp. 131–84.

15. Alan Ware, *Political Parties and Party Systems* (Oxford: Oxford University Press, 1996), p. 167.

16. Arend Lijphart, *Electoral Systems and Party Systems: A Study of Twenty-Seven Democracies 1945–1990* (Oxford: Oxford University Press, 1994), p. 96.

17. Pettai and Kreuzer, "Party Politics in the Baltic States," p. 164.

18. Nørgaard et al., *The Baltic States after Independence*, p. 97.

19. Arter, *Parties and Democracy in the Post-Soviet Republics,* p.20.

20. Pettai and Kreuzer, "Party Politics in the Baltic States," p. 161.

21. Sartori, *Parties and Party Systems,* pp. 132–33.

22. Arter, *Parties and Democracy in the Post-Soviet Republics*, pp. 194–205.

23. Ibid., p. 194.

24. Marti Taru and Rein Toomla, *Ülevaade avaliku arvamuse uuringust,* June 1998, unpublished paper, p. 9.

25. Taru, Toomla, *Ülevaade valijaskonna eelistustest Tartu linnas;* "Valimispäeva küsitluse tulemusi."

26. Ibid.

27. Arter, *Parties and Democracy in the Post-Soviet Republics,* p. 17.

28. Herbert Kitschelt, "Formation of Party Cleavages in Post-communist Democracies: Theoretical Propositions," *Party Politics* 1, October 1995: 458.

29. Arter, *Parties and Democracy in the Post-Soviet Republics;* Nørgaard et al, *The Baltic States after Independence,* p. 85ff; Pettai and Kreuzer, "Party Politics in the Baltic States."

CHAPTER 9

1. Seymour Martin Lipset and Stein Rokkan, "Introduction," in *Party System and Voter Alignments: Cross-National Perspectives,* ed. Seymour Martin Lipset and Stein Rokkan (New York: The Free Press, 1967), p. 6.

2. Ole Nørgaard, Dan Hindsgaul, Lars Johansen, and Helle Willumsen, *The Baltic States after Independence* (Cheltenham and Brookfield: Edward Elgar, 1996).

3. Joseph LaPalombara and Weiner Myron, "The Origins of Political Parties," in *The West European Party System,* ed. Peter Mair (Oxford: Oxford University Press, 1990), p. 25.

4. J.C. Thomas, *The Decline of Ideology in Western Political Parties* (London: Sage Publications, 1975).

5. Alesandro Pizzorno, "Parties in Pluralism," in *The West European Party System,* ed. P. Mair (New York: Oxford University Press, 1990), p. 61.

6. Quoted from Andris Runcis, "The Citizenship Issues as Creeping Crisis," in *Crisis Management in a Transitional Society: The Latvian Experience*, ed. Eric K. Stern and Dan Hansen. Vol. 12. (Stockholm: Försyarshögskolan, 2000).

7. Osvalds Freivalds, *Latviešu politiskās partijas 60 gados* (Stockholm: Imanta, 1961), pp. 83–147.

8. Imants Mednis, "Politiskās Partijas Latvijas Republikā," *Latvijas Arhīvi* (3), 1995.

9. Juris Dreifelds, *Latvia in Transition* (Cambridge: Cambridge University Press, 1996); Ilmārs Mežs,. "Pārmaiņas Latvijas Iedzīvotāju Etniskajā Sastāvā 20.gadsimtā," *Latvijas Zinātķu Akadēmijas Vēstis* (5/6), 1995.

10. Juris Dreifelds, "Demographic Trends in Latvia," *Nationalities Paper*, vol. 12, no.1 (Charleston: IL, 1984).

11. Heinrihs Strods, "Genocīda Galvenās Formas un Mērķi Latvijā, 1940–1985," in *Komunistiskā Totalitārisma un Genocīda Prakse Latvijā* (Rīga: Zinātne, 1992); Egils Levits, "Latvija Padomju Varā. Stagnācijas Periods no 1960. līdz 1985.gadam," *Latvijas Vēsture* (3), 1991.

12. Latvijas Republikas Valsts Statistikas Komiteja. Rīga, 1992.

13. Graham Smith, *The Nationalities Question in Soviet Union* (Cambridge: Cambridge University Press, 1990).

14. Nils Muiznieks, "Latvia: Origins, Evolution and Triumph," in *Nations and Politics in the Soviet Successor States*, ed. Ian Bremmer and Ray Taras (Cambridge: Cambridge University Press, 1993).

15. Donald L. Horovitz, *Ethnic Groups in Conflict* (Berkeley and Los Angeles: University of California Press, 1985).

16. Ilga Apine, "Staļinisma Recidīvs," *Horizonts* (4), R'iga, 1989.

17. Romuald Misiunas and Rein Taagepera, *The Baltic States: Years of Dependence 1940–1990* (London: University of California Press, 1993).

18. B. Wessels and H-D.Klingemann, *Democratic Transformation and the Prerequisites of Democratic Opposition in East and Central Europe* (Berlin: WZB, 1994).

19. See the Web site of the Saeima: http://www.saeima.lv/

20. Kārlis Dišlers, *Ievads Valststiesību Zinatnē* (Rīga: A. Gulbis, 1930), p. 102.

21. *Political Transformation and Electoral Process in Post-Communist Europe.* Web site of the Project Based in the Department of Government at the University of Essex, United Kingdom. See http://www2.essex.ac.uk/elect/electjp/lv_el93.htm

22. *Political Transformation and Electoral Process in Post-Communist Europe.* See http://www2.essex.ac.uk/elect/electjp/lv_lcec.htm

23. See the Web site collection of Latvian laws: http://www.likumi.lv/ALikumi/public_organiz.htm

24. Levits, "Latvija Padomju Varā. Stagnācijas."

25. Lipset and Rokkan, "Introduction."

26. Juan J. Linz and Alfred Stepan, *Problems of Democratic Transition and Consolidation: Southern Europe, South America, and Post-Communist Europe* (Baltimore, MD: John Hopkins University Press, 1996).

27. Lipset and Rokkan, "Introduction."

28. Martin Harrop and William L.Miller, *Elections and Voters: A Comparative Introduction* (London: Macmillan, 2001).

29. Herman Smith-Sivertsen, "Latvia," in *Handbook of Political Change in Eastern Europe*, ed. Sten Berglund, Tomas Hellen, and Frank Aarebrot (London: Edward Elgar, 1998), p. 89.

30. Ian-Eke Dellenbrant and Ole Norgaard, eds., *The Politics of Transition in the Baltic States. Research Reports N2* (Umea: Umea University, Department of Political Science, 1994): p. 120.

31. Ilona Runce and Andris Runcis, "Political Parties in Latvia during the Transition from Totalitarianism to Democracy," in *The Transition Towards Democracy: Experience from Latvia and in the World* (Rīga: University of Latvia, 1994).

32. Dzintra Bungs, "The Shifting Political Landscape in Latvia," *RFE/RL Research Report* 2 (12), 1993: p. 30.

33. Maurice Duverger, "Caucus and Branch, Cadre Parties and Mass Parties," in *The West European Party System*, ed. Peter Mair (Oxford: Oxford University Press, 1990): pp. 41–42.

34. Guillermo O'Donnell and Philippe C. Schmitter, *Transitions from Authoritarian Rule: Tentative Conclusions about Uncertain Democracies*, 3rd ed. (Baltimore, MD and London: The John Hopkins University Press, 1991), p. 57.

35. Maurice Duverger, *Political Parties: Their Organization and Activity in the Modern State* (London: Methuen, 1954; New York: John Wiley and Sons, 1955).

36. O'Donnell and Schmitter, *Transitions from Authoritarian Rule*, part IV.

37. Valdis Blūzma, "Politisko partiju veidošanās Latvijā pirmsākumi," in Valdis Blūzma et al. *Latvijas valsts atjaunošana 1986–1993*, Rīga: Latvijas Vesture, 1998, pp. 264–65.

38. Smith-Sivertsen, "Latvia."

39. Brigita Zepa, "Kad vēlēšanu kaislības pierimušas," *Diena*, 20 April, 1999.

CHAPTER 10

1. On the relationship between the mode of transition and party options also see: Herbert Kitschelt, Zdenka Mansfeldova, Radoslav Markovsky, and Gabor Toka , *Post-Communist Party Systems: Competition, Representation, and Inter-Party Cooperation* (New York: Cambridge University Press, 1999), pp. 36–37.

2. Seymour M. Lipset and Stein Rokkan, "Cleavage Structures, Party Systems, and Voter Alignments: An Introduction," in *Party Systems and Voter Alignments: Cross-national Perspectives*, ed. S.M. Lipset and S. Rokkan (New York: The Free Press, 1967), pp. 1–64.

3. Alfred E. Senn, "Lietuvos partinės sistemos formavimasis," *Politologija* 2 (8): 3–4.

4. Ibid., p. 10.

5. Jan-Erik Lane and Svante Ersson, *Politics and Society in Western Europe*, (London: Sage, 1994), p. 103.

6. On the changing character of democratic elections see: Algis Krupavičius, "Political Results of the Seimas Elections of 1996 and the Cabinet Formation," in *Lithuania's Seimas Election of 1996: The Third Turnover*, ed. A. Krupavičius (Berlin: Ed. Sigma, 2001), pp. 137–39.

7. See: Hermann Smith-Sivertsen, *Towards Parties of Elites—or Populism?*, paper presented at the Second Symposium of the IPSA "The Challenge of Regime Transformation: New Politics in Central and Eastern Europe," Vilnius, December 10–15, 1996, p.7.

8. Excluding the membership of the Union of ex-Political Prisoners and Deportees, which was an interest group rather than a party.

9. A. Brazauskas, after his election as the President of Lithuania in 1993, suspended his membership in the LDLP, but the party was still identified with his name in the following years.

10. *Lietuvos Respublikos Konstitucija* (Vilnius: LR Seimo leidykla, 1993), p. 22.

11. Ibid., p. 51.

12. See Lietuvos Kelias (1990). Vilnius: Viltis, p. 31.

13. Alvidas Lukošaitis, *Parlamentarizmo raidos etapai Lietuvoje 1990–1997m* (Vilnius: LR Seimas, 1997), pp.19–20.

14. Michael D. Simon and David M. Olson, *Parliamentary Committees and Parliamentary Development in Poland's Democratic Transition,* paper delivered at the Annual MidWest Political Science Association Meeting, Chicago, April 18–22, 1996, p. 1.

15. *Lietuvos Respublikos Seimo Statutas,* (Vilnius: LR Seimas, 1998) pp. 18–19.

16. Russell J. Dalton, *Citizen Politics: Public Opinion and Political Parties in Advanced Industrial Democracies* (Chatham: Chatham House Publishers, 1996), p. 152.

17. Lane and Ersson, *Politics and Society in Western Europe,* p. 175.

18. Maurice Duverger, Political Parties: Their Organization and Activity in the Modern State (London: Methuen, 1954). Lithuanian scholars tend to evaluate party systems exclusively on the basis of Sartori's typology; see: Jūratė Novagrockienė, "Partinės sistemos ir jų tipologija," *Politologija* 1 (6): 54–72.

19. Lane and Ersson, *Politics and Society in Western Europe,* pp. 177–79.

20. The institutional attributes of voter turnout are analyzed in detail in: Robert W. Jackman and A. Miller Ross, "Voter Turnout in the Industrial Democracies During the 1980s," *Comparative Political Studies* 4: 468–77.

21. In econometric literature, this index was originally known as the Herfindahl-index.

22. Darius Žėruolis, "Rytai tampa Vakarais?" *Politologija* 1 (7): 38.

23. Lane and Ersson, *Politics and Society in Western Europe,* p. 184.

24. It was about 15 percent in 1992.

25. Lane and Ersson, *Politics and Society in Western Europe,* p. 183.

26. Žėruolis, "Rytai tampa Vakarais?" p. 38.

27. See Adam Przeworski, "Institutionalization of Voting Patterns, or Is Mobilization the Source of Decay?" *American Political Science Review* 69: 47–67.

28. Data from: Kenneth Janda, *Restructuring the Party Systems in Central Europe,* paper prepared for the International Symposium *Democratization and Political Reform in Korea,* Seoul, November 19, 1994, pp. 13–16.

29. Jūratė Novagrockienė, "Seimo rinkimai 2000: Partinės sistemos evoliucija ar transformacija?" in *Lietuva po Seimo rinkimų;,* ed. Algimantas Jankauskas (Kaunas: Naujasis Lankas, 2000), p. 55.

30. See data in Stefano Bartolini and Peter Mair, *Identity Competition, and Electoral Availability: The Stabilisation of European Electorates, 1885–1985* (Cambridge: Cambridge University Press, 1990), p. 69.

31. For instance, the volatility score of the HU(LC) is +4.6, but the actual increase in the electorate was only 3.9 percent in the Seimas elections of 1996.

32. Paul Pennings, Hans Keman, and Jan Kleinnijenhuis, *Doing Research in Political Science* (London: Sage Publications, 1999), p. 232.

33. Calculated from: Mindaugas Degutis, "Seimo rinkimai 2000: Nauji Lietuvos rinkėjo portreto bruožai," in *Lietuva po Seimo rinkimų 2000,* ed. Jankauskas Algimantas (Kaunas: Naujasis Lankas, 2000), p. 17.

34. Dalton, *Citizen Politics*, p. 210.

35. Ibid., p. 204.

36. Lester W. Milbrath, "Political Participation," in *The Handbook of Political Behavior*, vol. 4, ed. S. E. Long (New York: Plenum Press, 1981), pp. 197–240.

37. Russell J. Dalton, *Democracy and Its Citizens: Patterns of Political Change*, The Center for the Study of Democracy, http://www.oac.uci.edu.

38. A larger urban-based electorate might also be an encouraging factor for the parties' extensive use of the Internet.

39. Giovanni Sartori, *Parties and Party Systems. A Framework for Analyses* (Cambridge: Cambridge University Press, 1976), pp. 42–44.

40. In 1992 it was achieved by the Democratic Labour Party, and in 1996 by the Homeland Union.

CHAPTER 11

1. G. Hermet, "Disenchantment of the Old Democracies," *International Social Science Journal* 43: 451.

2. See, for example, R. L. Tokes, "Transitology: Global Dreams and Post-Communist Realities," *Central Europe Review* 2 (10), 13 March.

3. See, for example: D. Collier and St. Levitsky, "Democracy with Adjectives: Conceptual Innovation in Comparative Research," *World Politics* 49, April, 1997; T. Inoguchi, E. Newman, and J. Keane, eds., *The Changing Nature of Democracy* (Tokyo: United Nations University Press, 1998); R. Dahl, *On Democracy* (New Haven, CT: Yale University Press, 1999); A. Przeworski, "Minimalist Conception of Democracy: A Defense," in *Democracy's Value*, ed. J. Shapiro and C. Hacker-Cordon (Cambridge: Cambridge University Press, 1999), pp. 23–53; Ch. Mouffe, "For an Agonistic Model of Democracy," in *Political Theory in Transition*, ed. N. O'Sullivan (New York: Routledge, 2000), pp. 113–30; L. Diamond,"Thinking about Hybrid Regimes," *Journal of Democracy* 13 (2), April, 2002: 21–35.

4. Th. Carothers, "The End of the Transition Paradigm," *Journal of Democracy* 13 (1).

5. F. Zakaria, "The Rise of Illiberal Democracy," *Foreign Affaires* (76), November-December 1997.

6. S. Levitski and L A. Way, "The Rise of Competitive Authoritarianism," *Journal of Democracy* 13 (2), April 2002, pp. 51–65.

7. K. R. Luther and F. Müller-Rommel, "Political Parties in a Changing Europe," in *Political Parties in the New Europe*, ed. K. R. Luther and F. Müller-Rommel (Oxford: Oxford University Press, 2002), pp. 3–16.

8. I speak here about a concrete historical model of democracy realized in the modern West in political forms of pluralistic representation. Just this very real democracy has been imitated. The philosophical discussion about democratic values, which could be realized in various political forms, is not the case here.

9. P. Mair, "Introduction," in *The West European Party System*, ed. P. Mair (Oxford: Oxford University Press, 1990), p. 1.

10. Ibid., p. 1.

11. Ibid., p. 2.

12. See Kay Lawson, Andrea Roemmele, and Georgi Karasimeonov (eds.), *Cleavages, Parties, and Voters: Studies from Bulgaria, the Czech Republic, Hungary, Poland, and Romania* (Westport, CT, London: Praeger, 1999).

13. See J. J. Linz, "The Perils of Presidentialism," *Journal of Democracy* 1, Winter 1990: 51–70.

14. About similar problems in the states of East and Central Europe that developed parliamentary systems, see: A. Innes, "Party Competition in Post Communist Europe: The Great Electoral Lottery," *Comparative Politics* 35 (1), 2002: 85–104.

15. J. Bugajski, *Political Parties of Eastern Europe: A Guide to Politics in the Post-Communist Era* (New York: M.E.Sharpe, 2002), p. xxiv.

16. A. Panebianco, *Political Parties: Organization and Power* (Cambridge: Cambridge University Press, 1988).

17. See S. Pshizova, "Representative Rule or the Rule of Representations: The Case of Russian Political Parties," in *How Political Parties Respond: Interest Aggregation Revisited*, ed. Kay Lawson and Thomas Poguntke (New York: Routledge, 2004), pp. 227–49.

18. See R. Williams (ed.), *Party Finance and Political Corruption* (London: Macmillan Press, 2000); K-H. Nassmacher (ed.), *Foundations for Democracy: Approaches to Comparative Political Finance* (Baden-Baden: Nomos Verlagsgesellcshaft, 2001); S. Pshizova, "Finansirovanije politicheskogo rynka: teoreticheskije aspekty prakticheskich problem," [Financing Political Market: Theoretical Aspects of Practical Problems] *Polis* (1) 2002: 18–30, (2): 31–43.

19. J. Blondel, "Party Government, Patronage, and Party Decline in Western Europe," in *Political Parties: Old Concepts and New Challenges*, ed. R. Gunther, J. Ramón-Montero, and J. J. Linz (Oxford: Oxford University Press, 2002), p. 233.

20. J-E. Lane and S. Ersson, *Politics and Society in Western Europe* (London: Sage, 1999); P. Mair and I. Van Biezen, "Party Membership in Twenty European Democracies, 1980–2000," *Party Politics* 7 (1) 2001: 5–21; R. Katz, "The Internal Life of Parties," in *Political Parties in New Europe: Political and Analytical Challenges*, ed. K. R. Luther and F. Müller-Rommel (Oxford: Oxford University Press, 2002), pp. 87–118.

21. See, for example, J. Hopkin, "Bringing the Members Back In?" *Party Politics* 7 (3), 2001: 343–61; R. Katz, "The Problem of Candidate Selection and Models of Party Democracy," *Party Politics* 7 (3), 2001: 277–96; P. Pennings and R. Y. Hazan, "Democratizing Candidate Selection: Causes and Consequences," *Party Politics* 7 (3)3, 2001: 267–75; T. Poguntke, "Party Organizational Linkage: Parties without Firm Social Roots?" in *Political Parties in New Europe: Political and Analytical Challenges*, ed. K. R. Luther and F. Müller-Rommel (Oxford: Oxford University Press, 2002), pp. 43–62.

22. Panebianco, *Political Parties*; R. Katz and P. Mair, "Changing Models of Party Organization and Party Democracy: The Emergence of the Cartel Party," *Party Politics* 1 (1), 1995: 5–28; J. Hopkin and C. Paolucci, "The Party As Business Firm: Cases from Spain and Italy," *European Journal of Political Research* 35, 1999: 307–39; S. Wolinetz, "Beyond the Catch-All Party: Approaches to the Study of Parties and Party Organisation in Contemporary Democracies," in *Political Parties: Old Concepts and New Challenges*, ed. R. Gunther, J. Ramón-Montero, and J. J. Linz (Oxford: Oxford University Press, 2002), pp. 136–65.

23. S. Huntington, *The Third Wave: Democratization in the Late Twentieth Century* (Norman: University of Oklahoma Press, 1991), p. 101.

24. Ibid., p.102.

25. Ibid., p. 105.

26. Ibid.

27. Lawson et al., *Cleavages, Parties, and Voters*, p. 33.

28. J. Grugel, "Democratization Studies: Citizenship, Globalization and Governance," *Government and Opposition* 38 (2), 2003: 239.

29. For democratization rankings see Freedom House project: www.freedomhouse.org/research/nattransit.htm.

30. Ph. C. Schmitter, Presentation at the Conference "Democracy's Future," commemorating the fifth anniversary of the "Journal of Democracy," Washington, April 1995.

References

Aarebrot, Frank, and Terje Knutsen. "Comparative Perspectives." In *Politics and Citizenship on the Eastern Baltic Seaboard*, ed. Frank Aarebrot and Terje Knutsen, Kristiansand: Nordic Academic Press, 2000.

———. "Introduction." In *Politics and Citizenship on the Eastern Baltic Seaboard: The Structuring of Democratic Politics from North-West Russia to Poland*, ed. Frank Aaarebrot and Terje Knutsen. Kristiansand: Nordic Academic Press, 2000.

Aaskivi, Signe. "Parteiregistrid võrdluses." *Sõnumileht*, October 26–30, 1998.

Apine, Ilga. "Staļinisma Recidīvs." *Horizonts* (4). R'iga, 1989.

Arter, David. *Parties and Democracy in the Post-Soviet Republics. The Case of Estonia*, Aldershot: Dartmouth, 1996.

Bartolini, Stefano, and Peter Mair. *Identity Competition, and Electoral Availability: The Stabilisation of European Electorates, 1885–1985*. Cambridge: Cambridge University Press, 1990.

Berglund, Sten, Tomas Hellen, and Frank Aarebrot(1998). "Foundations of Change." In *The Handbook of Political Change in Eastern Europe*, ed. Sten Berglund, Tomas Hellen, and Frank Aarebrot. London: Edward Elgar, 1998.

Beyme, Klaus v. *Political Parties in Western Democracies*, Aldershot: Gower, 1985.

Blondel, J. "Party Government, Patronage, and Party Decline in Western Europe." In *Political Parties: Old Concepts and New Challenges*, ed. R. Gunther, J. Ramón-Montero, and J.J. Linz. Oxford: Oxford Univ. Press, 2002.

Blūzma, Valdis. "Politisko partiju veidošanās Latvijā pirmsākumi," in Valdis Blūzma et al. *Latvijas valsts atjaunošana 1986–1993*, Rīga: Latvijas Vesture, 1998.

Bogdanor, Vernon. "Founding Elections and Regime Change." *Electoral Studies* 9 (4), 1990.

Bottolfs, Heidi. "Latvia." In *Politics and Citizenship on the Eastern Baltic Seaboard: The Structuring of Democratic Politics from North- West Russia to Poland*, ed. Frank Aarebrot and Terje Knutsen. Kristiansand: Nordic Academic Press, 2000.

British Helsinki Committee Report on 2000 elections at http://www.bhhrg.org/belarus/belarus%202000/startpage.htm, retrieved in June 2001.

Bugajski, J. *Political Parties of Eastern Europe: A Guide to Politics in the Post-Communist Era.* New York: M.E.Sharpe, 2002.

Bungs, Dzintra. "The Shifting Political Landscape in Latvia." *RFE/RL Research Report* 2 (12), 1993: 30.

Carothers, Thomas."The End of the Transition Paradigm." *Journal of Democracy* 13 (1), January 2002, pp. 5–21.

Central Electoral Commission, http://www.izbirkom.ru/izbirkom_protokols/sx/page/protokolin.

Choe, Yonhyonk. *Institutional Trust in East- and Central Europe: A Macro Perspective.* Paper prepared for the ECPR General Conference, 6–8 September, 2001, Canterbury, UK.

Collier, D. and St, Levitsky. "Democracy with Adjectives: Conceptual Innovation in Comparative Research." *World Politics* 49, April 1997.

The Constitution of the RF, 1993, http://www.constitution.ru/en/.

Country Studies by The Library of Congress. Moldova. http://lcweb2.loc.gov/frd/cs/mdtoc.html.

Dahl, R. *On Democracy.* New Haven, CT; Yale University Press, 1999.

Dahrendorf, R. Reflecţii asupra Revoluţii in Europa" [Reflections on the Revolution in Europe], In *Editura Humanitas.* (Bucureşti, 1993).

Dalton, Russell J. *Citizen Politics: Public Opinion and Political Parties in Advanced Industrial Democracies.* Chatham: Chatham House Publishers, 1996.

———. *Democracy and Its Citizens: Patterns of Political Change.* The Center for the Study of Democracy, 1996.- http://www.oac.uci.edu

Degutis, Mindaugas. "Seimo rinkimai 2000: Nauji Lietuvos rinkėjo portreto bruožai." In *Lietuva po Seimo rinkimų 2000,* ed. Jankauskas Algimantas. Kaunas: Naujasis Lankas, 2000.

Dellebrant, Ian-Eke and Ole Norgaard, eds. *The Politics of Transition in the Baltic States.* Research Reports 2. Umea: Umea University Press, Department of Political Science, 1994.

Diamond, L. "Thinking about Hybrid Regimes." *Journal of Democracy* 13 (2), April, 2002, pp. 21–35.

Dišlers, Kārlis. *Ievads Valststiesību.* Zinatnē Rīga: A. Gulbis, 1930.

Dix, R.H. "Democratization and the Institutionalization of Latin American Political Parties." *Comparative Political Studies* 24, 1992: 488–511.

Dmitriev, A. "Korrupciya i vlast' v sovremennoi Rossii'," in *Tehnologiii vlasti i upravleniya v sovemennom gosudarstve.* Moscow: MGU, 1999.

Dreifelds, Juris. "Demographic Trends in Latvia." *Nationalities Paper* 12 (1), Charleston: IL, 1984.

———. *Latvia in Transition.* Cambridge: Cambridge University Press, 1996.

———. "Latvian National Rebirth." *Problems of Communism* 38, (4), 1989.

Duverger, Maurice. *Political Parties: Their Organization and Activity in the Modern State.* London: Methuen, 1954.

Eagles, M. and L. Johnston. *Politics: An Introduction to Modern Democratic Government.* Peterborough, Ontario: Broadview Press. 1999.

Eesti Vabariigi põhiseadus, Olion ja Eesti Entsüklopeediakirjastus, Tallinn, 1992.

Elections for President 26 March 2000, The State Duma Elections 19 December 1999. Foundation For Effective Policies. http://www.election.ru/eng_index.html.

Erakonnaseadus, Riigi Teataja, nr. 40, 6. June 1994.

Fedor, Helen, ed. *A Country Study: Moldova.* The Library of Congress. http://lcweb2.loc.gov/frd/cs/mdtoc.html.

Final official results of the Duma elections on the whole Russia at December 29, 1995 —http://www.nns.ru/elects/izbobyed/res-eng.html.

Fond Obschestvennoiye mneniye [Public Opinion Fund], Database: http://www.fom.ru.

Freivalds, Osvalds. *Latviešu politiskās partijas 60 gados.* Stockholm: Imanta, 1961.

Furman, D. et al., *Belorussiya i Rossiya: Obschestva i Gosudarstva* (Belarus and Russia: Societies and States). Moscow: Prava Cheloveka, 1998.

Gel'man, Vladimir, Grigorii Golosov, and Elena Meleshkina (eds), *Pervyi elektoral'nyi cikl v Rossii (1993–1996).* Moscow: Iz-vo "Ves' mir", 2000 (The First Electoral Cycle in Russia, 1993–1996).

Gel'man, Vladimir, Grigorii Golosov, and Elena Meleshkina (eds), *Vtoroi elektoral'nyi cikl v Rossii (1999–2000).* Moscow: Iz-vo "Ves' mir", 2002 (The Second Electoral Cycle in Russia, 1999–2000).

Goodin, Robert E., and Hans-Dieter Klingemann. "Political Science as a Discipline." In *A New Handbook of Political Science,* ed. Robert E. Goodin and Hans-Dieter Klingemann. New York: Oxford University Press, 1996.

Gorbachev, Mikhail. "Mnogopartiinost': istoriya i sud'ba." In *Parlamentarizm i mnogopartiinost' v sovremennoi Rossii,* ed. V. Lysenko. Moscow: ISP, 2000, pp. 135–141 (Multiparty System: A History and a Fate. In Parliamentarianism and Multiparty System in Contemporary Russia).

The Government Courier June 24, 1997 [In Ukrainian].

Grugel, J. "Democratization Studies: Citizenship, Globalization and Governance." *Government and Opposition* 38 (2), 2003.

Guthier, S.L. "The Belorussians: National Identification and Assimilation, 1897–1970." *Soviet Studies* 29(1,2), 1997.

Harrop, Martin, and William L.Miller. *Elections and Voters. A Comparative Introduction.* London: Macmillan, 2001.

Hellen, Tomas, Sten Berglund, and Frank Aarebrot "The Challenge of History in Eastern Europe." In *The Handbook of Political Change in Eastern Europe,* ed. Sten Berglund, Tomas Hellen, and Frank Aarebrot. London: Edward Elgar, 1998.

Hermet, G. "Disenchantment of the Old Democracies." *International Social Science Journal* 43, 1991.

Hopkin, J. "Bringing the Members Back In?" *Party Politics* 7 (3), 2001: 343–61.

Hopkin, J., and C. Paolucci. "The Party As Business Firm: Cases from Spain and Italy." *European Journal of Political Research* 35, 1999: 307–39;

Horovitz, Donald L. *Ethnic Groups in Conflict.* Berkeley and Los Angeles: University of California Press, 1985.

Huntington, S.P. "Political Development and Political Decay." *World Politics* 17, 1965.

———. *The Third Wave: Democratization in the Late Twentieth Century.*(Norman: University of Oklahoma Press, 1991.

Inglehart, R, "How Solid Is Mass Support for Democracy—And How Can We Measure It?" *Political Science and Politics* 36 (1), 2003.

Innes, A. "Party Competition in Post Communist Europe: The Great Electoral Lottery." *Comparative Politics* 35, (1), 2002, pp. 85–104.

Inoguchi, T., E. Newman, and J. Keane (eds.). *The Changing Nature of Democracy.* Tokyo: United Nations University Press, 1998.

Jablons'kyi V. and J. Latko. *Suchasni politychni partii Ukrainy: politykam i pochatkivcjam* [Modern Political Partiess of Ukraine.] Kiev: Alterpres, 1999 [In Ukrainian].

Jackman, Robert W., and Ross A. Miller "Voter Turnout in the Industrial Democracies during the 1980s." *Comparative Political Studies* 4, 1995, pp. 468–77.

Janda, Kenneth. Comparative Political Parties: Research and Theory. In: Finifter, A. *Political Science: The State of the Discipline* 2. Washington, DC: Amer. Politic. Sci. Ass., 1993. pp. 163–191.

———. *Political Parties: A Cross-National Survey.* New York: Free Press, 1980.

———. *Restructuring the Party Systems in Central Europe.* Paper prepared for the International Symposium *Democratization and Political Reform in Korea,* Seoul, November 19, 1994.

Jelgavas ziņotājs. 1989.gada 10.jūnijs.

Katz Richard S. "The Internal Life of Parties." In *Political Parties in New Europe. Political and Analytical Challenges,* ed. K.R. Luther and F. Müller-Rommel. Oxford: Oxford Univ. Press, 2002, pp. 87–118.

———. "The Problem of Candidate Selection and Models of Party Democracy." *Party Politics* 7 (3), 2001: 277–96.

Katz, Richard S., and Peter Mair. "Changing Models of Party Organization and Party Democracy." *Party Politics* 1 (1), 1995, pp. 5–28.

Kitschelt, Herbert. "The Formation of Party Systems in East Central Europe." *Politics and Society* 20 (1), 1992: 7–50.

———. "Formation of Party Cleavages in Post-communist Democracies: Theoretical Propositions," *Party Politics* 1(4), 1995: 447–73.

Kitschelt, Herbert, Zdenka Mansfeldova, Radoslav Markovsky, and Gabor Tokar. *Post-Communist Party Systems: Competition, Representation, and Inter-Party Cooperation.* New York: Cambridge University Press, 1999.

Kohaliku omavalitsuse volikogu valimised 17. oktoober 1993, Dokumente ja materjale, Eesti Vabariigi Riigikogu Kantselei, Valimiste osakond, Tallinn, 1993.

Kohaliku omavalitsuse volikogu valimised 20. oktoober 1996, Vabariigi Valimiskomisjon, Tallinn, 1997.

Korgunyuk, Yurii. *Sovremennaya rossiiskaya mnogopartiinost'.* Moscow.: INDEM. 1999. (Current Russian Multiparty System).

Korosteleva, E. *Explaining Party System Development in Post-Communist Belarus,* Ph.D. thesis, University of Bath, 2001.

Korosteleva , E. et.al. (eds.), *Contemporary Belarus: Between Democracy and Dictatorship.* London: Curzon Press, 2002.

Krupavičius, Algis. "Political Results of the Seimas Elections of 1996 and the Cabinet Formation." In *Lithuania's Seimas Election of 1996: The Third Turnover,* ed. A. Krupavičius. Berlin: Ed. Sigma, 2001.

Kulik, Anatoly. "To Prosper in Russia: Parties Deep in the Shadow of the President.". In *When Parties Prosper,* ed. Kay Lawson and Peter Merkl. (In progress).

Kulik, Anatoly, and Susanna Pshizova. "Political Parties in the Post-Soviet Space: A Unique Response to the Context or a Future of the Western Model?" prepared for the XVIII World Congress of the International Political Science Association, 1–5 August 2000, Quebec.

Laakso, M., and R. Taagepera, "Effective Number of Parties: A Measure with Application to West Europe." *Comparative Political Studies* 12 (3), 1979.

Lagerspetz, Mikko, and Henri Vogt. "Estonia." In *The Handbook of Political Change in Eastern Europe*, ed. Sten Berglund, Tomas Hellen, and Frank Aarebrot. London: Edward Elgar, 199p.

Lane, J.-E., and S. Ersson. *Politics and Society in Western Europe*, 2nd ed. London: Sage Publications, 1999.

LaPalombara, Joseph, and Myron Wiener. "The Origin and Development of Political Parties," In *Political Parties and Political Development*, ed. Joseph LaPalombara, Myron Wiener. Princeton, NJ: Princeton University Press, 1966, pp. 7–21.

———. "The Origins of Political Parties." In *The West European Party System, ed.* Peter Mair. Oxford: Oxford University Press, 1990.

———. *Political Parties and Political Development.* Princeton, NJ: Princeton University Press, 1966.

Latvijas Republikas Valsts Statistikas Komiteja. Rīga, 1992.

Lawson, Kay. *The Human Polity.* Boston, New York: Houghton Mifflin Company, 1999.

Lawson, Kay, ed. *Political Parties and Linkages: A Comparative Perspective.* London: Yale University Press, 1980.

Lawson, Kay, Andrea Roemmele, and Georgi Karasimeonov, eds.. *Cleavages, Parties, and Voters. Studies from Bulgaria, the Czech Republic, Hungary, Poland, and Romania.* Westport, CT, London: Praeger, 1999.

Lawson, Kay, and Peter Merkl, eds.. *When Parties Fail: Emerging Alternative Organizations.* Princeton, NJ: Princeton University Press, 1988.

Levits, Egils. "Latvija Padomju Varā Stagnācijas Periods no 1960. līdz 1985.gadam." In *Latvijas Vēsture* (3), 1991.

Levitski, S, and L.A. Way L. "The Rise of Competitive Authoritarianism." *Journal of Democracy* 13 (2), April, 2002, pp. 51–65.

Lietuvos Respublikos Konstitucija (1993). Vilnius: LR Seimo leidykla, p.22.

Lietuvos Respublikos Seimo Statutas (1998). Vilnius: LR Seimas, pp.18–19

Lijphart, Arend. "Constitutional Alternatives for New Democracies." *Polis* (2), 1995 [In Russian].

———. *Democracies: Pattern of Majoritarian and Consensus Government in Twenty-One Countries.* New Haven, CT: Yale University Press, 1984.

———. *Electoral Systems and Party Systems: A Study of Twenty-Seven Democracies 1945–1990.* Oxford University Press, 1994.

Linz, J.J. "The Perils of Presidentialism," *Journal of Democracy* 1, 1990, pp. 51–69.

Linz, J.J., and A. Stepan. *Problems of Democratic Transition and Consolidation: Southern Europe, South America and Post-Communist Europe.* Baltimore, MD: John Hopkins University Press, 1996.

Lipset, Seymour, and S. Rokkan, *Party Systems and Voter Alignments: Cross-National Perspectives.* New York: Free Press, 1967.

Lipset, Seymour, and Stein Rokkan. "Cleavage Structure, Party System and Voter Alignments: An Introduction." In *Party Systems and Voter Alignments: Cross-National Perspectives,* ed. Seymour Lipset and Stein Rokkan. New York, London: The Free Press, 1967.

Lipset, Seymour, and Stein Rokkan. "Introduction." In *Party System and Voter Alignments: Cross-National Perspectives*, ed. Seymour Lipset and Stein Rokkan. New York: The Free Press, 1967.

List of All-Russian Political Public Associations as of January 1, 1999. Institute for Election Systems Development (IESD). http://www.democracy.ru/english/history/eng_1999–36.html.

Litvin, V. *Political Arena of Ukraine:Persons and Doers.* Kyiv: Abris, 1994.

Lukošaitis, Alvidas. Lietuvos Respublikos politinės partijos. Vilnius: LR Seimo kanceliarija. 1993, 1994, 1995, 1996, 1998, 1999, 2000.

———. Parlamentarizmo raidos etapai Lietuvoje 1990- 1997m.Vilnius: LR Seimas, 1997.

Luther, K.R., and F. Müller-Rommel. "Political Parties in a Changing Europe." In *Political Parties in the New Europe*, ed. K.R. Luther and F. Müller-Rommel. Oxford: Oxford University Press, 2002.

Lysenko, Vladimir. "Desyat' klyuchevyh let rossiiskogo parlamentarizma." In *Parlamentarizm i mnogopartiinost' v sovremennoi Rossii*, ed. Lysenko, V. Moscow: ISP, 2000, p. 14–20. (Ten Key Years of Contemporary Russian Parliamentarianism)

———. ed. *Parlamentarizm i mnogopartiinost' v sovremennoi Rossii.* Moscow: ISP. 2000.

Mainwaring, S. "Presidentialism in Latin America." *Latin American Research Review* 29(1), 1990: 157–79.

———. *Rethinking Party Systems in the Third Wave of Democratisation. The case of Brazil.* Stanford, CA: Stanford University Press, 1999.

Mair P. "Introduction." In *The West European Party System*, Mair P. (ed.). Oxford: Oxford University Press, 1990.

Mair P. and I. Van Biezen. "Party Membership in Twenty European Democracies, 1980–2000." *Party Politics* 7 (1), 2001: 5–21.

Manaev, O. "Belorusskii Electorat: Za i Protiv Presidenta" (Belarusian Electorate: For and Against the President), *NISAPI News* 1.

Marples, D, *Belarus: The Denationalized Nation. Post-Communist States and Nations.* Amsterdam: Harwood Academic Publications, 1999.

McFaul Michael. *The Fourth Wave: Democracy and Dictatorship in the Post-Communist World.* Paper prepared for delivery at the Annual APSA meeting, San Francisco, August 30–September 2, 2001.

McFaul, Michael, and Andrei Ryabov, eds. *Russian Society: The Establishment of Democratic Values?* Moscow Carnegie Center. Moscow: Gendalf, 1999. http://pubs.carnegie.ru/english/

McFaul, Michael, Nikolai Petrov, and Andrei Ryabov, eds. *Russia in the Course of 1999–2000 Election Cycle.* Moscow Carnegie Center. Moscow: Gendalf, 2000. http://pubs.carnegie.ru/english/ p. 611

McGrath, Troy. "Russia." In *Nations in Transit 2002. Country Reports.* New York,Washington, Budapest, Bucharest, Belgrade, Kiev, Warsaw: Freedom House, 2003. http://www.freedomhouse.org/research/nattransit.htm

Mednis, Imants. "Politiskās Partijas Latvijas Republikā." *Latvijas Arhīvi* (3). 1995.

Mežs, Ilmārs. "Pārmaiņas Latvijas Iedzīvotāju Etniskajā Sastāvā 20.gadsimtā." *Latvijas Zinātņu Akadēmijas Vēstis* (5/6), 1995.

Milbrath, Lester W. "Political Participation." In *The Handbook of Political Behavior*, ed. S. E. Long. Vol. 4. New York: Plenum Press, 1981, p. 197–240.

Misiunas, Romuald, and Rein Taagepera. *The Baltic States: Years of Dependence 1940–1990.* London: University of California Press, 1993.

Monitoring VZIOM: Monitoring Obschestvennogo Mneniya: Economicheskiye I Sozial'nye Peremeny [The Monitoring of the Public Opinion: Economic and Social Changes], 2(22), Moscow: VZIOM, 1996.

Morlino, Leonardo "Political Parties and Democratic Consolidation in Southern Europe." In *The Politics of Democratic Consolidation: Southern Europe in Comparative Perspective,* ed. Richard Gunther, Nikiforos P. Diamandorous, and Hans-Jurgen Puhle. Baltimore, MD: The John Hopkins University Press, 1995.

Mosneaga, V. "Parliamentary (1998) Elections and Consolidation of Democracy in Moldova." *Moldova-98: Political Realities and Parliamentary Elections.* Chisinau: East West Parliamentary Practice Project, 1998 (in Russian).

———. "Political Parties and Parliament of Moldova: Juridical Aspects of Connection." *Aspects of Parliamentary Practice: Relations between Parliament and Government. (Republic of Moldova).* Chisinau: East West Parliamentary Practice Project, 1997 (in Romanian).

———. *Moldova-96: Presidential Elections, Political Parties and Elective Technologies.* Chisinau: MSU, 1997 (in Russian).

Mosneaga, V., and G. Rusnac. *Parliamentary (2001) Elections in Republic of Moldova: Specificity, Results, Elective Strategy and Technologies.* MOLDOSCOPIE (Problems of Political Analysis). Part XVI. Chisinau: MSU, 2001 (in Russian).

Mosneaga, V., and G. Rusnac. *Political Parties and Political Movements in the Context of the Development Political Independence in the Republic of Moldova.* MOLDOSCOPIE (Problems of the Political analysis). Part III. Chisinau: MSU, 1993 (in Romanian and Russian).

———. *Republic of Moldova and Parliamentary Elections (1994) Political Geography of Electorate.* Chisinau: MSU, 1997 (in Romanian).

Mouffe, Ch. "For an Agonistic Model of Democracy." In *Political Theory in Transition,* ed. N. O'Sullivan. London, New York: Routledge, 2000, pp. 113–130;

Muiznieks, Nils. "Latvia: Origins, Evolution and Triumph." In: *Nations and Politics in the Soviet successor states,* ed. Ian Bremmer and Ray Taras. Cambridge: Cambridge University Press, 1993.

The Multiparty System in Moldova: Essence and Specifics of Formation. Coord. V.Mosneaga.—Chisinau: CAPTES, 2000. (in Romanian).

Nassmacher, K-H., ed. *Foundations for Democracy: Approaches to Comparative Political Finance.* Baden-Baden: Nomos Verlagsgesellcshaft, 2001.

Nations in Transit 2002. Country Reports. New York, Washington, Budapest, Bucharest, Belgrade, Kiev, Warsaw: Freedom House. 2003. http://www.freedomhouse.org/research/nattransit.htm.

Nations in Transit 2003, Table 4. Nations in Transit 2003 Democratization Rankings. http://www.freedomhouse.org/research/natransit/2003/2003table4.pdf.

Nations in Transit 2004, Moldova Country Report by Freedom House. http://www.freedomhouse.org/research/nattransit/2004/Moldova2004.pdf.

*Nezavisimaya gazeta,*12 July 2000. http://ng.ru/politics/2000–07–12/3_show.html.

Nørgaard, Ole, Dan Hindsgaul, Lars Johansen, and Helle Willumsen, *The Baltic States after Independence,* Cheltenham and Bookfield, Edward Elgar, 1996,

Novagrockienė, Jūratė. "Partinės sistemos ir jų tipologija." *Politologija* 1 (6), 1995, pp. 54–72.

———. "Seimo rinkimai 2000: Partinės sistemos evoliucija ar transformacija?" In *Lietuva po Seimo rinkimų 2000*, ed. Jankauskas Algimantas. Kaunas: Naujasis Lankas, 2000.

Obshestvennoe mnenie—2002. Moscow: VCIOM, 2002 (Public opinion—2002). http://www.wciom.ru/vciom/info/cnew/opinion2002.htm.

O'Donnell, Guillermo. "Delegative Democracy" *Journal of Democracy* 5(1), 1994: 55–69.

O'Donnell, Guillermo, and Philippe C. Schmitter. *Transitions from Authoritarian Rule: Tentative Conclusions about Uncertain Democracies.* 3rd ed. Baltimore, London: The John Hopkins University Press, 1991.

Offe, Claus. "Capitalism by Democratic Design? Democratic Theory Facing the Triple Transition in East-Central Europe." In *Economic Institutions, Actors and Attitudes: East Central Europe in Transition*, ed. Lengyl Gyorgy, Offe Claus, and Tholen Jochen. Budapest: University of Economic Sciences, 1992.

Official Internet site of the State Duma, http://www.duma.ru/deputats/fraction.htm.

On Basic Guarantees of Electoral Rights and the Right of Citizens of the Russian Federation to Participate in a Referendum—Federal Law No. 124-FZ of September 30, 1997. Amended March 30, 1999, No. 55-FZ.

On the Election of Deputies of the State Duma of the Federal Assembly of the Russian Federation—Federal Law No. 121-FZ of July 1, 1999.

On the Election of the President of the Russian Federation—Federal Law No. 228- FZ. of December 31, 1999.

On Political Parties—Federal Law No.95-FZ of July 11, 2001. *The above referred laws are available at* http://www.democracy.ru/english/library/laws/.

Panebianco, A. *Political Parties: Organization and Power.* Cambridge: Cambridge University Press, 1998.

The Parliament of the Republic of Moldova. http://www.parlament.md/en.html.

Pennings, Paul, and R.Y. Hazan "Democratizing Candidate Selection: Causes and Consequences." *Party Politics* 7 (3), 2001, pp. 267–75.

Pennings Paul, Hans Keman, and Jan Kleinnijenhuis. *Doing Research in Political Science.* London: Sage Publications, 1999.

Pettai, Vello, and Marcus Kreuzer. "Party Politics in the Baltic States: Social Bases and Institutional Context," *East European Politics and Societies* 13 (1), Winter 1999.

Pizzorno, Alesandro. "Parties in Pluralism." In *The West European Party System*, ed. P.Mair. New York: Oxford University Press, 1990.

Poguntke, T. "Party Organizational Linkage: Parties Without Firm Social Roots?" In *Political Parties in New Europe: Political and Analytical Challenges*, ed. K. R. Luther and F. Müller-Rommel. Oxford: Oxford Univ. Press, 2002, p. 43–62.

Politicheskaya istoriya: Rossiya—SSSR—Rossiiskaya Federaciya: V 2 t. T. 1.—M.: TERRA, 1996. 720 s. (Political History: Russia—USSR—Russian Federation. In 2 volumes. Vol. 1.)

Political calendar: information-analytical review (1999) No. 1–12. [In Ukrainian].

Political Parties of the Republic of Moldova by Association for Participatory Democracy (Political Parties, Legislation, Elections, Electoral Blocs). http://www.parties.e-democracy.md/en/.

Political Transformation and the Electoral Process in Post-Communist Europe. Web site of the Project Based in the Department of Government at the University of Essex, UK. Legislation, Election Results, Constituency Data, Candidate Data. *http://www2.essex.ac.uk/elect/database/indexCountry.*

Pozniak, Zenon. "PraektČyhir," *Naviny* 12, March 1999.

Pribylovsky, Vladimir. *Russia's Political Parties and Electoral Associations.* December 1995. http://www.panorama.ru:8100/.

Przevorski, Adam. *Democracy and Market: Political and Economic Reforms in Eastern Europe and Latin America.* Cambridge University Press, 1992. Russian translation, Moscow, 1999.

———. "Institutionalization of Voting Patterns, or is Mobilization the Source of Decay?" *American Political Science Review* 69, 1975: 47–67.

———. "Minimalist Conception of Democracy: A Defense." In *Democracy's Value,* ed. J. Shapiro and C. Hacker-Cordon. Cambridge: Cambridge Univ. Press, 1999, pp. 23–53.

Pshizova S. "Finansirovanije politicheskogo rynka: teoreticheskije aspekty prakticheskich problem." [Financing Political Market: Theoretical Aspects of Practical Problems] *Polis,* 2002, (1): 18–30; (2): 31–43.

———. "Representative Rule or the Rule of Representations: The Case of Russian Political Parties." In *How Political Parties Respond: Interest aggregation revisited,* ed. Kay Lawson and Thomas Poguntke. London, New York: Routledge, 2004, pp. 227–49.

The Public Opinion Foundation, a nonprofit organization for conducting public opinion surveys in Russia in fields: Politics, The state, Society, Persons and some others. http://english.fom.ru/.

Public Opinion Foundation poll from 4 November 2000, http://www.fom.ru/reports/frames/d002932.html.

Putin, Vladimir. Speech to Campaign Supporters, February 12, 2004 (In English), http://putin2004.ru/english/authorized/402D773F.

Renney, A. *Governing of Men.* Manchester: Manchester University Press, 1989.

Riigikogu valimine 7. märts 1999, Vabariigi Valimiskomisjon, Tallinn, 1999.

Riigikogu valimised 1995, Dokumente ja materjale, Eesti Vabariigi Valimiskomisjon, Tallinn, 1995.

Rimskii, Vladimir. "Nuzhny li Rossii politicheskie partii?" In *Parlamentarizm i mnogopartiinost' v sovremennoi Rossii* (Whether Political Parties Are Needed in Russia?), ed. V. Lysenko, Moscow: ISP. 2000, pp. 151–52.

———. "Parlamentarizm v poskommunisticheskoi Rossii: nadezhdy i razocharovaniya," In *Parlamentarizm i mnogopartiinost' v sovremennoi Rossii,* (Parliamentarianism in Post-Communist Russia: Expectations and Disillusion) ed. V, Lysenko. Moscow: ISP, 2000.

ROMIR Research Group (Russian Public Opinion & Market Research), an independent research agency, conducting both social/political studies and full scope of market research. http://www.romir.ru/eng/.

Rose, Richard. "Living in an Antimodern Society." *East European Constitutional Rev.* 8 (1–2). Winter/ Spring 1999. http://www.law.nyu.edu/eecr/vol8num1-/special/living.html.

———. "A Supply-Side View of Russian's Elections. Forthcoming in: *East European Constitutional Review.* http://www.law.nyu.edu/eecr/.

Rose, Richard, Neil Munro, and Tom Mackie. *Elections in Central and Eastern Europe since 1990.* Glasgow: University of Strathclyde, 1998.

Rose, Richard, and T.M. Mackie, "Do Parties Persist or Fail? The Big Trade-Off Facing Organizations." In*When Parties Fail: Emerging Alternative Organizations,* ed. K. Lawson and P.H. Merkl. Princeton, NJ: Princeton University Press, 1988.

Rossi'skoe obshestvo nakanune prezidentskih vyborov. Moscow: VCIOM, 2004. http://www.wciom.ru/files/040212.doc, p. 31.

Rossiya: partii, associacii, soyuzyi, klubyi. Spravochnik. T.1. Chast' 1. 1991. M.: Izdatel'stvo "RAU-PRESS" (Russia: Parties, Associations, Unions, Clubs. Guidebook. Vol. 1. Part 1).

Rotman, D.G. "Kakoi mi vidim Belarus?"[What Belarus Can We See?], *Narodnaya Gazeta* [People's Paper], 21 October, 1997, p. 1, 3;

———. *Sociological Report 1998–99* Minsk: Belarusian State University, 1999.

Rotman, D.G., and A. Danilov, "President and Opposition: Specific Features of the Belarusian Scene," in *Contemporary Belarus: Between Democracy and Dictatorship,*ed. E. Korosteleva et al. London: Curzon Press, 2002.

Rotman, D.G., E.A. Korosteleva, et al. *Kakoy Mi Vidim Nashu Belarus? Dannye operativno-socioloogicheskisch oprosov 1994–1995"* [What Kind of Belarus Do We See? The results of sociological observations 1994–1995] (Minsk: Belarusian State University, 1996).

Runce, Ilona, and Andris Runcis. "Political Parties in Latvia during the Transition from Totalitarianism to Democracy." In *The Transition towards Democracy: Experience from Latvia and in the World.* Rīga: University of Latvia, 1994.

Runcis, Andris. "The Citizenship Issues as Creeping Crisis." In *Crisis Management in a Transitional Society: The Latvian Experience,* ed. Eric K.Stern and Dan Hansen. Vol.12. Stockholm: Försvarshögskolan, 2000.

Rusnac V., and G. Rusnac. *The Party System of Moldova: Essence and Features.* MOLDOSCOPIE (Problems of Political Analysis). Part III. Chisinau: MSU, 1993 (in Romanian and Russian).

Ryabov, Andrei. *The Outlook for the Russian Multi-Party System in the New Political Context.* The Carnegie Moscow Center: Briefing Paper: Issue 8, August 2001. http://pubs.carnegie.ru/english/.

———. *Political Stability and an Agenda for Putin's Next Presidency.* The Carnegie Moscow Center: Briefing Paper: Issue 8, August 2002. http://pubs.carnegie.ru/english/.

"Rossiiane o vyborakh v Gosdumu" (Russians on the Elections to the State Duma), VCIOM-A Press release #27, 21 November,2003, www.vciom-a.ru

Rupnik, Jacques. "The Postcommunist Divide." *Journal of Democracy* 10(1): January 1999, pp. 57–62.

Russia Votes 2003/2004—a joint project of Centre for the Study of Public Policy, U. Strathclyde (Director: Professor Richard Rose) and VCIOM Analytic Agency (Director: Yuri A. Levada). http://www.russiavotes.org/.

Sakwa, Richard. *Regime Change from Yeltsin to Putin.* Manuscript prepared for *Politicheskaya nauka.* Moscow: INION RAN. 2003.

———. "The Regime System in Russia." *Contemporary Politics* 1 (3), 1997: 7–25.

Sartori, Giovanni. *Parties and Party Systems.* Vol. 1: *A Framework for Analysis.* Cambridge: Cambridge University Press, 1976.

Satversme of the Republic of Latvia. Riga, 1996.

Schattschneider, E. E. *Party Government*. New York: Rinehart and Winston, 1942.

Schmitter Ph. C. 1995. Presentation at the Conference "Democracy's Future," commemorating the fifth anniversary of the "Journal of Democracy," Washington, April 1995. http://www.ned.org/publications/publications.html.

Schnetzer, Amanda. "Nations in Transit 2003: Milestones." In *Nations in Transit 2003: Democratization in East Central Europe and Eurasia*. Rowman & Littlefield Publishers, Inc. Co-published with: Freedom House, 2003. http://www.freedomhouse.org/research/nattransit.htm p. 9.

Senn, Alfred E. "Lietuvos partinės sistemos formavimasis." *Politologija* 2(8), 1996.

Sheinis, Viktor. "Konstitucionnyi process na sovremennom etape." (Constitutional Process at the Current period). In *Kuda idet Rossiya?*. ed. Zaslavskaya, T. Moscow: MVShSEN, 1997, pp. 114–25

———. "Rossiiskii parlament: desyat' let trudnogo puti" [Russian Parliament: Ten Years of the Hard Way]. In Lysenko ed., *Parlamentarizm i mnogopartiinost v sovremennoi Rossii*. Moscow: ISP, 2000: p. 75

Shevtsova, Lilia. "Between Stabilization and a Breakthrough: Interim Results of Vladimir Putin's Presidency." *Briefing Paper*, Issue 1, January, 2002. The Carnegie Moscow Center: http://pubs.carnegie.ru/english/.

———. Dilemy postkommunisticheskogo obshestva. (Dilemmas of the Post-communist Society). "*Polis*," # 5,1996, p. 80–92

Silitski, V, "Explaining Post-Communist Authoritarianism in Belarus." In *Contemporary Belarus: Between Democracy and Dictatorship*, ed. Korosteleva , E. et.al. London: Curzon Press, 2002.

Simon, Michael D., and David M. Olson. *Parliamentary Committees and Parliamentary Development in Poland's Democratic Transition*. Paper delivered at the Annual MidWest Political Science Association Meeting, Chicago, April 18–22, 1996.

Smith, Graham. *The Nationalities Question in Soviet Union*. Cambridge: Cambridge University Press, 1990.

Smith-Sivertsen, Herman. "Latvia." In: *Handbook of Political Change in Eastern Europe*, ed. Sten Berglund, Tomas Hellen, and Frank Aarebrot. London: Edward Elgar, 1998.

———. "Towards Parties of Elites—or Popularism?" *Revue Baltique*, (8), 1997.

———. *Towards Parties of Elites—or Populism?* Paper presented at the Second Symposium of the IPSA "The Challenge of Regime Transformation: New Politics in Central and Eastern Europe," Vilnius, December 10–15, 1996.

Sogrin, Viktor. *Politicheskaya istoriya sovremennoi Rossii. 1985–2001: ot Gorbacheva do Putina*. (Political History of Contemporary Russia). Moscow: Izdatel'stvo "Ves' Mir," 2001.

Steen, Anton. "Elites, Democracy and Policy Development in Post Communist States: A Comparative Study of Estonia, Latvia and Lithuania."*Research Report 02/96*, Department of Political Science, University of Latvia.

Strods, Heinrihs. "Genocīda Galvenās Formas un Mērķi Latvijā, 1940–1985." In *Komunistiskā Totalitārisma un Genocīda Prakse Latvijā*. Rīga: Zinātne, 1992.

Strokanov, Alexandre. *An Analysis of the Programs of the Major Political parties and Electoral Blocs in the State Duma Elections in December 1999*. http://www.panorama.ru:8100/.

Sege, Hans Petter, and Christer D. Daatland. "Estonia." In *Politics and Citizenship on the Eastern Baltic Seaboard: The Structuring of Democratic Politics from North-West Russia to Poland,* ed. Frank Aaarebrot and Terje Knutsen. Kristiansand: Nordic Academic Press, 2000.

Taagapera, R., and M. Shugart, M. *Seats and Votes: The Effects and Determinants of Electoral Systems.* New Haven, CT: Yale University Press, 1989.

Taru, Marti. "Valimispäeva küsitluse tulemusi" In R. Toomla et al., eds., *Riigikogu valimised 1999.* Tartu: Tartu Ülikooli kirjastus, 1999.

Taru, Marti, and Rein Toomla. *Ülevaade valijaskonna eelistustest Tartu linnas, oktoober 1999,* Unpublished paper

———. *Ülevaade avaliku arvamuse uuringust,* June 1998, unpublished paper.

Thomas, J.C. *The Decline of Ideology in Western Political Parties.* London: Sage Publications, 1975.

Tkachuk, A. "Deputy Faction and Groups in Ukrainian Parliament: Political orientation. Change Dynamics." *Citizen Voice* (4), 1997 [In Ukrainian].

Tokes, R.L. "Transitology: Global Dreams and Post-Communist Realities." *Central Europe Review* 2 (10), 13 March 2000.

Tomenko, M. "Results of Parliamentary Elections in Ukraine: Political Orientations and Preferences of the Population." *Polis* (3), 1998 [In Russian].

Toomla, Rein. *Eesti erakonnad.* Tallinn: Eesti Entsüklopeediakirjastus, 1999.

Traynor, I. "Belarusian Foils Dictator-Buster … for Now," *Guardian,* 14 September 2001.

Tsibenko, A. *Political Party in Parliament of Ukraine: The Principals of Organization and Functioning.* Kiev: KIS, 1997.

Vabariigi Presidendi ja Riigikogu valimised 1992, Dokumente ja materjale, Eesti Vabariigi Valimiskomisjon, Tallinn, 1992.

Verkhovna Rada of Ukraine: Paradigms and Paradox 1, 1995 (Kyiv: Ukrainian perspective) [In Ukrainian]..

*Verkhovna Rada of Ukraine: Paradigms and Paradox,*Issue 4, 1996 (Kyiv: Ukrainian Perspective, 1996) [In Ukrainian].

Verkhovna Rada of Ukraine: Informational reference (1998). Kyiv: NISD. [In Ukrainian].

"Vlast' i narod. Chto pokazal vserossiiskii opros," *Rossiiskaia Federatsia,* No18/94, 9–11.

Vybory '98: Yak Ukrania Holosuvala [Elections '98: As Ukraine Voted]. Kiev: KIS, 1998.

Wallerstain, M. "Electoral Systems, Parties and Political Stability." *Polis* (5–6), 1992 [In Russian],

Ware, Alan. *Political Parties and Party Systems,* Oxford University Press, Oxford, 1996.

Wessels, B. and H-D. Klingemann. *Democratic Transformation and the Prerequisites of Democratic Opposition in East and Central Europe.* Berlin: WZB, 1994.

Williams, R., ed. *Party Finance and Political Corruption.* London: Macmillan Press, 2000.

Wolinetz, S. "Beyond the Catch-All Party: Approaches to the Study of Parties and Party Organisation in Contemporary Democracies." In *Political Parties. Old Concepts and New Challenges,* ed. R. Gunther, J. Ramón-Montero, and J.J. Linz. Oxford: Oxford University Press, 2002.

The World Factbook by CIA. Moldova http://www.cia.gov/cia/publications/factbook/geos/md.html.

Zakaria, F. "The Rise of Illiberal Democracy." *Foreign Affaires* (76), November–December 1997.

Zaprudnik, J. *The Historical Dictionary of Belarus.* Lahman, MD, London: The Scarecrow Press, 1998.

Zepa, Brigita. Kad vēlēšanu kaislības pierimušas. *Diena,* 20.aprīlis, 1999.

Žėruolis, Darius "Rytai tampa Vakarais?" *Politologija* 1 (7), 1996.

———. "Lithuania." In *The Handbook of Political Change in Eastern Europe,* ed. Sten Berglund Tomas Hellen, and Frank H. Aarebrot. London: Edward Elgar, 1998.

Index

About the Contributors

VOLODYMYR FESENKO is chairman of the Board of the Center for Political Studies "Penta" (Kiev, Ukraine). Among his recent publications: "Politichni partiï—providnii chinnik rozvitku politichnoï sistemi Ukraïni" [Political Parties—A Leading Factor of the Development of Political System in Ukraine] in *Ukraïna: strategichni prioriteti: analitichni ocinki—2004*. Za red. A.S.Gal'chins'kogo [A.S.Gal'chins'kii (ed.) Ukraine: Strategic Priorities: Analytical Estimations], (2004); "Peizazh pered pochatkom bataliï (konfiguraciya politichnih sil naperedodni prezidents'koï viborchoï kampaniï v Ukraïni)" [Landscape before the Fight (An Alignment of Political Forces on the Eve of Presidential Elections in Ukraine)] in *Politichnii portret Ukraïni* [Political Profile of Ukraine], 2004, No. 29.

ELENA A. KOROSTELEVA is now Lecturer in European Politics, Department of International Politics, University of Wales, Aberystwyth. She earned her degree and began her career in Minsk State University. Dr. Korosteleva's recent publications include *The Quality of Democracy in Post-Communist Europe* (2005, with Derek Hutcheson) and *Postcommunist Belarus* (2005, with Stephen White).

ALGIS KRUPAVIČIUS is Professor and Director of Policy and Public Administration Institute at Kaunas University of Technology. He is co-editor of *Lietuvos politinė sistema: sąranga ir raida* [Lithuanian Political System: Structure and Change] (2004), which was recognized the best book in political science for the year 2004 in Lithuania. Among his other publications: *Lithuania's Seimas Election 1996: Analyses, Documents and Data* (2001); "The Left-wing Parties in Lithuania, 1990–2002," in Curry J.L., Urban J.B. (eds.) *The Left Transformed in Post-Communist Societies* (2003); "Political Parties and Elite Recruitment in Lithuania," in Berglund S., Duvold K. (eds.) *Baltic Democracy at the Crossroads. An Elite Perspective* (2003, with Giedrius Žvaliauskas).

ANATOLY KULIK is a senior research fellow at the Department of Political Science, Institute of Scientific Information in Social Sciences, Russian Academy of Sciences. His research interests comprise: comparative party politics, Russia's transformational politics, e-democracy and e-government, government in America. Among his most recent publications are: "Politicheskie partii" [Political Parties] in *Bol'shaya Rossiiskaya enciklopediya: V 30 t. T. "Rossiya"* [Great Russian Encyclopedia: In 30 vol. Vol. "Russia"] (2004); "Teoriya razmezhevanii v rossiiskom kontekste: ispytanie politicheskimi realiyami" [The Theory of Cleavages in Russia's Context: Verification by Political Realities] in *Politicheskaya nauka*. Vyp. 4. [Political Science, Issue 4.] (2004); *Electronic Democracy for Russia: A View on the State of Art, Problems and Prospects.* Paper for 13th Annual EINIRAS Conference, London, 2003 http://www.einiras.net/publications/publications.htm.

VALERIU MOSNEAGA is head of the Department of Political Science at the State University of Moldova. The area of his scientific interests includes political parties and party systems, elections and electoral behavior, problems of migration. Among his publications: *The Parliamentary Election-94* (1997); Election *and the Political Geography of Vote* (1999, with Gh.Rusnac); *Independent Moldova and Migration* (1999); *Labor Migration of Moldavian Population* (2000).

SUSANNA PSHIZOVA is associate professor at School of Public Administration, Lomonosov Moscow State University. She is member of the Editorial Board of the International Political Science Review. Her main research interests are: comparative analysis of political parties and transformations of political regimes. Among her publications: "Representative Rule or the Rule of Representations: The Case of Russian Political Parties" in Lawson K., Poguntke T. *How Political Parties Respond* (2004); "Finansirovanyje politicheskogo rynka: teoreticheskije aspekty prakticheskich problem" [The Political Market Finance: Theoretical Aspects of Practical Problems] in *Polis,* N 1,2,2002; "Demokratiya I politicheskyi rynok v sravnitel'noj perspective" [Democracy and Political Market in Comparative Perspective] in *Polis,* N 2,3, 2000.

ANDRIS RUNCIS is associate professor at the Department of Political Science, University of Latvia, Riga. His main research interests are: elections and political parties in postcommunist countries and the process of decision making. His recent publication is: "La formationdes clivages et les parti politigues en Lettonie apres l'independance" in Jean-Michel De Waele (ed.) *Les clivages politigues en Europe centrale et orientale* (2004).

ANDREI TARNAUSKI holds a Ph.D. in Sociology, Byelorussia State University, Minsk. He is co-author of *Politika, vybory i elektoral'noe povedenie (metodologiya operativnogo sociologicheskogo issledovaniya)* [Politics, Elections and Electoral Behavior (Methodology of Sociological Analysis)] (2000, with Elsukov A.N., Rotman D.G. at al.); Elektoral'nye sociologicheskie issledovaniya" [Electoral Sociological Studies] (2002, with Rotman D.G ., Levickaya I.V. at al.); "Ispol'zovanie analiticheskih modelei v elektoral'nyh issledovaniyah" [Application of Analytical Models in Electoral Studies] in *Sociologiya*, 2001, No. 2 (with Rotman D.G.).

REIN TOOMLA is the head of the Department of Political Science, University of Tartu, Estonia. He is author of *Estonian Political Parties*, 1999 [in Estonian] and editor of *Elections to Riigikogu*, 1999 [in Estonian]; *Presidential Election in Estonia*, 2002 [in Estonian]; *Elections to Riigikogu*, 2003 [in Estonian].